THE DORSET YEAR BOOK FOR 2018

ONE HUNDRED AND NINTH YEAR OF ISSUE

First published in Great Britain in 2017 by The Society of Dorset Men

Copyright © 2017 The Society of Dorset Men

All rights reserved.
No part of this publication may be reproduced, stored in a retrieval system, or transmitted, in any form or by any means, without the prior permission in writing of the publisher, nor be otherwise circulated in any form of binding or cover than that in which it is published and without similar condition including this condition being imposed on the subsequent purchaser.

A CIP catalogue record for this book is available from the British Library.

Paperback ISBN 978-0-9926594-6-2
Price £8.00

Edited by Selwyn Williams

Printed and bound in Great Britain by
Print Team (Dorset) Limited
www.printteam.co.uk

Our Cover:
A view of Milton Abbey, where John Damer was buried on 21st August 1776, by courtesy of: Andrew Hepburn (heppydog@hotmail.co.uk)

George Albert Hotel and Spa
... definitely more than just a great night's sleep

An Ideal Wedding *Venue*

- From 4 to 400 Guests
- Ceremony Room
- Exclusive Use Possible
- In-House Hair, Nail & Spa Treatments
- Exceptional Accommodation
- Pre-Wedding Taster Menu
- Personal Wedding Co-ordinator

Bespoke Weddings Tailor-Made to Your Dreams

www.gahotel.co.uk

T: 01935 483430
F: 01935 483431
E: events@gahotel.co.uk

George Albert Hotel,
Wardon Hill, Evershot,
Dorset DT2 9PW

INDEX

ARTICLE TITLE	AUTHOR	PAGE No.
Needless to say, there were no prosecutions	Maurice Hann	1
A Walking Lifetime	Eric Gosney	3
Alonjg the Dorset Stour in Blackmore Vale	Philip Knott	5
Editor's Note and Thanks	Selwyn Williams	14
From the Colonies to Die	Greg Schofield	15
The Church 'as Lost its Flock	Chris Slade	18
Portland Prison Roll of Honour	Susan E. Dean	19
Jo Draper	John Travell	22
Hardy Annual	Helen Lange	25
William Barnes	Albert Douglas Gillen	30
Arthur J Hare (1855-1931)	John Dennett	31
The William Barnes Society	Brian Caddy	35
"Headless"	Mark Vine	37
WW2 Plane Found Off Chesil Beach	Selwyn Williams	45
Colmer vs Cumulus	Chris Slade	51
Keep Changing: Military Museum News	Christopher Jary	52
HMS Vanguard	Greg Schofield	54
It Came to the Crunch	Albert Douglas Gillen	56
Breakout	Jack W. Sweet	57
Major-General Colin Shortis CB CBE	Christopher Jary	58
Wey/Melcombe & Monmouth Rebellion	Greg Schofield	60
Jurassic Storm	Kay Ennals MBE	66
Dorchester Company & John White's Vision	David Cuckson	67
Stone Unveiling /Wrackleford Auxiliary Unit	David Downton	75
The Wrackleford Zev'n	Devina Symes	80
Bridport's First Firework Demonstration	Jack W. Sweet	82
Two Moonfleet Churches – and a Mystery	Michael Ward	85
Moreton Church	Fran Gardner	89
From the Year Book 100 Years Ago	Rev. Dr. John Travell	90
Wildlife in Fortuneswell	Chris Preece	95
Christmas Eve Service, Whitcombe Church	Marion Tait	97
The Family View	Chris Slade	100
The Dorset Regiment's Bugle	Brian C. Moore	101

ARTICLE TITLE	AUTHOR	PAGE No.
At Maiden Castle	Mark Duxbury	104
The Charm	Hayne Russell	106
Witches and Wizards	Hayne Russell	107
Root and Branch	Chris Slade	108
The Blackmore Vale Trip	Marion Tait	109
40 Years of Dancing in Dorset	Chris Preece	112
The Hardy Tree – St. Pancras	Graham R. Allard	116
The Royal Navy's Forgotten Graves	Kevin Patience	119
Book Review - 'Yells, Bells and Smells'	Christopher Jary	124
Dorset Christmas 1950's	Bev Lenthall	126
The Vikings on Portland	Paul Snow	128
First Blood	Paul Snow	129
King Solomon's Pillars/Masonic Symbols	Selwyn Williams	131
A-Maze-Ing	Adrian Fisher	138
Alan's adventures in Newfoundland	Roger Guttridge	139
Something Fishy Going On	Chris Slade	149
Weymouth Men and Q-Ships	Greg Schofield	150
The Story of John Damer 1744-1776	Kay Ennals, MBE	152
Statues: Contrast and Compare	Chris Slade	154
Lady of the Black Horse - Mabel Stobart	Graham Allard	157
The Sweet Smell of Mill Street	David Forrester	160
In Harmony With Dorset	Kay Ennals, MBE	162
Major-General Mark Bond		163
A Blue Plaque for Mill Street	David Forrester	164
Gentleman Pyrate, Henry Strangways,	Fabyan Hodder	166
The Western Front 1917 - Weymouth's Dead	Greg Schofield	169
Sturminster Mill	Fran Gardner	175
Surdly Sam	David Downton	176
On first visiting Kingcombe Ponds	David Downton	176
Dorchester – Stories from the Great War	Brian Bates	177
Robert Hudson - The Man who Saved the Ryder Cup	Peter Fry	194
County Dinner 2017	Hayne Russsell	197
In Memoriam		199
The Society's Rules		200

Needless to say, there were no prosecutions....!

"The face of one of the angels has been replaced at a later date, it seems, with inferior glass."

Maurice Hann

(Quote from A Guide and History of St Michael & All Angels Parish Church, Verwood), page 6

It would appear that nobody in Verwood has any idea how damage was caused to the face of the angel. I cannot be sure how it happened, but I am willing to have a good guess. Sometime in the early 1950s my Dorset-born grandfather Francis Richard Hann told me all he knew about this percussion-cap pistol. I was a young teenager, and he was a retired master-carpenter. I had seen this pistol amongst his carpentry tools in his garden shed and had asked if he would allow me to have it. I was told that he would give it to me if I remembered the story behind it. He reminded me that his father was Richard Lane Hann, one of the first police officers in the Dorset Police Force, and that his number had been "P.C.1". Richard had been stationed at thirteen villages or towns during his service of twentyeight years. Grandfather continued his story by adding "One day Richard heard from the

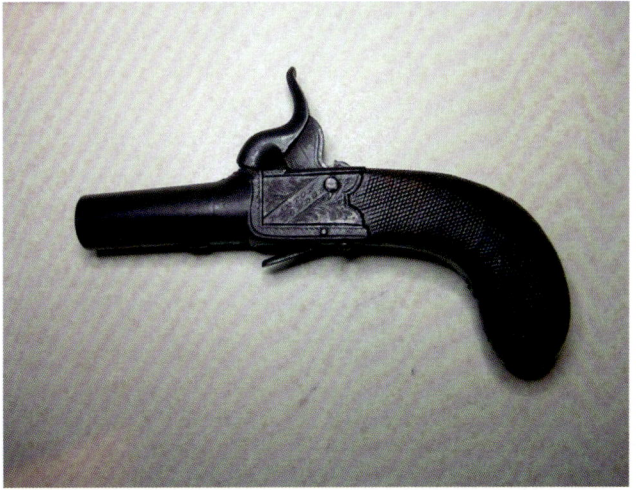

local vicar that the church windows had been broken, and on investigation he found that the damage had been caused by this pistol being fired by his own son George, in league with the vicar's son!" Many years later, in the late 1980s I decided to find all I could about my great-grandfather's history, and in particular his police career. This eventually led to a book being published in 1989 "Policing Victorian Dorset". After it was published, my wife and I continued to holiday in Dorset and started to visit some of the villages and towns where Richard had worked. This included Verwood, and the site of the old station and Albion Hotel. We then visited St Michael & All Angels, and picked up a church guide. That guide mentioned the damaged stained glass window. However, at that stage there was little I could do to prove who was responsible.

Another twenty-six years on, and having retired to Dorset, I decided I must investigate further. Assuming George was between ten and fourteen years old when the window was damaged, I concluded that this must have happened in Piddlehinton, Blandford, Cranborne or Verwood. Who was the vicar circa 1868 in Verwood? Did he have a son similar age to George? In those years Verwood came under the Parish of Cranborne, and the incumbent was the Revd John Carnegie, born in Ireland. The 1861 census returns show him with sons John, aged 3, George aged 2 and William, three months. Hence in 1868 when PC.1 was moved from Cranborne to Verwood John Carnegie Jnr would have been about eleven or twelve years old, and George Hann about fourteen. In 1868 there was no official police station or house in Verwood, and therefore PC.1 and his family were given accommodation in the Albion Hotel. Richard Hann had been stationed at Cranborne before moving to Verwood, so he and Revd Carnegie would have known each other very well, for a police officer was required to "Attend Divine Service at least once on a Sunday, and to be in full uniform". Maybe I have not proved the case, — but I'm pretty sure George Hann and John Carnegie Jnr were responsible! Oh, if you are wondering what happened to George ….. He joined Dorset Police Force in 1878 and retired as Sergeant in 1905!

Richard Lane Hann, (circa 1904) PC.1. Dorset Constabulary 1859-88

Richard's son George, (circa 1878) Promoted to sergeant 1902

A Walking Lifetime

Eric Gosney - 93 year old kid.

Here, from my kitchen window, oft I stare.
    This view produces pleasure, - and despair!
That lengthy Ballard Down before my eyes
    I've walked so often under windy skies.

This pleasant sight brings memories to me
    Of walks I did in former years, you see.
Advancing years have caused my steps to slow;
    I'm doleful now, on long walks I can't go!

In Dorset, my home-county, I declare
    Just name a lovely spot, and I've walked there!
Bulbarrow and on Cranborne Chase I've trod.
    Lulworth to Osmington, - my favourite plod.

I've walked the whole length of The Isle of Wight,
    And Beachy Head, in Sussex, chalky-white.
From Winchester to Salisbury's slender spire.
    Such memories delight me, and inspire.

The borderlands of Wales meant much to me,
    The Brecon Beacons, Malvern Hills to see;
Ludlow and Knighton, lengthy Offa's Dyke-
    Much beauty there surrounds a healthful hike.

From Harrogate I've walked the Yorkshire Dales,
    Those great, green slopes whose beauty never fails
Or North York Moors stretched round me, heather-clad
    O! What a splendid walking life I've had!

On Bodmin Moor in Cornwall I have been.
    And from Land's End surveyed the ocean scene.
Speaking of Cornwall, though I mustn't boast,
    I've walked great lengths along its rocky coast.

Thatched cottages, church towers, my memory fills,
    And lonely rambles over gorse-clad hills.
I've sung my songs on many a grassy down,
    And sunk a pint in many a country town.

Sadly it's over, - my old legs are weak,
    Such walks are 'out of bounds', the outlook bleak.
Around the stone quay to the pier I go;
    It's only safe to walk that far, I know.

Now snapshot and guide-books bring back to me
    Fond memories of walks that used to be.
If I had never done them, - stayed at home,
    No longer through sweet memory could I roam.

In spite of all those great walks I have done
    In frosty weather or in summer sun
The walks that I most treasure were near here,
    It's where I started, down in Dorset dear.

For Swanage was my birthplace, near the sea.
    What views, what treasure trove lay there for me!
Corfe Castle, Worth Matravers, Kimmeridge shore,
    Creech Barrow, Chapman's Pool and Durdle Door.

The Caves at Tilly Whim, fair Studland Beach
    Though I'd no car, were still in easy reach
So you may guess those early walks I did
Inspired me much when I was still a kid!

Editor's note: - I recently had the news that Eric died on 2nd March 2017 but he has left us with such an optimistic view of his rich life and the Dorset he loved. I will really miss his articles, RIP Eric.

The Coppleridge Inn

Cosy, candlelit restaurants with light bites, smaller portions, contemporary specials and traditional pub favourites

Delicious Sunday Lunch

Cocktails, premium wines, special gins and quality beers and ales

Children's Garden, tennis courts & 15 acres of land to explore

Private dining, parties and weddings

The Coppleridge Inn, Motcombe, Shaftesbury, Dorset, SP7 9PA ~ 01747 851980
thecoppleridgeinn@btinternet.com ~ www.coppleridge.com

Along the Dorset Stour in the Blackmore Vale

by Philip Knott

The Source of the Stour

The Stour receives water from ten main tributaries during its journey through the Blackmore Vale. All of these tributaries, and the smaller brooks and streams that feed into them, play a vital role in draining the vale, to maintain the land in a suitable condition for cultivation, for arable crops, and to provide pastureland for cattle grazing. The sources of these ten tributaries define the perimeter of the Blackmore Vale. On three sides, the boundary can be clearly identified by the chalk downlands that enclose the vale. In the north-west the boundary is less clearly defined, but can be identified as the parish boundary between Stourton and Purse Caundle at Haddon, with the springs rising to the west, just within the parish of Purse Caundle, flowing towards Sherborne to join the river Yeo and at Frith, where the spring rising just to the south feeds the Bibberne Brook and the spring at Frith Farm feeds into the River Yeo, and at Copse House, Landshire Lane. Parishes located on the north western boundary of the vale are Stowell, South Cheriton, North Cheriton and Holton.

The source of the Dorset Stour is usually identified as being in the wooded valley in the parkland to the north of the formal gardens. At the head of the valley, St Peter's Pump, standing at 662 feet above sea level, is a Celtic style rock structure surmounted by a 1474 market cross.

Although St Peter's Pump stands at the source of the Stour, the remaining well at its base is normally dry. The spring now first appears above ground when it arrives at the top end of the highest pond at Six Wells Bottom, due to a drop in the water table in the Upper Greensand springs and the underlying chalk aquifer, as the result of bore-hole abstraction. The water produced by the spring flows into the northern end of the lake in the ornamental gardens, after passing through the ponds. This spring is one of five that contribute to the fledgling Stour. Two springs flow directly into the main lake at the Grotto, in the ornamental gardens. One cascades over a sleeping nymph on a marbled stand into a shallow pool, and flows out into the lake via a stone conduit. The other flows from a white-painted lead statue of the River God Ariadne. Two springs meet at Top Lane Farm in Gasper; one rising in woodland just to the south of King Alfred's Tower, and the other just to the east of Aarons Hill just inside the Wiltshire county boundary with Somerset. The water produced from them flows directly into the northern end of Gasper Lake.

Gasper Lake, formerly a medieval fishpond, was extended in the 19th Century. The lake was reconstructed after its dam was destroyed: as the result of a huge storm in 1917. The reconstruction of the dam was completed in 1920. The Stour starts on its journey to the English Channel from the Gasper Lake outlet.

The Upper Stour

The Stour flows away from Gasper Lake along a deep tree-lined valley, listed as an Area of Outstanding Natural Beauty, which forms the county boA large slab of lichen-covered green sandstone, known as Egbert's Stone, stands above the river near the rear of the millpond. King Egbert, the first King of Wessex, raised the stone to mark the boundaries of Dorset, Somerset and Wiltshire when he divided the land into shires, hence its alternative name of the Three Counties Stone. The stone has been moved up the slope from its original location at the meeting point of the county boundaries, and is now located inside the Bulpits golf course, adjoining the narrow lane known as Pen Mill Hill. Near this spot, King Alfred the Great mustered his army on the eve of the Battle of Edington, when in May 878 he defeated the invading Danes. The battle took place close to Edington Hill near Westbury.

On arriving at the millpond at Bourton Mill, the Stour crosses the county boundary into Dorset. Bourton Mill dates back at least to 878. A map of 1610 shows Longlane Myll approximately on the site of the current mill. In the middle of the 18th Century, an industrial spinning process was invented and Daniel Maggs built a mill for the processing and spinning of flax. This was on the site of what is now Bullpits and was powered by a waterwheel driven by the Stour. The mill produced bed linen and supplied canvass to the Royal Navy.

In 1820, a completely new factory driven by two waterwheels was built on the site. In 1821, it became Maggs and Hindley, and in 1837, the famous 60-foot diameter overshoot waterwheel was built in the foundry to power the flax mill. A year later in 1838 a descendant, Oliver Maggs, built a new foundry with a blast furnace powered by two more, smaller waterwheels. The foundry produced water wheels for other mills, agricultural tools and equipment, including threshing machines, cheese presses, portable and stationery steam engines and later some of

the first steam-driven cars. The foundry had its own showrooms in Queen Victoria Street, London and its products, including portable steam engines and boilers, were exported to agricultural communities throughout the British Empire and beyond, giving many years of reliable service. Still little more than a brook, the Stour flows through the village of Bourton, passing along the front of Riverside Cottage and under the former A303 trunk road, constructed of steel and concrete. This bridge replaces the original bridge washed away when the dam burst at Gasper in 1917.

Located close to the A303 by-pass, Silton Mill had the river on one side and the mill leat on the other. Zeals Estate abandoned the mill and eventually the roof and walls fell down covering the wheel. Maggs and Hindley of Bourton, who made the wheel, were the first manufacturers in the country of this type of wheel. The Poncelet wheel had specially shaped buckets to give it extra power and the one at Silton is the only wheel of its kind left on the Stour. When other iron mill wheels were taken for scrap during the Second World War, Silton was overlooked. The wheel was only rediscovered when the mill house was being renovated in 1974. The restored mill and mill house at Silton is now a private residence. A little further on in Church Lane Silton is a small stone hump-backed bridge and the first to bear the name of the river. The Stour then arrives at a narrow lane where Fitz Farm ford provides a crossing point.

Waterloo Mill, located in the parish of Silton, survives as a private residence. Waterloo Bridge has two small stone arches and an 1820 date stone and brick parapets.

The Stour passes Pierston Farm on its approach to Milton-on-Stour. The village stands between the Stour and its tributary, the Shreen Water. The Stour then flows through the Peacemarsh area of Gillingham, where a large area of public open-space land, between recent housing development and the river, provides both a recreational area and a floodplain. A single-arch brick bridge at Wavering Lane provides a pedestrian crossing. The road has been closed to through traffic, following the construction of the relief road at Rolls Bridge. The Stour then crosses under Wyke Road and Le Neubourg Way, before the Shreen joins the Stour at the rear of the Waitrose store. The Stour then re-crosses Le Neubourg Way, flowing past the Brickfield Trading Estate, Withy Wood and under the railway line, on its way to Eccliffe Mill. Eccliffe Mill, a 19th-century mill, has now converted to a private residence. The mill carries a date stone 'C.E.M.1904' suggesting a rebuild. Beyond Eccliffe Mill the Stour begins its meandering passage through the pastoral tranquility of the Blackmore Vale, merging into the rolling rural landscape on its way to former West Stour Mill. The former mill, located on the East Stour side of the river at Highbridge Mill Farm, between East and West Stour survives. The farm generates its own electricity by means of a water turbine. The Stour then passes under the A30 near West Stour Filling Station, heading for Stour Provost Mill.

Stour Provost Mill is listed in the Domesday Book. Records also list a mill on the site in 1570, 1640 and 1747. The mill retains a working waterwheel capable of producing electricity. The mill wheel, which dates from 1886, was restored in 1998. Until 1925, the mill, along with most of the village, belonged to King's College, Cambridge.

Around the Corallian Outcrop

The Stour passes under Trill Bridge on a lane linking Fifehead Magdalen with Stour Provost. A limestone ridge obstructs the Stour on its approach to Marnhull, diverting it around the western side, after passing through a gap in the limestone ridge on its way to Lower Fifehead. At Lower Fifehead are the surviving remains of the former fulling mill complex. In 1840, the Mill House was occupied by Thomas Dowding and his son, also named Thomas, who ran the mill. The tenancy then changed hands every few years and the mill was still recorded as operating until 1899. At the 1904 sale of the Manor estate, the dwelling house and mill were described as being in ruins. The stone tiles were removed and transported to Fifehead Magdalen in 1906, to be used for repairing the church roof. After leaving Lower Fifehead, the Stour meanders through low-lying fields at Marnhull Ham which provide a flood plain, passing Hamwood, Crib House and Gomershay farms on its way to Kingsmill.

The weir at Marnhull Ham was constructed in 1942, when the Stour was realigned to bypass West Mill. The purpose of the scheme was to reduce the level in the Stour by 3ft, in order to reduce the flood risk to the nearby Royal Naval Air Training Station, HMS Dipper, under construction at the time.

The present mill building at Kingsmill dates from 1829 and worked until 1935. A mill was recorded on this site in the Domesday Book, in the ownership of the Abbott of Glastonbury.

The building has been restored and structurally is in very good condition, housing three pairs of

stones and some ancillary machinery. A mill was in operation at Kings Mill at the time of the Domesday Book. In Norman times, all land and property was divided into Manors and the miller at Kings Mill had to pay rent to the Lord of the Manor, the Abbott of Glastonbury. With the dissolution of the monasteries, in the reign of King Henry VIII, the mill passed into private ownership, but later ownership transferred to the Crown and during the reign of Elizabeth I the mill became a Crown grant. Records, for the period of around 1816 show the mill in the ownership of a Robert Toogood, followed by his son William. Sometime after 1833, the mill and surrounding land was sold to the Duke of Westminster, who also held the title Lord Stalbridge. The farmhouse and farm buildings were then constructed. At the time of the 1859 Enclosures Act for Marnhull Common, the then Marquess of Stalbridge was granted half an acre of land, in lieu of previous rights, to excavate clay soil at Marnhull Common for repairing the mill, dams, banks, hatches and sluices at King Mill.

W G Johnson purchased the mill at the time of the 1918 dispersal sale of property in the ownership of Lord Stalbridge. The mill closed in the mid-1930s, and in 1941 the hatches and weir were removed as part of the scheme to reduce the water table at Gibbs Marsh prior to the construction of the Royal Navy Fleet Air Arm base in 1941.

The mill had an undershot waterwheel. The water strikes the paddles at the bottom of the wheel, making it less efficient than the overshot wheel, where the water strikes the wheel at the top, creating more head, resulting in greater efficiency and more power being generated. The undershot is cheaper, and easier, to build and is especially suitable for low-lying flat areas such as Kings Mill. However, the reduced power output will create problems in providing sufficient power to operate the machinery in the mill during periods of low flow encountered in the summer months. There is now very little left of the original undershot type water wheel and the weir will need to be rebuilt if the mill is to be restored to working order.

Members of the Stalbridge Angling Club fish in the millpond at Kings Mill. Kings Mill Bridge, constructed in 1823 by a John Stone of Yarcombe, replaced an earlier bridge dating from 1673. The Lydden, with its catchment area in the western side of the vale around Buckland Newton, joins the Stour beyond Kings Mill Bridge, on the opposite side of the road to the mill.

Marnhull to Sturminster Newton

The Stour then leaves Kingsmill, meandering through the meadows on its way to Cutt Mill at Hinton St Mary. Part of this section of the Stour, along with its tributary the Cale, forms the parish boundary between Stalbridge and Marnhull.

The remains of the present building at Cutt Mill, badly damaged by fire in 2003, date

from the 18th Century, with 19th and 20th-century additions. However there has been a mill on this site for many hundreds of years.

The Domesday Book of 1086 lists Hinton St Mary as a working watermill. The earliest known millers were John Rake and his son, Ambrose, who died in 1752 and 1789, respectively. The remains of the waterwheel, not replaced with a water turbine, as at Sturminster and Fiddleford mills. This was due to the low head of water available to power the mill. The first Ordnance Survey maps of Dorset, published in 1811, clearly show the mill and miller's cottage and spell it 'Cut Mill'. The name comes from the Middle English 'cut', meaning water-channel. Wooden hatches were replaced with iron hatches in 1908.

The 2003 fire was not the first. In March 1817, the local papers advertised the sale of 'the site of Cutt Mills, which were lately destroyed by fire'. Coincidentally in the same year, Stephen Scorey, 'miller and baker, late of Hinton St Mary', was reduced to petitioning for 'insolvent relief' from his debtor's cell in the King's Bench Prison. The mill was re-built but the next miller, Henry Newman, fared little better and was declared bankrupt in 1828. Less than three years later, 'Cutt Mills' were offered for sale again and described as 'all that newly-erected and well-accustomed water grist mill, at present only working two pair of stones, with a powerful and constant supply of water capable of working four pair'.

By 1848, George Jeffery was the miller and Cutt Mill was entering what was to be the most stable period of its recorded history. Jeffery was there at least seventeen years and by 1867 had been succeeded by Robert Hunt, whose family was to remain there for more than a century. Robert was succeeded between 1907 and 1911 by his widow, Eliza. By 1920, their son Herbert was the miller. Commercial milling at Cutt Mill was to stop before the end of this decade largely due to the low head of water available to turn the wheel, which

meant that the mill was not updated, or a water turbine installed to replace the wheel during the late 19th Century early 20th Century, leaving the mill unable to compete with nearby mills at Sturminster Newton and Fiddleford. The Divelish, with its catchment area under Bulbarrow Hill, joins the Stour midway between Hinton St Mary and Sturminster Newton.

The Stour then flows between the curtailed arches of the bridge that took the Somerset and Dorset railway into Sturminster Newton.

Colber Bridge is a Grade II-listed cast iron footbridge, constructed in 1841 by J

Conway to link Sturminster Newton with Stalbridge Lane and Bagber. Thomas Hardy's one time residence is just visible between the trees.

Sturminster Newton mill is now a working museum. A working mill is recorded on this site in the Domesday survey of 1086. The present building, dating from around 1650, closed as a working mill in 1970. A miller's cottage once stood where the car park and picnic area is now located. A surge of floodwater in the winter of 1926-27 washed away the cottage and the rolling bay. The stone from the cottage was used to rebuild the rolling bay.

In 1904, my grandfather's cousin Sidney Knott, who was the leaseholder and Master Miller of Sturminster Mill at this time, installed a 24-horsepower 45-inch 'British Empire' turbine, providing double the power generated by the waterwheel. From 1925 until its closure, the mill was leased to Blandford and Webb Ltd, corn and seed merchants, to produce animal feed.

Sturminster Newton to the Stour Gap

Fiddleford Mill, rebuilt in the late 18th Century, has a dated inscription of 1566 on two stone blocks that have been reset into the wall. The last Fiddleford miller, Rupert Rose, was a great-grandson of Job Rose, the model for William Barnes' 'Worthy' Bloom the Miller. In 1906, a turbine was installed to replace the water wheel. Water turbines were first used in the 1880s.

The ancient and the modern, with the former mill to the left and the new hydro-generating plant, with the end of its Archimedes Screw just visible in the water.

Job Rose took over the lease for Fiddleford Mill in 1855 at an annual rent of £70. He had previously worked at Sturminster Mill as the assistant to the miller Mr. Roke before taking over as the miller on Mr. Roke's retirement. He married his wife Hannah in 1838 and they lived in a small terrace cottage near Sturminster Newton Bridge, where their two eldest children Samuel and Mary were born. In 1844, he had moved to Woodbridge Mill at Bedchester to take over the running of the mill. In the 1861 census, Henry Fudge is listed as the miller at Fiddleford Mill, with Job Rose still residing at Woodbridge Mill along with his wife and eight children. Job Rose was a larger than life character, epitomised by his weight reputed to be in excess of 31 stones. He was immortalised in the William Barnes poem 'John Bloom in London'. Job's eldest son Samuel took over as miller at Fiddleford and his second son James took over Sturminster Mill. James died in 1875 at the age of 32, leaving a widow Matilda and four children. Matilda married Sydney Knott, who was a cattle and hay dealer, in 1883 and Sydney took over as the master miller at Sturminster Mill. Job Rose died in 1871 and is buried at Hartgrove Methodist Chapel. The graveyard has now been de-consecrated and the railings and memorial stones removed, leaving no indication that here is the final resting place of a well-known Blackmore Vale character in the 19th Century.

A memorial tablet was removed from the interior of the chapel prior to its conversion to a private residence and fixed on the interior of the rear wall at Fontmell Magna chapel. Samuel Rose remained at Fiddleford Mill until his death in 1892. His widow Mary took over the lease until her death in 1913 when the lease transferred to her son Sidney. A water turbine had been installed in 1906 and Sidney changed the mill's main output from the production of flour to the milling of wheat and barley for animal feed. Sidney died in 1946 and his two sons Rupert and Howard took over the running of the mill. Sidney, who was a bachelor, died in 1975 leaving Rupert to continue as miller, with the assistance of his son, until he retired in 1977. His son Sidney, who was farming at Higher Farm Manston, did not take on the lease of Fiddleford Mill and the 120-year association of the Rose family with Fiddleford Mill came to an end. Brian Young took over at Fiddleford for a while before transferring to Sturminster Mill, ending 700 years of continuous operation of Fiddleford Mill.

The Domesday Book recorded the existence of a large house on the bank of the River Stour at Manston, demolished in the latter part of the 17th Century to make way for a new building. An inscription in the chancel of the nearby Church of St Nicholas states that the yew trees, which are now a feature of the grounds of the house, were planted in 1690, about the same time as the house was built. The Dibbens sold Manston House to Henry Kaines, the celebrated diarist, and it then passed to Thomas Barnabas Hanham, youngest son of Sir James Hanham, the 7th Baronet of Deans Court in Wimborne. Hanham probably acquired Manston House in the 1850s. In 1857, the Dorset County Chronicle of 12th February reported that 'on Friday morning last, soon after 4 o'clock, Manston House, the seat of T.B Hanham Esq., was discovered to be on fire.' The fire was disastrous, destroying most of the building and its contents, although no lives were lost. The report concludes with the melancholy news that 'the insurance will not cover above a moiety (half) of the pecuniary loss.'

Hanham, then in his early thirties, started building a new house. The old rear wing, which had survived the fire, was incorporated into the design, completely undetectable from the north-facing front, on the east and west sides, however the join is clearly visible. Hanham had joined the Royal Navy as a young man, achieving the rank of Lieutenant in 1847 and Commander in 1864. He became a Justice of the Peace and a Deputy-Lieutenant of Dorset and rose to the height of Past Provincial Senior Grand Warden as a Freemason.

He was less fortunate when it came to the longevity of his wives, all three of whom predeceased him. The second of these, Josephine Ida Dodson, died in 1866 had expressed a dislike for the churchyard, which was regularly flooded by the Stour, so Hanham had a waterproof vault built next to his private aisle in the church. When the vault was opened up on the death of his only child, Maud, in 1869, he found it flooded to a depth of 19 inches. This distressed both Hanham and his new wife Edith so much that she made him promise that he would have her body cremated if he survived her and Edith promised to do the same for him. Cremation was not legal in Britain at the time. After Edith died in 1876, Hanham, being a Justice of the Peace and a law-abiding citizen, was not prepared to break the law, so he had her body stored in a lead-lined coffin while he had a mausoleum built in the grounds of Manston House. The coffin of his late wife was placed in the mausoleum while he negotiated with the authorities to have cremation legalised.

It was not until 8th October 1882 that Hanham could legally consign her body to a cremation, following legislation and after having a small crematorium built in the grounds of the house. His mother had died by then and she followed her daughter-in-law the next day. These were the first legal cremations in the country. The crematorium has now been dismantled and the building converted to a garden store. The mausoleum is now in pristine condition as the result of a refurbishment in 1985; the lead from its domed roof was stolen in the 1960s and the building had deteriorated badly.

The 2nd Viscount Portman, who built Bryanston House, also built a hunting lodge facing the Stour at Hammoon, for the use of his family and guests when hunting with the Portman Hunt. The lodge provided a convenient destination for a morning's ride, or a location to change horses during a day's hunting. Hammoon House remained part of the Portman estate until 1923 when it was sold as East Farm, together with 323 acres of land. A recording station at Hammoon Bridge monitors the flow rate and level of potential flooding during periods of heavy rainfall.

The Stour between Hammoon and Fontmell Parva with the cattle grazing peacefully on the river bank and the field covered in golden buttercups.

The Stour then flows past the rear of Fontmell Parva House on its way to Bere Marsh. The Bower family bought the house in 1864. In the 19th Century, the house was enlarged on both sides and to the rear. At Bere Marsh, the mill closed in 1925 and was later demolished. The Stour then crosses Haywards Lane Bridge. A new bridge, completed in 2016, has replaced the former bridge, which was constructed of cast iron and concrete. An Act of Parliament in the reign of Elizabeth I established a charity to fund the construction and maintenance of the original bridge, paid for by rental income from cottages at Bere Marsh and Cookswell.

The Stour meanders through the meadows on its way to the gap in the chalk escarpments at the foot of Hod Hill. Hambledon Hill, with its Iron Age ramparts, dominates this section of the Stour valley. This section of the Stour forms the parish boundary between Shillingstone and Child Okeford. The Stour leaves the Blackmore Vale through a gap in the chalk escarpment at the foot of Hod Hill to continue on its journey to the English Channel, a total distance of around 61 miles from its source to the sea. The Stour joins the Hampshire Avon at Christchurch before it reaches the sea at Mudeford.

Despite the significant residential and light industrial development which has taken place in the towns, and to a lesser extent the villages, in the Blackmore Vale, to accommodate an ever-increasing population and to provide much needed employment, along with the changes resulting from modern farming methods, the rural landscape of the vale remains remarkably well preserved. A walk along the banks of the River Stour today, through the meadows at Colber between Sturminster Newton and Hinton St Mary, where my great-grandfather made hay and grazed his cattle during the early part of the 20th Century, will reveal a landscape that has not changed dramatically since the days of Thomas Hardy and William Barnes.

Editor's note & thanks.

Thank you to all the contributors who provide the content, to Chris Smith of Print Team (Dorset) Ltd for his expertise, to Hayne Russell, Shaun Cregan, Stuart Adam and especially to Peter Lush for his great help in proof reading the many articles. I again think there is something for everybody in this Dorset Year Book and I am delighted that this year we have the first full colour edition, though some of the most remarkable photos are b&w.

Please note all articles are printed in good faith and opinions expressed are solely those of the individual contributors and do not necessarily reflect the opinions of the editor or the Society of Dorset Men.

From the Colonies to Die

Greg Schofield

During the First World War, many Weymouth men who had emigrated to the colonies, returned with the colonial forces to take part in the struggle against Germany and her allies, and many of them died. Most came back from Canada or Australia, but New Zealand, Rhodesia and India were also represented.

1915:

In an attempt to force Turkey out of the war, in April 1915 the Gallipoli Peninsula was invaded by the British, French and the 'Australia and New Zealand Army Corps' (ANZACS). During that campaign, Arthur George BANKS, a Private in the Wellington Regiment NZEF, aged 26, died of wounds at Gallipoli on 15th August, 1915. He was the 4th son of Faithful Annie Banks, 78, Walpole Street.

In Belgium, during the Second battle of Ypres, which is most famous for the first use of poison gas, the Germans attacked east and west of St Julien, and were repulsed by the Canadians, during which Ernest WEEKS, aged 42, a Lance Corporal in 16th Canadian Infantry (Manitoba) died on 23rd April, 1915. He had been apprenticed to a photographer, Mr Cox of St Mary Street, Weymouth, and after went into business with his brother.

1916

This year was dominated by the Battle of the Somme, which lasted for nearly five months and saw hundreds of thousands of allied troops killed. Amongst them from the colonies was:-

- W. SLADE, aged 38, Private in 3rd Canadian Infantry (Central Ontario Regiment), died 8th October, 1916. Son of Edward and Cornelia Slade, 54, Ranelagh Road

- Frederick James CURTIS, aged 39, Private in 15th Australian Infantry, died 25th August, 1916. Son of William & Maud Curtis, 19, Hardwick Street.

1917

This was a year of fierce fighting on a number of fronts for the allied forces, although it was dominated by the terrible Third Battle of Ypres, sometimes known as the Passchendaele Campaign.

In April, the Canadians were given the responsibility of taking Vimy Ridge, which was captured in a brilliant campaign, during which, Sydney HAYMAN, aged 23, a Private in Canadian Infantry (Manitoba Regiment) Machine Gun Section, died on 28th April, 1917. Fourth youngest son of Henry Hayman, 58, St Thomas Street.

Also in April, the Second Battle of Arras (Battle of the Scarp) was taking place, during which Charles Henry William ALP, aged 21, a Private in 51st Australian Infantry, died 2nd April, 1917. Son of Charles and Ada Alp.

In June, as a prelude to the Third Battle of Ypres, in what was arguably the most efficient campaign of the war, the Messines Ridge was captured. But it did see the death of:-

- James Chester BADGLEY, aged 29, a 2nd Lieutenant in 6th Wiltshire Regiment, died 7th June, 1917. He had enlisted in the Canadian Contingent at Quebec in 1914, and transferred to the Wiltshires, his father's regiment in which he was a Colonel, on being commissioned.

- Ronald Coode C SHIELD, aged 34, a Private in 1st Wellington NZEF, died 8th June, 1917. Son of Mr & Mrs Shield, Dorchester Road.

The Third Battle of Ypres is a by-word for mud, misery, suffering and bitter fighting, During that campaign three Weymouth men from the colonies died:-

- Richard Luther GEDDES, aged 37, Lieutenant in Canadian Infantry (Central Ontario Regiment), was killed by a sniper on 7th September, 1917. He had been promoted from the ranks, and his father, was an Abyssinian War veteran, and RE officer at Nothe Fort (Died July 1917). He had two brothers serving in a Labour Battalion and the Dorset Yeomanry.

- Alec LOWE, aged 26, Private in Canadian Infantry (Quebec Regiment), died 6th November, 1917. Only son of Mr & Mrs Lowe, 4, Gloucester Terrace.

- Henry Ernest WHETTAM, aged 28, 2nd Corporal Australian Engineers, was killed in action on 24th October, 1917. His brother, Frank Charles WHETTAM in the Royal Engineers, also died. They were the sons of John and Annie Whettam, 'Elmhurst', Carlton Road.

In the Middle East, fighting the Turks in the Mesopotamian Campaign, Arthur Edward LE MESURIER, aged 21, 2nd Lieutenant 6th Gurka Rifles, died 9th March, 1917. Son of Haviland and May Le Mesurier.

In Africa the brilliant German General, von Lettow, with his Askari army and using German East Africa as a base, tied down hundreds of thousands of British and Commonwealth troops for the duration of the war. During that fighting, Arthur Rowland CARTER, aged 35, a Sergeant in 2nd Rhodesian Regiment, was killed in action on 12th February, 1916. He had spent his boyhood in Weymouth, served in the Boer War, and then joined the South African Police for 10 years. In 1914 he bought Odzi Rapids Farm in Rhodesia, and then signed up again with a colonial regiment fighting in a German Colony. He was the eldest son of 'Deputy Surgeon General' Rowland and Louisa Carter, 'Hadley House', 11, Dorchester Road.

Also killed in that year, in what was chillingly known as 'natural wastage' was Arthur Frederick JACKSON, aged 24, Private in Canadian Cycle Corps. He died on 19th January,

1917 at Tranqueville, British Columbia, from the affects of gas poisoning at Hill 60. Son of James and Kathreen Jackson, 7, Dorchester Road.

1918

This year was marked by huge campaigns and a change from static trench warfare to return to a war of movement. It began in March with two huge German attacks, during the course of which the allied lines retreated to breaking point, but were ultimately to hold. During those retreats, James Finch NOBBS, aged 25, a Driver in 2nd Australian Infantry, died 13th March, 1918. Son of the late John Nobbs and Jessie, 'Egerton House'.

The Germans having run out of steam, the British and French launched a series of coordinated counter-attacks which culminated in the brilliant breaching of the Hindenburg Line. During those attacks six Weymouth men from the colonies died:-

- Arthur James BAGGS, aged 23, Private (Bugler) in 12th Australian Infantry, died 25th August, 1918.

  Charles Henry BRANSON, aged 28, Private in 41st Australian Infantry, died of wounds 14th October, 1918. Only son of Henry and Marion Branson, Glendinning Avenue.

- William George BRINKLEY, aged 26, Private in Lord Strathcona's Horse (Canadian), killed in action 9th October, 1918. Only son of George and Mary Brinkley, 43, Brownlow, Street.

- George Eaton GROVES, aged 27, a Private in 10th Australian Infantry, died 31st July, 1918. He was recommended for the Military Medal on 13th July, 1918 and it was awarded on 21st October, 1918, nearly 3 months after his death.

- James Robert HARRIS, of 3rd Canadian Infantry (Central Ontario Regiment) Medical Corps, was killed in action by a sniper whilst on a mission of mercy on 30th August, 1918. Only son of Mr & Mrs Harris, 2, Eldon Villas, Westham.

- Sydney Percival HUMPHREY, aged 31, Private in the Canterbury Regiment NZEF. Killed in action on 4th September, 1918. He relinquished a good position and prospects at the Penang Straits settlement and enlisted at Wellington, NZ.

Walhachin was a small fruit-growing settlement near Ashcroft, planned as a progressive scientific model of the most advanced agricultural science. Historian Elsie Turnbull wrote that 97 of its 107 men enlisted. One was Gordon Flowerdew, the storekeeper. His sister, Eleanor, ran the Walhachin Hotel. He was a horseman of skill and dash.

In 1911, riding his horse Dixie, he won most of the honours in races held for King George V's coronation. In 1914, he joined a cavalry regiment. He never returned, leading a heroic but doomed cavalry charge against German machine guns in 1918 for which he would win the Victoria Cross, having denied the enemy a crucial height of land.

Nor did the other men come home to what was supposed to be an Eden in the desert. The women there struggled a while, then they, too, left. All that remained of Walhachin was a decaying irrigation flume on a hillside. The dream of progress had perished along with other illusions.

Editor's Note. I visited my brother in Canada in 1982 and we travelled past Kamloops down to Vancouver and passed the irrigation flume stretching along the nearby hills and my brother told me the story. Gone but not forgotten.

The Church 'as Lost its Flock

by Chris Slade

Us 'ad a lovely little pleace
Aside the river Winterbourne
Our Church was tiny but was nice
But now three of the walls be gorn.

We'd chalky hills to meake cob walls
An' lynchetts to grow grain and thatch
To keep warm and dry our modest halls
An' from the stream small fish we'd catch.

But then the changes came along:
A trade began in weaving wool,
So sheep upon our fields did throng.
No more was corn the measter's jewel.

He didn't need no working men.
We lost our jobs and got no pay.
'Twas just a shepherd now and then.
The rest of us could go astray.

With nobody within the Church
There was no need to keep it up.
The roof and walls o'er time did lurch.
No one on bread and wine could sup.

The Church walls didn't go to waste.
There's stepping stones cross which we'd trip.
The south bank of the stream was faced,
And for the sheep they built a dip.

Portland Prison Roll of Honour

Susan E. Dean

During a visit to the Portland Prison Museum I noticed a framed 'Prison

Service Roll of Honour' for World War One. Although clear to read still through the glass it saddens me to see how little was known of these courageous men. I resolved to use the information on the 'Roll' to help me find each person on the website www.livesofthefirstworldwar and improve their records so that they were suitably remembered in our national digital memorial. The product of this work is a sixteen page index, with years of birth and death, places of birth and soldier numbers, in addition to the details in the roll of honour. The community I have created on the website is called 'PRISON OFFICERS of WW1' and it contains the details of 116 men.

The index is available to search at Portland Prison Museum and the Somerset and Dorset Family History Society headquarters in Sherborne, check the opening times at their respective websites. The following nine men with connections to Dorset are examples of what you can find on the website:

Harry Arthur W. ATKIN, listed as a Warder at Portland. He was born in Lincoln, Lincolnshire during 1883, the son of Harriett and Samuel Atkin. He was awarded the Belgian Croix de Guerre whilst serving with the 9th Cheshire Regiment as solider number 24714, reaching the rank of Regimental Sergeant-Major. Harry survived the conflict and died during 1961 in Birmingham.

Horace Vernon BARNES, born at The Grove, Portland in 1883 to Jane and Richard Barnes, he is listed as a Warder at Canterbury, Kent. On census night 1891 the Barnes family is at home in The Grove, Portland. In 1909 he married Amy Maria KEMPSTER at Sculcoates, Yorkshire. He served with the Sherwood Forrester's as soldier number 6745, reaching the rank of Sergeant and was awarded the Distinguished Conduct Medal. The medal citation reads 'For gallantry and good work on reconnaissance duties near Frelingheim on 21st February 1915.' Horace died in France on the 7th May 1917.

George James J. BLANDFORD, is listed as a Warder at Portland but was born in Bromley, Kent during 1890 to Agnes. On census night 1911 George is a lodger with the Lillywhite family at 81 Easton, Portland his occupation is Clerk. Four years later, 1915 at Weymouth, George marries Mary L. WASKETT. George was promoted to Staff Captain during his service with the Royal Garrison Artillery. He survived the conflict and died in the Isle of Wight in 1967.

George Fenton BROCKELSBY, is also listed as a Warder at Portland Prison but was born in Boston, Lincolnshire during 1881 the son of Eliza. Between 1901 and 1911 George worked at various jobs on the railway in Doncaster living with wife Beatrice Lily but I have been unable to discover the date they married or her maiden name. During his WW1 service with the Royal Field Artillery as Farrier Sergeant 18454 he was awarded the Military Medal, announced in the gazette on 6th August 1918. Amongst the duties of the Farrier was dispatch injured and dying horses. George survived the war and died during 1963 in the Chichester, registration district of Sussex.

William Stuart Cooke CHICK, was born during 1881 in Melcombe Regis, Dorset the son of Ellen M. and Joseph C. Chick. The family is at Myrtle Terrace, Weymouth in 1881 and William has left home and is a lodger at the CROCKER family home in West Parade, Weymouth on census night 1901. In 1911 William is now a married man living with wife, Ellen Annis nee LONGMAN on the Isle of Wight and working as a Warder at Parkhurst Prison.

The Roll of Honour lists him as a Warder at Wormwood Scrubs Prison. During his WW1 service with the Military Mounted Police as Lance Corporal P/20907 he was awarded the Belgian Croix de Guerre and promoted to Sergeant. William died on the Isle of Wight during 1952.

Otho Richard ELLIOTT, is listed as a Warder at Portland Prison but was born in Manchester during 1878. On census night 1911 he is a married Assistant Warder living at the Grove, Portland with wife Annie Maud, nee CARTER whom he married in Weymouth during 1907. When Otho left to fight, his home was to remain in Dorset as he appears on both the 1918 and 1919 Absent Voters lists. During his service in the East Lancashire Regiment as soldier number 31559 he reached the rank of Sergeant and was awarded the Distinguished Conduct Medal. The medal citation reads: 'For conspicuous gallantry and devotion to duty. On one occasion during an attack he personally rushed an enemy post and bayoneted three of the enemy. He rendered great assistance to the platoons on both his flanks by his able co-operation and the skilful manner he directed fire to cover their advance, and his initiative and good leadership enabled his own men to inflict heavy casualties on the enemy. He was subsequently wounded but declined to leave his platoon until forced to do so, exhausted by loss of blood. He set a very fine example of courage and fortitude to all around him. 30th October 1918.' Otho died in Weymouth during 1963.

Thomas Charles Moore PHIPPEN, is listed as a Warder in Portland Prison but was born during 1885 in Swansea, Glamorganshire the son of Alma and Gilbert Phippen. In 1908 he married in Swansea Sarah Jane JONES and three years later the couple are living in Block 16E Princetown, Devon. Thomas is employed

as a Warder at the prison. The couple have three daughters including Elsie who was born in Weymouth on 26th July 1913. His military service in the 1st Battalion, Grenadier Guards as soldier number 11467 seems to have been action packed as he reached the rank of Sergeant, was mentioned in despatches and awarded both the Distinguished Conduct Medal, announced in the London Gazette on 28th January 1918, and the Military Medal on 30th October 1916.

The medal citation reads: 'For conspicuous gallantry and devotion to duty. In spite of constant shelling, by which the cable was frequently broken between Brigade and Battalion headquarters, he personally organized a party and laid five lines himself, maintaining communication at a critical time by his gallant and prompt action. On the following day he displayed similar initiative and skill in connecting up the forward companies with the Battalion Headquarters.' A closer look at his service record shows that Thomas had completed several years in the reserve before war broke out and was de-mobbed in 1920. However, when the Governor of Winchester Prison enquired of the Royal Hospital Chelsea in 1937 if Thomas Phippen was to receive a pension he was told no! Thomas Charles Moore Phippen died during 1955 in the Bridgwater registration district of Somerset.

Alfred B. WILLIAMS, is also listed as a Warder at Portland but was born on Jersey in the Channel Islands during 1879 to Matilda Angelina Williams.
On the night of Alfred's first census in 1881 his father is not present as he is employed as a Master Mariner. In 1911 Alfred and Charlotte, his wife of two years who had been born in Afghanistan, are living at Block 35E, Alma Terrace, The Grove, Portland with their son Edward; Alfred is a warder at the prison. He served in the Royal Garrison Artillery as soldier number 30736, reaching the rank of Lieutenant. Alfred died in the Bournemouth registration district of Dorset during 1935.

Frederick Richard YEOMAN, listed as a Warder at Portland was born in Canterbury, Kent the son of Mary and Frederick Yeoman during 1881. In the 1911 census Frederick is with his Battalion in India, so his first career was in the army. The following year, 1912 Frederick spends some time back in England as his marriage to Susannah BUSH in Canterbury is registered during that year. He served as soldier number S/12560 in the Seaforth Highlanders and during the First World War conflict he was mentioned in despatches. Frederick died during 1945 in the Canterbury registration district of Kent.

If you have a family member who served during the First World War please go to www.livesofthefirstworldwar and improve their record for all who are interested in reading about them.

Jo Draper

John Travell

Jo Draper, one of the best-known historians and writers about all things Dorset, died on 24 June 2017.

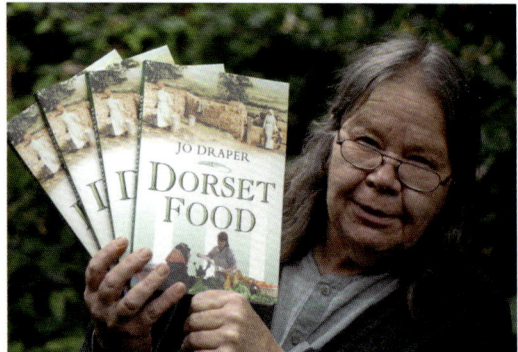

Jo was born in Hampshire in February 1949, where her family had been long established as smallholders and blacksmiths. When she was fifteen, she was persuaded to take part in an archaeological dig at Ports Down during the deep snows of the winter of 1964. She was immediately fascinated by this digging up of ancient history and artifacts and from then on she attended digs at every opportunity, to the extent that she neglected her other school subjects, which meant that she failed to qualify to go to a university. But she had already come to know the eminent archaeologist, Professor (now Sir) Barry Cunliffe of Southampton University, who was so impressed by her keenness, ability and intelligence that he became her mentor. He invited her to work with him on many of his major excavations, such as that at Danebury Hill, which she did for several years, becoming a considerable expert herself, and particularly an authority on ancient pottery and ceramics.

Jo moved to Dorset with her husband Chris Chaplin, in 1967 to work on archaeological excavations, and Chris, who was a fine artist and cartographer, became employed at the Ordnance Survey establishment in Southampton. Chris, with his long beard and bicycle, became a well-known local personality, and worked together with Jo providing maps and illustrations for a number of her books.

Jo quickly became involved in the life of the town and county. For fifteen years she edited the Proceedings of the County Museum, and worked there on medieval and post-medieval pottery for exhibitions and displays, and produced more than sixty articles and monographs. All aspects of Dorset's history and life interested her, from the Tolpuddle Martyrs and the conditions of the Dorset farm labourers and their families during the 19th Century, to Dorset food. She wrote several books about the county town, on 'Dorchester Past', 'A Dorchester Camera', and another of photos of Dorchester going back 150 years for the Archive Series. She famously collaborated with her friend John Fowles for a book on 'Thomas Hardy's England' and Fowles contributed the Foreword to her outstanding book, 'Dorset: the Complete Guide' which is a detailed, scholarly and comprehensive account of the whole county. For many years Jo was the archivist for the Lyme Regis Museum, and mounted exhibitions there on Lyme's most celebrated resident, the pioneer fossil hunter Mary Anning.

Jo and Chris were a very close couple, and Jo was deeply affected when this kind and gentle man was taken ill and after several operations was subsequently bedridden at home for many months, where he died in August 2015. He was buried at Higher Ground Meadow outside the village of

Corscombe, and this is where Jo's ashes were taken to be placed beside him on 24 July, 2017. A large number of Jo's friends and those who had known and worked with her over the years came together there to celebrate her life and to share their memories of her. Barry Cunliffe, who was unable to be present, had written a letter addressed to Jo, which was read on his behalf.

Several of those who came to know Jo in different spheres of her life, have paid their personal tributes to her. Helen Gibson, the curator of the Hardy Collection at the County Museum spoke of Jo's great contribution to local history and her particular interest in country people. "Her knowledge of both Thomas Hardy and Dorset made her an authority on both subjects. She was a most enthusiastic person and most wonderful scholar." David Burnett, the owner of the Dovecote Press, who published many of her books, said, "She was the most kind and generous person. She was always there for you." Dr. Alan Chedzoy of the Barnes Society wrote, "Somewhat eccentric in her appearance and manner, she was essentially kindly and her infectious laugh on a Dorchester street corner, will long sound in the memories of those who knew her."

A well-known figure in the town for many years, she was an active supporter of the County Museum and of the Lyme Regis Museum. Jo's enthusiasm for matters concerning Dorset was unrivalled. She is said to have published eight books on the county, mostly for the Dovecote Press. Chief among these is 'Dorset: The Complete Guide', introduced by her friend, John Fowles, with its terse but vivid descriptions of the county's landscape, architecture and history.

Fowles wrote:- "I know Jo Draper has indefatigably visited and revisited, and re-assessed, everywhere she has described in the writing of the guide; and no one has better credentials to be its author…most visitors are not serious scholars and need a concise friend…This is not simply a guide to the county; but like all good books, a guide to the greater freedom of anyone who reads it." First published in 1986, the Guide is still unrivalled. It remains by far the most authoritative account of the county and will be, as Fowles wrote, a friend for many years to come for all those who love Dorset.

Of her other publications, Thomas Hardy's England, beautifully illustrated with photographs from the nineteenth-century, provides a vivid introduction to the fast-vanishing rural society that Hardy described in his novels. For young readers who find it hard to picture that world, this book is a godsend. But Jo was never deferential even to this great man. She was quite prepared to criticise where appropriate, as in her sharp note on Hardy's 'snobbery'…(He was) '..careful to entertain his brother and sisters only when there were no 'important' guests present.'

Jo was a prolific and meticulous scholar of Dorset history. Her death, at a comparatively early age is a great loss to all who love and want to know more about our county.

I knew Jo as a neighbour and friend. She was very helpful to me with her suggestions and criticisms when I was preparing a book for publication, and I will never forget the very quick response from both Chris and Jo when my wife suddenly collapsed and I needed their help in contacting the emergency services and to get her to hospital. All those who are interested in and care about our county owe Jo a great debt of gratitude, and she deserves to be remembered by the institutions she contributed so much to, and surely has earned her own place along with Hardy, Barnes, Powys and Hutchins in the Writers' Gallery in the Dorset County Museum.

We are a Commercial and Personal Insurance Brokers based in Blandford Forum. We have 28 years experience and offer a first class personal customer service to all our clients.

 PROPERTY
- BLOCKS OF FLATS
- SHOPS
- OFFICES
- HOTELS
- PUBLIC HOUSES
- CARE HOMES
- FACTORIES
- WAREHOUSES
- MOTOR TRADE

 MOTOR
- COMMERCIAL VEHICLES
- MOTOR FLEET

 BUSINESS INSURANCES

 LIABILITIES
- CONTRACTORS/TRADESMEN
- PROPERTY
- EVENT
- PROFESSIONAL INDEMNITY
- DIRECTORS & OFFICERS
- GOODS IN TRANSIT

 PERSONAL
- KIT & CONTENTS
- HOME
- TRAVEL
- PRIVATE MOTOR FOR DIRECTORS & FAMILIES
- YACHT/BOAT
- BUY TO LET PROPERTIES
- HOLIDAY LETS

Unit 2b Clump Farm Industrial Estate, Blandford Forum, Dorset DT11 7TD.
Tel: 01258 488879 Fax: 01258 480629
www.allinsureservices.co.uk
All Insure Services Ltd is authorised and regulated by the FSA - No 568982

Hardy Annual

Helen Lange

As the ninth person to chair the Thomas Hardy Society since its foundation in 1968 and the first woman so to do, I take particular pleasure in reporting on the Society's activities for 2017, (our first Hardy Annual for a while), in the publication of The Society of Dorset Men.

Wreath Laying Ceremony at Westminster Abbey

We began the year with our annual Wreath Laying Ceremony at Hardy's grave in Poets' Corner in Westminster Abbey, to commemorate the 89th anniversary of Hardy's death on 11th January 1928. The ceremony followed its traditional pattern, beginning with a welcome from The Revd. Anthony Ball, Canon in Residence, and continuing with prayers and with readings from Hardy's work. On this occasion, for the first time, the area around Hardy's memorial stone was roped off. This had the odd effect of bringing more people, who were not Hardy Society followers, into the area – a positive outcome in terms of promoting Hardy, our principal mission. 2018, being the 90th anniversary of Hardy's death, will be one of our main aspects of celebration in what will be the 50th anniversary of the foundation of the Society in 1968.

An unusual event took place on 1st February, when we were invited to join the Dorset County Boundary Research Group, for their annual indoors event. Entitled 'Boundless Wessex', the event began with an introductory talk by Katherine Barker, co-founder of the Dorset County Boundary Group, which was followed by a presentation on the literature and landscape of Dorset and its neighbouring counties. This also examined the Thomas Hardy connections and in particular, references to Tess of the D'urbervilles and especially the area of Pentridge near Cranborne.

My predecessor as Chair of the Hardy Society, Dr. Tony Fincham, gave a talk on the Wessex of Hardy's novels and poems. In the course of his argument he provided strong evidence that the setting of the house Hardy calls 'The Slopes' in Tess of the D'urbervilles, where Tess is sent to meet the D'urberville family, is in the Boveridge area, not Pentridge. Despite this refutation of the previous speaker's argument, this session ended happily with a sociable break for coffee and much interesting conversation.

After the break we turned our attention to Hardy's poem 'The Trampwoman's Tragedy', which is set in Wynyard's Gap, a historically and geographically important place on the Dorset boundary and from where five counties can be seen. I read this ballad whilst Tony Fincham showed images appropriate to the story.

Finally, we had a fascinating presentation by Andrew Morgan, from the Boundary Group, on the way in which the boundary is walked regularly and systematically and how the research on its features and significance are explored and recorded.

Something which we had never previously done was to have a Thomas Hardy Study Day. This took place on Saturday 22nd April at the Corn Exchange in Dorchester and was the brainchild of our Student Representative, Tracy Hayes. As 2017 was the 130th anniversary of the publication of The Woodlanders, the focus was on this novel. As well as a keynote lecture, a presentation on the manuscript and papers on different aspects of the work and appropriate folk music by the 'New Hardy Players' Tatterdemalion group, there was a most interesting account of current research taking place at the Dorset County Museum on letters written to Hardy. These included the long-term correspondence with Florence Henniker, who remained a close friend of Hardy until his death. This event, having proved highly successful and popular, will be repeated annually.

The Woodlanders was celebrated not only in the Study Day, but also in two very different walks. In May we explored the Melbury Osmond area, beginning at Evershot and going on to Hintock House and Park, taking in four churches en route. In June, as part of the Birthday Weekend, we enjoyed a very gentle walk around Sherborne town, noting the several Woodlanders references, but we also visited Sherborne Old Castle, the setting for 'Anna, Lady Baxby', one of Hardy's 'Group of Noble Dames.' There was also a Portland coastal walk in July, celebrating the 120th anniversary of the publication of The Well-Beloved.

The Birthday Weekend at the beginning of June each year, celebrating Hardy's birth on the 2nd of that month, is always a major event for the Society. This year the annual Birthday Lecture, 'Landscape Painting in Hardy Country' was given by Gwen Yarker and was followed by the well-established, traditional performance by the New Hardy Players and the wreath-laying ceremonies at Hardy's statue and William Barnes' statue. On the Saturday evening we always have a social event and this year that was an entertainment created by Andrew and Marilyn Leah which also featured our Town Crier, Alistair Chisholm. The entertainment centred around Theodore Wirgman's beautiful portrait of Agatha Cox (later Thornycroft) 'her on whom I thought when I wrote Tess,' as Hardy said to Edmund Gosse.

The Sunday of the Birthday Weekend also takes a very traditional shape, with a service at Stinsford Church and a visiting preacher, who this year was the Rector of the Dorchester Benefice, Canon Thomas Woodhouse.

In September we celebrated another short story, 'A Waiting Supper', on its 130th anniversary. This story is set in Stafford House, now the home of our President, Lord Fellowes. We were privileged to enjoy not only walking to and in the park, having started from Athelhampton House, also a setting in the story, but were then generously hosted by Lady Fellowes to a champagne and cream tea. We then held our AGM in the very elegant dining room, with our President duly presiding.

Since the Dorchester Literary Festival began, in 2015, the Hardy Society has been a sponsor and has organised a Hardy event, taking the form of a panel discussion with contemporary writers. As usual Tony Fincham led that discussion. On the Sunday morning after the official end of the Festival Tony, together with Alistair Chisholm, led a Hardy Walk beginning at Max Gate.

Each year we have a Thomas Hardy London Lecture, which is sponsored by Birkbeck College. This year Mark Ford, Professor of English and American Literature at University College, London, gave the lecture, 'Thomas Hardy – Half a Londoner', which is also the title of the book he published in 2016, an excellent work which skilfully blends biography and analysis and has clearly established the importance of London in Hardy's life and work, especially his poetry.

Our final event of 2017 was 'Going the

Rounds' which we do every other year, in between the Conference years. This comprises a walk by torchlight in and around Kingston Maurward, re-enacting scenes from Under the Greenwood Tree and singing carols. The event now ends in Stinsford Church, where we manage to accommodate nearly a hundred people and where we have a Mummers Play and consume mulled wine and mince pies in this glorious setting.

Hardy's reredos design

Windsor church doorway resembling that at Max Gate

A glimpse of the reredos behind a later altarpiece

Something which goes back to 2016 but is of great importance to us, is the discovery of a hidden altarpiece designed by Hardy, a design which in living memory had never been thought to have been realised.

We were contacted by All Saints Church in Windsor to tell us that this reredos had been discovered hidden behind a 1930s rather plainer altarpiece. Fund raising was organised by the church and the Hardy Society contributed a third of the £12,000 needed. The appeal was successful and so this year the reredos has been revealed in all its ornate Victorian glory. A re-consecration of the restored altarpiece took place on 26th November, a service led by the Bishop of Reading and many Hardy Society members attended that event.

At the time of writing we are in the midst of preparing for the 50th anniversary of the foundation of the Society in 1968. This

Detail of marble in reredos

Festival and Conference will take place from 14th to 21st July, based at Kingston Maurward for the opening weekend and then at the United Church in Dorchester after that.

We have a full and varied programme of celebratory events planned and look forward to publishing those early in 2018.

The Centrepiece

A J Wakely & Sons

Family Funeral Directors
and
Monumental Mason

Established 1897

7 North Street, Beaminster	Tel: 01308 862358
91 East Street, Bridport	Tel: 01308 423726
33 Sparrow Road, Yeovil	Tel: 01935 479913
16 Newland, Sherborne	Tel: 01935 816817

www.ajwakely.com

A private family business giving personal service at all times. Please contact Clive Wakely, Simon Wakely or a member of their dedicated team for any advice or guidance.

William Barnes

by Albert Douglas Gillen

A bronze turned green as Dorset field
In church courtyard, a book does wield
It's William Barnes, off High West Street
Pray turn your head, his stare you'll meet

So close to earth, benign and kind
A man of stature, lively mind
Philologist, historian, poet, teacher
A keen musician, engraver, preacher

In plain English, or dialect
His poetry accorded great respect
Whether County, field, or village green
He vividly described the scene

Julia Miles, his supportive wife
The love of William Barnes's life
Till her last breath, she fought for him
From her death's day, his light grew dim

Good friends, William justly won
In Hardy, Arnold, Tennyson
Hopkins, Gosse, Browning, Palgrave
To his great works, respect they gave

This Dorset poet of Blackmore Vale
Throughout his life, trials did assail
Now each good school beneath the sun
Holds 'Linden Lea' to name but one

In modern times good folk do strive
To keep the famous poet alive
Chedzoy, and Laycock, do ensure
That Barnes's memory will endure.

Arthur J Hare (1855-1931)

John Dennett

A Shining Colonial Dorset

My great granduncle Arthur John Hare was born at Blandford in 1855. He was the sixth of nine children to Alfred and Maria (nee Best) Hare, who were married in 1843. The Bests from Durweston, and the Hares from northern Dorset and the Blackmore Vale, originated primarily from rural working families. From time to time however, they conducted their own operations including innkeeping and general carrying businesses.

Alfred Hare conducted a small carpentry and joinery business in Blandford. He and his wife Maria struggled to provide for their growing young family and in 1856 did what many in their position did - emigrated. Southern England in mid-Victorian times saw its generous share of rather aggressive migration agents from the colonies. With the support of the Colonial Office in London, the New World was often sold as a panacea to a gloomy future in rural parts of the south west counties as the country underwent unprecedented social change.

In 1856 the Hare family emigrated to Australia on the Plantagenet. Their fare of £54 was paid by Maria's brother George Best who along with his wife and young family had emigrated to Sydney from dire conditions in Durweston in 1849. Arthur was one year old on his arrival in Sydney. The family settled close by the Bests and had another three children after arrival.

Emigration had certainly lifted the fortunes of the Best family. After seven years working as orchardists in the Ryde district of Sydney they were able to save enough to financially sponsor the Hare family's passage. If this example of success and a better life was a motivation for the Hare family then it certainly worked. The children of Alfred and Maria Hare grew up in and about Sydney, married and had successful lives and careers. Many married and moved into rural New South Wales and their descendants grew in number and became widely scattered.

The successful life of Arthur J Hare is worthy of special mention and one can only wonder how its course may have been different had the family not emigrated. Young Arthur was a talented child and he was selected to attend the prestigious Fort Street school in Sydney The school was one of Australia's first high schools and was established in 1849 as a Model School, to serve as an exemplar for all other government schools. Many Fort Street students went on to make significant contributions to the growth of the colony and in the federation of the states to nationhood in 1901. Arthur J Hare was one of these.

On completion of his secondary school studies in 1872, Arthur at the age of 17, successfully passed a competitive examination and was recruited as a cadet survey draughtsman with the NSW Department of Lands (the equivalent to the HM Land Registry in England). NSW was at the time, and remains, the most populated state in Australia. The responsibility of the Department extended to the administration of all state land titles covering an area of approximately 310,000 square miles, more than three times the size of the United Kingdom. The sheer size of the task of surveying and draughting the countless number of small and exceedingly large parcels of land kept a growing team of survey draughtsman busy for decades.

DORSET MEN BEYOND THE SEAS.
The First Executive of the New South Wales Society of Dorset Men and Women, SYDNEY, 1912-1913.

Arthur remained with the Department of Lands all of his working life of nearly fifty years. He ultimately became head of the Department when he was appointed its Under Secretary in 1911. From his early days as a cadet draughtsman he set about learning his profession and systematically cut out an exemplary career. Within ten years he headed up his first division. He became draughtsman in charge of the Department's regional survey offices in Moree, Orange and Wagga Wagga. At the age of 46 in 1901 he was appointed the Department's chief draughtsman. He was soon elevated to the role of Inspector then Senior Inspector, assistant Under Secretary and at the age of 56 ultimately reached the top rung being appointed Under Secretary. He was now in charge of the Department he joined as a junior thirty nine years before and was directly responsible to the Minister of Lands. He remained in that position until his retirement in 1920.

In addition to an illustrious professional career, Arthur made a considerable contribution to his community in a variety of other ways. Throughout his working life and afterwards he maintained a high public profile and discharged numerous civil duties outside work. He was appointed a Justice of the Peace, was a trustee of both the Sydney Cricket Ground Trust and the National Park Trust and also managing trustee of the Northern Suburbs Cemetery in Sydney. In addition he enjoyed the role of joint editor of the NSW Government Gazette.

He lived through a momentous time, arriving in the colony 70 years after its establishment, witnessing the transition to nationhood in 1901 and the calamity of the first world war. Although born in Dorset he knew no country other than his adopted Australia. But for all this and for all his professional and civil energy, he harboured a longing for his county of birth and particularly for Dorset. In a speech he made in 1923, he said: *"I was born in Blandford... and came to NSW when very young and consequently remember nothing about the beauty of Dorset. Its flowering lanes, its beautiful fields, its quaint dialect, its literature, its great men, its war tradition are only known to me by reading and illustrations.*

I love Australia; it is the land of my adoption; the only land indeed, that I know: but I am English born - both parents were Dorsets - I have read all I can about the dear old County, and am proud of the English blood in my veins, and am prouder still of the County from which I came and which claims me as its own".

Apart from his reading, as a youngster he would have lived and breathed the life of an extended Dorset family in exile, coming to grips with the strangeness of a new world half a world away. The habits and characteristics of those family members and indeed the pervading Dorset dialect he heard every day would surely have made an impression that was to last throughout his life.

In 1911, the same year he reached the pinnacle of his profession, Arthur J Hare together with four other local Dorsets established the NSW Society of Dorset Men Beyond the Seas. The Society was granted affiliation by and with the Society of Dorset Men in London, only seven years after its own establishment. Arthur J Hare was elected the Society's inaugural President, a position he maintained for twenty years. The Society went on to become the Dorset Society of NSW and since its inauguration included men and women.

Under his Presidency the Society grew to over 220 members and flourished despite the ravishing effects of the first world war upon the new nation and indeed elsewhere. The arrival of the Year Book each year was met with great enthusiasm by the growing flock of antipodean Dorsets. Despite the war, in his 1918 annual report he states: *"The Year Book is undoubtedly a valuable asset to our Society. This year's production exceeds all expectation. Many members have expressed their pleasure in reading and have said "It is interesting from cover to cover"".*

It is comforting to know that some things remain the same, and that as his great grandnephew, I share the same sentiments one hundred years later.

During the war years the NSW Department of Lands became the subject of a prolonged controversy. As the new nation battled overseas, it also battled on the home front with the question of how to treat Australian citizens of German origin, particularly within the public service. German immigrants had played a considerable role in the expansion of the colony and many held important public positions at the outbreak of war. Their loyalty and/or sympathy to their mother country which was now at war with England, and supported by Australia, became a concern to the state and federal parliaments. The press had a field day with cartoons and running spurious stories of the Department's maps being stolen and dispatched to the enemy to assist in a possible invasion. Arthur J Hare became embroiled in a very public controversy with some Department draughtsmen of German origin who had expressed sympathy or "disloyal utterances" for their homeland. The NSW parliament exhaustively debated the issue, the Prime Minister of Australia Andrew Fisher called for the file and was briefed and the press wrung the matter out to dry. The imbroglio effectively ended when, in accordance with government policy, he dismissed a fellow draughtsman of German origin who had been a long term employee with the Department. This unwelcome incident saw the end of a colleague's career due to the expression of national pride. At the same time it involved Arthur J Hare who was just as proud of his homeland but was able to enjoy freedom of expression. On reflection this irony may not have been lost by Arthur.

I have been interested in the life of Arthur J Hare for some time and the question of whether he returned to his beloved Dorset during his busy lifetime has persisted. Recently I have, to my pleasure, discovered that he did in fact return on two occasions but not until he was aged 69 and he had retired from a busy career. In 1923 he and his wife Anne made a two month visit which was followed up the following year with a visit lasting twelve months that took them through the United Kingdom and included an extensive tour of Dorset. He was welcomed by members of the Society of Dorset Men in London on more than one occasion and attended their dinners and other functions. He loved poetry and one of the highlights of the second trip was a special performance by Walter Bawler and his party from Dorchester reciting and singing the poems of William Barnes in King George's Hall before the Society of Dorset Men in London. After the presentation the President acknowledged the presence of the Hares from Australia and *'the universality of the influence of Dorset and the pride of the homeland which Dorset people carry with them to the remotest parts of the earth"*. After some applause, Mrs Hare was presented with a bouquet. Arthur was able to pack into his return luggage a wheel of Blue Vinny which survived two months on the sea and was made available to members of the NSW Society to share (with the traditional cider) at their next function. His accomplishment as a cheese importer is no mean feat. To this day my local cheesemonger cannot secure supply of that signature treasure into Tasmania, despite his best efforts.

The post war period witnessed major changes to Australian society, again as elsewhere, and the economic conditions in the early 1930s placed further pressure upon the lives of the Society's members. The strain of maintaining what was a successful Society of like-minded Dorsets proved too much for the individual members whose priorities turned to their own lives and survival and the Society collapsed under that dreadful weight.

After a prolonged illness Arthur J Hare died in March 1931 at the age of 76. He was survived by Anne, his wife of 53 years. There were no children to the marriage. Anne was a woman of great strength and a leader in her own right. In addition to taking an active role in the affairs of the Society since inauguration, and supporting her husband through his myriad of achievements and interests, she worked tirelessly to benefit her community. She was President of the Red Cross in Sydney and personally raised large sums of money to aid soldiers returning from the war. She died in 1945 at the age of 87.

Under Secretary for Lands, Arthur Hare, c.1917

State Records NSW NRS 4481

The William Barnes Society

Brian Caddy

The William Barnes Society has enjoyed another busy and successful year with all events well attended and the busiest year to date for what the society terms its outreach events.

A members evening in March featured performances of the majority of Barnes eclogues, while in April the Society welcomed Dr Martin Dubious, lecturer of Victorian Literature at Newcastle University, who spoke on Victorian Poetry and English Dialect in Sense of the Range of dialect poetry within Barnes lifetime. We were blessed with a beautiful April morning for the Annual Service of Remembrance at St Peter's Church, Winterborne Came, conducted by Allen Knott, Licensed Lay Minister. As is the tradition, the service included Barnes poems. The selection this year was 'Vok a-comen into Church' (Devina Symes), 'The Bwoat' (Rod Drew), 'May' (David Guy), and 'The Beam in Grenley Church' (Dr Alan Chedzoy), whilst the lessons were read by Keith Hooper and Helen Gibson. Floral tributes were laid on the graves of William Barnes, and his daughter Laura by Vice President Tim Laycock and his wife Angela.

Our Summer Lunch, held this year at Cerne Abbas Village Hall, proved to be one of the best attended ever. The speaker was Rev. Jonathan Still who compared Barnes time at Cambridge University whilst studying for his degree with his own all those years later. Musical entertainment was provided by that very fine folksinger Richard Buckland.

A beautiful summer afternoon in July brought a gathering of members to Pine Lodge, Higher Bockhampton, for a cream tea, and readings.

In September, in conjunction with the National Trust at Max Gate, Tim Laycock organised the annual afternoon of Barnes poetry. Again attended by record numbers it featured the Barnes poetry which Thomas Hardy included in his published tribute to his old friend.

On October 8th the Morning Service at St Peter's Church, Dorchester, commemorated the death of William Barnes on 7th October, 1886. The service was conducted by the Rev. Claire McClelland, and Rev Richard Franklin, who in his ministry had serviced in the Blackmore Vale where Barnes was born and grew up, gave a very informative and thought provoking sermon. Chairman of the Society Brian Caddy read 'Sleep did come wi the Dew'. Following the service the floral tribute was laid at the foot of the Barnes statue by David Downton, while the St Peter's Church choir sang Vaughan Williams setting to 'Linden Lea'. Dave Burbidge closed the ceremony by reading from the inscription on the plinth of the statue the words from Culver Dell, and the Squire: -

But now I hope his kindly feace,
Is gone to vind a better pleace,
But still, wi vok a-left behind,
He'll always be a kept in mind.

Our A.G.M in October was again well attended, with musical entertainment provided by our member John Blackmore in a programme entitled 'West Country Sound and Song'.

Among a very busy year our outreach events have included talks and readings to Fordingbridge U3A, St Georges Thursday Club, and Giant Festival at Cerne Abbas, Sherborne Literary Society, Oak Fayre, Crossways Library, Bridport Stroke Club, National Trust, Dorchester Literary Festival, and an evening of entertainment at Piddlehinton Village Hall.

Dr Alan Chedzoy, Dr Sue Edney and Dr Martin Dubious all travelled to Lille University in France to contribute to a conference entitled The Meanings of Dialects in English Poetry from late 19th to 21st Century.

One of the unexpected highlights of the year was the purchase by a Dorchester book dealer of a hand written framed poem by William Barnes in Nation English titled 'Solice of the Fields'. This was performed by our secretary Marion Tait on several occasions, in all probability for the first time. The actual framed poem was sold to the Cushing Library, University of Texas in May 2017.

Meanwhile the coming year promises to be an exciting one with a full programme of events plus the release of a CD by John Blackmore featuring some of his own compositions to Barnes poetry. The launch of a new collection of William Barnes poetry selected by Dr Alan Chedzoy is also eagerly anticipated.

For all further news and details of the Society visit www.williambarnessociety.org.uk

"Headless"

Mark Vine

Most people we meet on life's path leave little or no trace, either in real terms, or, in our memories. But very occasionally, we chance across a special soul, someone so different, so extreme, that their memory is etched into our hearts forever. Headless was one of those. He wasn't a Dorset man and he wasn't the most openly friendly person around either, but if he tolerated you, and you really needed help, he'd usually help you. If you needed your ego massaging, you'd best steer clear of 'Headless'. He was honest to a fault, right up to the point that many would consider rude and insulting. It was never a careless, unthinking or clumsy rudeness however; Headless was too sophisticated for that. It was far more controlled. A carefully selected observation or remark, wrought in a razor-sharp intellect, an aural exocet, faultlessly delivered with precise timing and tone, and always, always controversial.

I was privileged enough to know him for about twelve years, and during those halcyon times, I learned more about the countryside, the tides, history and human nature than I ever have, before or since. He was a tall, blonde, fierce looking Oxfordshire man, then in his mid forties with a full yellow/grey beard, a Viking in oilskins. His considerable and complicated character was a hybrid somewhere between James Robertson Justice and Jeremy Paxman, a formidable, opinionated and argumentative one-off.

We shared the same interest, metal detecting, and this inevitably brought us together after a chance meeting in the local library where Headless was looking for a book on the ceramics of Pablo Picasso. When I asked him why, he informed me that he had recently purchased a pot at auction and believed it to be made by the prodigious little Spaniard, and therefore worth a small fortune. He couldn't find an appropriate book to check his theory but just shrugged and said, "Oh well it's probably for the best". "Why"? I puzzled. He breathed in sharply and replied in a strong but resigned tone, "Well, if I'm not sure about it, I can carry on believing that I'm a rich man can't I".

I didn't know it then, but this was a typical Headless remark. His wonderfully inconcentric logic was, during the next few years, going to provide me with a wealth of similar quotes to commit to memory, voiced thoughts that on first airing sounded somewhat bizarre, but, usually contained more than an element of wisdom if one was willing to search hard enough for it and to view life from his somewhat offbeat angle. In his words I soon became his 'apprentice'. And we'd often venture out for the day in his distinctive little yellow and white van, off in to the peerless Dorset countryside in pursuit of our hobby, which as any aficionado will tell you, soon becomes an obsession. Headless loved old and ancient metalwork. Celtic, Roman, Saxon, Medieval, he craved it all if it was of acceptable quality.

This passion gave rise to the nickname that he was called at this time. The moniker 'Headless' came later as we shall discover, but in the early 1980s he was widely known as 'Mad Richard'. His unashamedly quirky manner alone could easily have spawned this less than flattering title, but in fact he got it because of his rather strange habit of exchanging artefacts that he desired and which were found by other detectorists, for the exact weight of the object in gold rings! These rings he would find with consummate skill at low tide on the numerous South Dorset beaches that became his hunting ground.

It didn't particularly matter to Headless what the objects were worth, if he liked them, he simply had to possess them and loved to marvel at the workmanship and technique involved in their making. He understood it. There seemed to be an unseen bond spanning the centuries between the ancient craftsman who created the piece, and this uncommon 20th century loner.

He was by necessity a beachcomber, one of a gaunt, driven breed of men who tirelessly scoured the seas off Dorset's beaches with their detectors, reaping a very lucrative golden harvest from the property lost by bathers in the waist-deep waters a few yards from shore. Rings very often detach themselves because the finger shrinks very slightly in cold water and the ring then slides off without being missed until it's too late.

He became such a proficient exponent of this art, working the various holiday haunts between Boscombe pier and Weymouth that he always had an excess of bullion with which to indulge his collecting passion. Each tourist year of course, this resource was renewed in time for the season of storms that followed. But of course, if the owners ever wanted their property back, then they could have it … for a price.

Accompanying him on one of his beach expeditions was a real education. Over the years Headless had honed his knowledge of wind and tide to such a degree that he intuitively knew when the optimum searching times were, and where best to maximise his chances of good finds depending on wind direction. He was also emphatic when it came to timing. If he said he would pick me up at eight minutes past nine, then that is exactly when he would appear. And if he then decreed that we would be leaving the first stretch of sands at 10:14 am to drive to another beach a few miles further along the coast, and arrive there at 10:32 am, then rest assured that is the precise time that those events would occur. Not a moment before, nor one minute after! Headless had become such a master of his art that he would even predict how many gold rings he would find on any given beach, and also what carat they were likely to be. And Headless was seldom wrong.

He always worked both sets of spring tides irrespective of what time of the day or night they occurred or how inclement the weather was. One was just as likely to see him gliding methodically through the swell at 3am as 3pm. The season for searching was roughly from September to April and the dramatic winter storms could be a beachcombers best friend if the wind was in the right direction, i.e. blowing off of the beach and out to sea. This would generally ensure that the tide stayed out a little longer, producing precious extra minutes in which Headless could ply his trade, searching the various gullies that the elements had fashioned into the seabed, before it finally turned and forced him reluctantly back to shore. Circular objects such as gold rings roll in the surf and currents, blundering straight in to these heaven-sent traps to be buried, awaiting the arrival of Headless, this 'hi-tech Neptune' of the Dorset coastline.

So complex was his character that he always refused to accept any donation from myself to help towards his petrol costs, saying that my extra weight in his vehicle actually meant that he used less petrol than if he were riding in it alone! It is a concept that I could never really get my head around, but, that was Headless for you and I never thought to question his knowledge.

One incident in particular though brought his idiosyncrasies in to sharp focus. One extremely stormy day in Weymouth, we were busy getting kitted up against the elements, taking what little shelter we could from the opened back door of his van, when I suddenly discovered that I had somehow broken a crucial component of my metal detector, namely the lid of the battery compartment. Without this, any ensuing rain or spray from the waves would certainly be able to seep in to the electrics and seriously damage the machine.

"I suppose you'll want to be borrowing some black tape to secure the top", droned Headless without even looking my way. "Well yeah, thank you", I replied. He slowly held out his hand, but as I reached for the 'lifesaving' roll, he quickly retracted it. A cat-like smugness spread across his face and in the same unemotional tone he casually announced, "That'll be £2.50 please". I laughed, but even as I did so, I knew that he meant it. "But I only need six inches of tape, not the whole roll", I whined. "That's right, £2.50 please", came the unsympathetic reply. I stared at my companion in pained disbelief, and then at the inviting shoreline that held so much promise of gold. "Well do you want it or not"? sighed Headless impatiently. Grudgingly, I delved in to my pocket and produced the necessary coinage. He nonchalantly tossed my hard-earned coins, gleaned from another beach on the previous day, in to his 'rubbish box', a kind of halfway house for the numerous non-gold items that he found each week, and said blandly… "Perhaps that'll teach you to come out well prepared in the future"… …
 … … It did.

How a man could, over the years, refuse what amounts to hundreds of pounds worth of petrol money in one breath and then turn around and charge £2.50 for a then 30p roll of tape is beyond comprehension, it was just the way he was and personally I wouldn't have had it any other way. But he did have a softer side too.

Soon after I met him in the early 1980s he suddenly turned up on my doorstep one day and sheepishly handed my wife, who is now a professional artist, a large carrier bag. As she peered inside, her jaw dropped open. It contained about £70 worth of brand new oil paints, acrylics, watercolours and brushes, a considerable amount in those far off days. She immediately said that she couldn't possibly accept such a gift, but Headless wouldn't hear of it and as he, almost apologetically made his excuses to leave added, "I've had a very good week on the beaches, and anyway, don't think that you're getting them for nothing, I want you to do me a little painting". The subject? What else but his favourite beach, Shell Bay at Studland.

By 1986 I had been working for almost three years as a field archaeologist with the local museum unit in Poole. This definitely did not sit well with Headless who considered all archaeologists to be pseudo academics and a drain on local council funds. In fact he thought that all of them should be immediately sacked and that they should "all be made to go out and get proper jobs". I could understand his animosity in one way as for many years those inside the closeted world of archaeology had wasted no opportunity whatsoever to decry and dishonour the hobby of metal detecting, which they viewed as nothing more than legalised theft and vandalism and Headless took this very much to heart, giving as much respect in turn as he received from them.

My unit were excavating a town site that used to be an old iron foundry near Poole Quay. Beneath it, all manner of archaeological treasures were coming to light. Foremost among these was an entire fourteenth century boat, in pieces. It had been left almost like a 'flatpack', under the shallow waters of what was then an inlet with a beach and boatyard. The timbers were apparently submerged as part of the medieval construction process, swelling the pieces to enable the shipwrights to fit them together more snugly.

Poole at that time was the homeport of the infamous Dorset pirate and adventurer, Harry Paye, a man who had no greater pleasure in life than to harass, board, plunder and if he could, steal any French or Spanish vessel that he chanced upon. The French and Spanish understandably took exception to young Harry's excesses and mounted a small 'armada' against the little seaport of Poole, and eventually after a hard fight, burned much of it to the ground killing, among others, Harry's brother in the melee. But they didn't catch Harry who, soon after, was back doing what he did best. The timbers of the boat that my unit had discovered had lain just under the water whilst this carnage ensued all around and were subsequently forgotten about in the panicked aftermath of the raid, until finally being rediscovered by us in 1986.

Any archaeological dig in a town naturally attracts the attention of the local populous, and this one was no exception. Unfortunately, it also attracted someone else! At the time I was busy working alone, finishing off the site plans at our previous dig, a Roman fort and Bronze Age cemetery in the countryside on the northern edge of Canford Heath, midway between Wimborne and Bournemouth. Sadly the area was earmarked for gravel extraction, and so with time at a premium, I was rarely able to get to the new site. The paradox being, that without the gravel extraction, there would have been no dig in the first place.

Occasionally though, reports reached me from Poole of a bleak spectral figure that had appeared on most days and had taken to wandering up and down along the perimeter fence muttering and cursing at the diggers. Once the site supervisor had given me a description of the 'apparition', my heart sank. "He's a tall chap, a bit like a tramp and quite fierce looking, blonde beard and moans and swears a lot".

That night, a phone call to Headless soon confirmed what I already knew to be true. He sounded very pleased with himself and took great delight in describing how he had been putting the diggers off their stroke. "Well, someone's got to make sure that they're doing their jobs properly and not wasting the taxpayers' money", he purred. The next time that I saw the supervisor I confessed that I knew the 'moaning phantom of the perimeter fence' and that if he actually took the time to engage it in conversation, he'd discover that he was quite a nice bloke, despite himself and even knowledgeable. The supervisor, an amiable little Welshman, took my advice and when Headless next resumed his 'haunting', he wandered over and introduced himself.

"I believe that we have a mutual friend", the Welshman started to say mentioning my name, but that was as far as he got. Headless merely stopped him in mid sentence saying firmly , "I don't have friends, only acquaintances" and with that turned on his heel and walked briskly away leaving the 'boy from the valleys' the way Headless left most people, open mouthed and staring in disbelief!

I did once manage to score something of a victory against him as far as archaeology was concerned, or at least an honourable draw. Looking through an old journal one day I was amazed to see a record of someone reporting the finding of several pieces of Roman pottery to the local museum. The address was Headless's house, which was built over a Roman road, and the name of the finder was the man himself. I photocopied this and sent it to him anonymously with just one word written on it, 'colaborator' . The next day we were due to go out to a beach, but Headless was strangely silent, a silence that grew in intensity as the journey progressed. Eventually he spoke, but only briefly… "There are actually two Ls in collaborator", he sighed. I tried to keep a dignified silence, but the equaliser had already been scored.

When the beaches were unavailable to us because of neap tides or the fact that wind and tide had combined to deposit too much sand offshore, thus burying the gold treasure we sought, we would travel inland to search the ploughed fields of Dorset, a brand of detecting that I personally preferred because the finds were invariably many centuries old, unlike most of those from beach detecting which were usually modern by comparison. As I mentioned, Headless was a mine of information about ancient artefacts, but also he had an extensive understanding of farming. He grew up on a farm and therefore knew how best to talk to farmers in their own language and they for their part appreciated it and responded by giving us plenty of fields to search. He also used to further endear himself to them by buying any produce that they might be selling and insisting that I did likewise.

But even in the tranquil pleasantness of the most beautiful County in Britain, Headless still kept up his never-ending war on archaeology and its minions. Several months in advance of a new road or bypass being built, he would always ensure that he had obtained written permission from the contractors to search the spoil heaps created by the upheaval, for any artefacts that might have been uncovered. When the work finally started, archaeologists were invariably present on a watching brief, closely observing what the JCBs were revealing for any signs of archaeological features they might uncover as the stratigraphy was stripped away layer by layer. Headless would then take great delight in parading up and down on top of the spoil heaps provocatively swinging his metal detector until one of the archaeologists inevitably questioned his legality to be there. Some were more 'bolshie' than others and these individuals came in for a particularly torrid time from the acid tongue of Headless, who always finished off with an artistic flourish of his written permission which came as an incontrovertible coup de gras to the engagement.

Headless later became quite a celebrity in the wider world of metal detecting. There are two monthly publications dealing with the ever popular hobby and one of these, 'The Searcher', were very happy to pay our hero handsomely for a yearly beachcomber's diary which they duly published in twelve interesting, informative and ultimately hilarious parts. In them Headless wrote about his finds for each day of the month, how he found them, the equipment he used, much of which he designed and built himself, and also and most importantly, his thoughts about the people he encountered and the world in general. Of course being Headless, a secretive and private man, he did not want his true identity known, and so all of the photographs that he sent in to illustrate his articles, first had to be 'doctored'. To this end, in those far off, pre-computer and photo-shop days, he simply cut the head from each one that contained an image of his face. The editor, with neither a name nor a face and, at a loss as to whom to attribute the articles, stared in bewilderment at the photos, but was then blessed with a moment of inspiration. He decided to publish them under the pseudonym of 'The Headless Hunter', and so, a metal detecting legend was born.

The column, sometimes three or four pages long each month, became, not surprisingly in view of its author, both infamous and controversial. Headless wrote it in exactly the same way that he spoke, and some subscribers simply couldn't handle that kind of honesty at all. Some wrote letters to the editor demanding that this crazy person be removed from its pages forthwith, while others, with a bit more about them, idolised him and hung on his every written word.

One of the things that the whingers complained most about was the fact that in the summer months Headless used to get to a popular nearby holiday beach very early in the morning to search the dry sand and 'hoover up' any coins or jewellery that may have been dropped the night before, during the numerous beach parties that occurred there. This deed was not the real source of contention however. What annoyed some readers was that Headless, having scoured the sands, would then place a sign on his windscreen advertising the fact that he would be willing to sell his pre-purchased, all day parking space for £5, (original price at that time, £1.50) to any holidaymaker desperate enough to want it.

Occasionally he would even conduct an auction right there in the car park in the event of more than one 'customer'. To me this was a perfectly sensible thing to do if you had the front to do it, and Headless most certainly did. And as he himself pointed out, it was normal to see three-mile traffic queues waiting for hours just to get vehicular access to the car park of this particular beach, so popular was it. Well-off tourists such as van loads of young surfers would consider themselves fortunate to be able to secure a spot right next to the beach wall, where they could easily unload their boards etc straight on to the golden sands of Shore Road at Sandbanks, even for more than three times the normal parking fee. Also, this money would then enable him to be able to take an 'acquaintance' all the way to Weymouth and back for nothing!

Plenty of other things from his articles also gave the moaners ample ammunition. Headless, worried that there were not enough pound coins being lost in the sand for him to find, had several hundred small stickers printed with the words 'Pound coins when dropped in the sand are impossible to find'. He stuck these on posts, railings and car park ticket machines etc, at all of his beaches, (he considered them HIS beaches and didn't really like to see any other detectorists on them) The logic of this behaviour being that, human nature being what it is, people would then read the stickers and immediately take out a pound coin and bury it in the sand, only to find, that yes indeed it is almost impossible to retrieve them without the aid of a metal detector. Headless maintained that after this superbly devious exercise in mind gaming, his finds rate did rise substantially. He also advised readers on how he ensured that he got something for his time. More often than not when searching a summer beach, someone would always approach him and ask if he would search for a lost item, some piece of gold jewellery, a ring, necklace or bracelet, lost in the deep dry sand. Headless's technique was to first ask the panicking holidaymaker where exactly they thought they had lost the item. That done and the spot firmly fixed in his mind, he would then enquire whether or not there was a reward for the recovery and then arrange the price, usually about one tenth of the retail value, gold prices being something that he was always particularly aware of. If the person then refused to negotiate, it was of little concern to Headless, who already new roughly where the object was hiding and would simply return later to recover it after the disgruntled holiday maker had vacated the beach! Harsh? It depends on your point of view. He treated the hobby as a business and while he was searching on someone else's behalf he would not be earning money for himself, unless there was a reward involved.

Sometimes these searches could take a considerable time, especially if the person losing the item was mistaken in where they thought they had lost it and, as he pointed out, if they refused to pay a small fee to get the object back, then it couldn't really have meant that much to them in the first place. All of this was obviously grist to the mill for his detractors who claimed that he was bringing the hobby in to disrepute, but his fans just could not get enough of his anarchic wit and behaviour, and I was very firmly numbered amongst them.

He even spawned adoring imitators. Soon, another diarist hit the pages of 'The Searcher', 'The Legless Hunter', who wrote of his never-ending quest to actually find and meet his hero, Headless. A thankless and fruitless task, if he but knew it as Headless never once divulged even which County he operated in, much less which beaches he frequented. A fact, which presumably drove poor old 'Legless' to drink, in his frustration!

His detractors though, didn't know the man as I did. They never saw the ill-disguised look of kindness on that weather-beaten old face, as he handed out silver rings to the plethora of kids that used to follow behind him on the sands like seagulls chasing a fishing boat. They never saw the look of contentment spread across those same craggy features as he stared in wonder at yet another prismed sunrise… And they never knew that instead of pocketing the hundreds of pounds that he earned for his writings, he told the editor to donate it all to a children's charity instead …. That was the kind of man my 'acquaintance' was.

The Last Sunrise:
In 1988 he was the best man at my wedding and in 1993 I moved from Poole to Weymouth. Through all of the years that I knew him, he was plagued with the misfortune of having a wife who was a paranoid schizophrenic. This was obviously not the fault of the poor woman herself, but probably went some way towards explaining his somewhat odd, almost nihilistic outlook on life.

I remember him once confiding to me that he fully expected to "wake up one morning with my throat cut". His wife was quite often confined to a special hospital in an effort to keep her illness in check but she then used to occupy her time by incessantly phoning him up, ten to twenty times a day, accusing him of the most ridiculously ludicrous things. His constant companion at home was a little Cavalier King Charles Spaniel, whom he idolised, but sadly, near the end of 1993, this little dog was killed by a car on the busy road outside of his home and Headless was heartbroken, although he did his best to hide it of course. Headless was 'old-school'.

One bright and very cold January day in 1994, I was walking along the Esplanade at Weymouth and, looking out to sea, I saw a familiar lone figure silhouetted against the chilly horizon. He was wading waist deep through the waves in his familiar, unhurried fashion with his self-designed sand scoop perched on his shoulder. Noting that the tide had turned, I knew that he would soon be heading back to shore and so I waited, eager to drink in some sadly-missed wisdom from a man whose company I had sorely lacked since moving the year before. We talked for a while about recent finds we'd made and hopes for the future, but I noticed there was something in his manner, something not quite right. Putting it down to the inclement weather and that for once he hadn't found any gold that day, I wished him good hunting and bade him farewell, little knowing that this was destined to be the last time that I would ever speak to this very special human being. When once more I reached the Esplanade, I glanced back across the lank, desolate sands and watched him for a while, before finally turning to go on my way. Small but distinct in the middle distance, Headless was doggedly trying his luck along the shoreline before calling it a day. I smiled to myself and turned away.

In February 1994 I was due to make a rare return to Poole and started to phone Headless to see if I could visit him when I got there. Half way through dialling though, I gave up, convincing myself that it was no use, and that even if he was in, he would only think it was his wife calling and, as usual, would not bother to pick up the phone. It was the worst decision of my life.

One week later I received a message from a fellow detectorist in Poole, informing me that Headless had taken his own life. He had apparently filled a bath with water, neatly folded a duvet and placed it on the floor next to the bath. He then removed his socks and shoes, rolled up his trouser legs, lay down on the duvet and, lifting his legs over the bath, immersed his feet in the water. He then deliberately pushed a live hot air paint stripper in to the bathwater, thereby putting an end to his very special, but seemingly very sad and troubled life. Headless had just had enough I suppose.

The inquest which I attended brought in a verdict of "suicide, whilst the balance of his mind was disturbed". The Coroner further noted that on the body, a large bag of gold rings had been found in one pocket. Grave goods?

Would it have made any difference if I had completed my phone call of the week before? Would Headless have picked up the phone and, would I have noticed that he was troubled and have been able to offer some kind words that may have calmed his self-destructive hand? Possibly, who knows? If I had, it certainly wouldn't have made matters any worse than they obviously were, and who knows, it might have made a big difference. That is something I have always had to live with and ponder ever since.

Headless was never really one who showed very much emotion, and would rarely mention his own troubles, even when encouraged by me to do so. Perhaps he just desperately needed someone to talk to at that time…but had no one.

Others who knew him have disagreed with me, but, I am very sure of one thing, a man who always planned everything so meticulously, and whose whole way of life had evolved around the application of electricity and water, had merely chosen to ritualistically leave this sad, sick world behind, using those very same two elements, a world that really would be so very much the poorer for his absence, and in his pocket, the means to pay the Ferryman.

If there is a heaven then it would be nice to think that Headless was up there somewhere in beachcombers' paradise, where every signal comes up as shining and as gold as every sunrise… … and all the seagulls are lousy shots.

One thing is very certain however, we shall never ever know the like of my 'acquaintance' again.

There was and could only ever be….. one Headless.

WW2 Plane Found Off Chesil Beach

Selwyn Williams

Chesil Beach is a volatile entity that changes with whatever weather nature throws at it. Each year a certain area of pebbles would be pulled out underwater after a storm and expose more of any wreckage. The changes were never uniform along the beach however in 1980 there was a very strong gale and the waves broke throughout the length of the beach, about a hundred yards off the shore. This unusual maelstrom caused pebbles to be picked up off the seabed and thrown further on shore than usual resulting in a whole swathe of the seabed being denuded of pebbles exposing the underlying solid clay bottom. The swathe was about 40 feet wide and centred at about the 40 feet depth. The adjacent areas of seabed inwards to the beach and further out had also lost a lot of the depth of pebbles leaving just a thin layer.

Where I had previously seen the odd anchor sticking out near the wreckage of a ship, now there were several exposed that I had never seen and a large part of the side of the iron ship ran towards the shore like the wing of a plane. I had also found previously unseen cannons lying on the clay.

One night in September 1980 I was doing an evening solo drift dive further along the swathe of clay towards Portland to see what other wreckage had been exposed. I drifted with the strong tide parallel to the beach towards Portland but not too far off the bottom purposely disturbing it with my fins. Visibility was only ever at best about 30 feet in each direction so as well as scanning visually side to side; I used the fact that any fish on nearby wreckage detecting this disturbed water would swim towards me thinking it was a source of food. All I then had to do was lie flat, wait and then follow them back and as you got nearer, the shoal of fish would become more abundant and then you would see the wreckage.

Sure enough after a fairly long swim I suddenly saw small fish where I had never found any wreckage before and I waited on the bottom then followed them back and the fish got bigger and the shoal became denser then all of a sudden out of the gloom ahead I could see a shadow coming up standing proud of the bottom. What was it? It was indeed some sort of wreckage and I managed to swim up and over the obstacle as the tide swept me towards it and as I did so I turned and grabbed hold of something to stop me being swept past it.

As I settled down on the bottom and let my breathing ease I could see it was a plane. I had strayed further out than the clay-only swathe onto the deeper seabed that still

Underneath wings showing wheel retracted

had a thin layer of pebbles. The plane was upside down with a wheel, with a seemingly inflated rubber tyre, still pulled up inside each wing and then I noticed twin machine guns in both wings. The nose was buried in the pebbles because of the weight of the engine and I had grabbed hold of one of the engine's two glycol radiators, which would have hung below the engine, but now stood proud of the seabed.

The fuselage was broken off behind the wing with quite a few tangled pieces of wire there; presumably they would have moved the ailerons. There was a large metal plate underneath the rear of the wing again presumably behind the pilot's seat in the buried cockpit. I looked around the remains of this plane and made a sketch on my diving slate then it was swim straight in to the beach to get some marks on the beach to be able to find it again.

Fuselage broken off behind wing showing pilot protection plate

When I went to work the next day I mentioned what I had found to one of my older colleagues and he turned out to be an expert on planes. I believed it was a World War 2 plane. I described the way the wheels and legs of the landing gear lay with the wheel towards the front of the wing and the strut or oleo going perpendicular to the wing, towards the rear of the wing. Most planes landing gear opened along the line of the wing, for example a Hurricane's wheels lay outwards toward the wing tips while a Spitfire's lay inwards towards the fuselage. He said there were only two planes with such landing gear that I described. It could be a P40 or a Corsair. "Did it have gull wings?" he asked. I said no they were flat so it was a P40.

As well as diving more and more on the wreck of the aircraft I started researching aircraft wrecks off Chesil Beach and looking in to history of the P40. There were various types, P40A, B and C and later ones. A & B only had one machine gun in each wing and did not have self sealing rubber over the wing fuel tanks that I had found on the wreck's tanks. Neither did they have a bullet proof back plate behind the pilot, the same plate I had found behind and under the wing.

Port machine guns

We spent a lot of time diving on the cannons wreck site but occasionally we dived on the plane wreck. One time we tied the boat onto the oleo, the leg of the landing gear. My friend Les was on the wreck when he suddenly saw the landing gear operating. The wheel was lifting up because the tide had come in and the boat was pulling it up but as it did so the gear was turning to align the wheel forward and aft for the first time in nearly 50 years. Les quickly relocated the rope to the boat. This was an example of the high quality materials this American built Curtis P40 was made from. I cracked the thin layer of crud off the oleo and it revealed a stainless steel mirror finish. A lot of ammunition chutes in the wings were stainless steel and were marked H81 confirming it was a P40.

For over ten years I tried to identify the individual aircraft but I could find no details of a plane crashing there save for one local fisherman saying a Spitfire went down thereabouts in November 1941 and I also remembered another fisherman saying there was a wreck of an American aircraft nearby. In 1992 the details of a series of aircraft types were published and all P40s were included in the book. I swiftly scanned the pages and sure enough there it was, a P40 numbered AH845, that had crashed off Chesil Beach during a training flight but the pilot was picked up by Seaplane tender ST 480 standing by the firing range off Chesil Beach.

P40s with French markings

What I didn't know was earlier versions of the P40 had been upgraded so where I thought it was a P40C it was indeed an earlier mark. The pilot was PO Harold Fraser English of 400 RCAF squadron, who had crashed into the sea on 8th November 1941. At last I could go through the RAF records and hopefully trace the pilot and present a trophy from his plane to him. Back came the records of the plane and of

Seaplane Tender ST 480 from Lyme Regis (Courtesy of Lyme Regis Museum)

The plane was a P40 Mark I Tomahawk, a P40B and it and 229 others were originally ordered by the French but with the fall of France they were diverted to the RAF so it had lots of French equipment, then other British equipment was added, all on top of its US origins. It also had several components revealing its common lineage with the previous Curtiss Mohawk radial engined fighter as there are several H75 (Mohawk model) and/or H81 marks on things like ammunition magazines and foot pedals.

PO Harold Fraser English

Pilot Officer English. Unfortunately it was not to be as he had been shot down off Etaples on the 13th December 1941 and reported as missing in action, again in a 400 RCAF squadron's P40. I tried to trace his family and left posts on Canadian War sites but without success.

I had advertised for help in possibly raising the aircraft once we knew there was no body on board and I had a response from an aircraft restorer who wanted it raised to give him patterns to rebuild a P40, as blueprints were no longer available for legal reasons. He paid us to undertake a survey of the wreck and wanted us to raise it as soon as possible so in 1993 I got in touch with the RAF to get permission to do so. That autumn we cleared the wings of pebbles ready to fit strops underneath the wings and the builder was ringing every week to see how things were progressing but the permission finally arrived after the winter gales put diving off until 1994.

I had arranged for a local salvage company of divers to handle the lift and the American had agreed to pay for them and a salvage vessel as well as us. We had a window of opportunity as the divers and salvage vessel were available on the weekend of the 50th commemorations of D Day, which also seemed apt for the WW2 plane to emerge from the depths. I kept emailing and phoning the American but there was no response.

What I didn't know was that because of Gorbachev's Glasnost, the P40s that had been lent to the Russians during the war and had since been abandoned on the ice were virtually intact apart from the engines having been removed. Tom had gone to Russia and he and others had several crated up and flown back to America.

With no news from him I told the divers and boat owner that there was no money but some of the divers and the boat owners were interested in the project so we went ahead. However when I went to buoy it the day before, the wings had gone. Obviously, lightened when we removed the pebbles from them the year before, a trawler must have caught the wings and pulled them off and dropped them in a spoil ground. Despite this further setback the lift went ahead.

The list of recoverigine areas included the two Glycol radiators we had removed previously, a British ICI fire extinguisher, some stainless steel 303 machine gun shell ejection chutes marked H75, electrics and some British broad arrow marked switches, the engine with engine mount plus the other engine mount, joy stick, instrument panel with the instruments. We recovered one set of engine exhaust stubs as well.

P40 Allison engine with one engine mount

We also recovered the rudder pedal marked H75, which was the identification plane number for the Curtiss Mohawk, (Hawk 75). The Tomahawk H81 (Hawk 81) was the successor to the radial engined Curtiss Mohawk plane but obviously used some of the same parts to speed up delivery during wartime.

These were all conserved and were later displayed in Weymouth Museum but I wanted to complete the story and find out more about PO English and 400 Squadron of the Royal Canadian Air Force. I found reference to him on the WW2 memorial and posted on the Squadron's web page but it wasn't until 2017 that his great-nephew Fraser Ash contacted me. His grandfather was Harold Fraser English's older brother who had flown DC3 aircraft during the war and Harold's other brother was a leading aircraftman. Fraser Ash sent me a wonderful treasure of photos and family details and I was able to reciprocate with underwater and other photos and information about his Great Uncle.

P40 showing 2 glycol and 1 lower oil radiators under the nose

I found out that the 'The Fighter Collection' at Duxford had taken delivery of a P40C and that was what the upgraded Mark 1 Tomahawk would have looked like, so I visited there to compare our salvaged items.

So we now had the full story and this was shared with 400 RCAF Squadron's Museum and in this Year Book. A full exhibition regarding his P40 aircraft and Harold Fraser English's history will be displayed at the Old Town Hall sometime in the next few months. The only thing still to be revealed is where his last aircraft remains off the French coast are, but PO Harold Fraser English is remembered at the Runnymede Memorial.

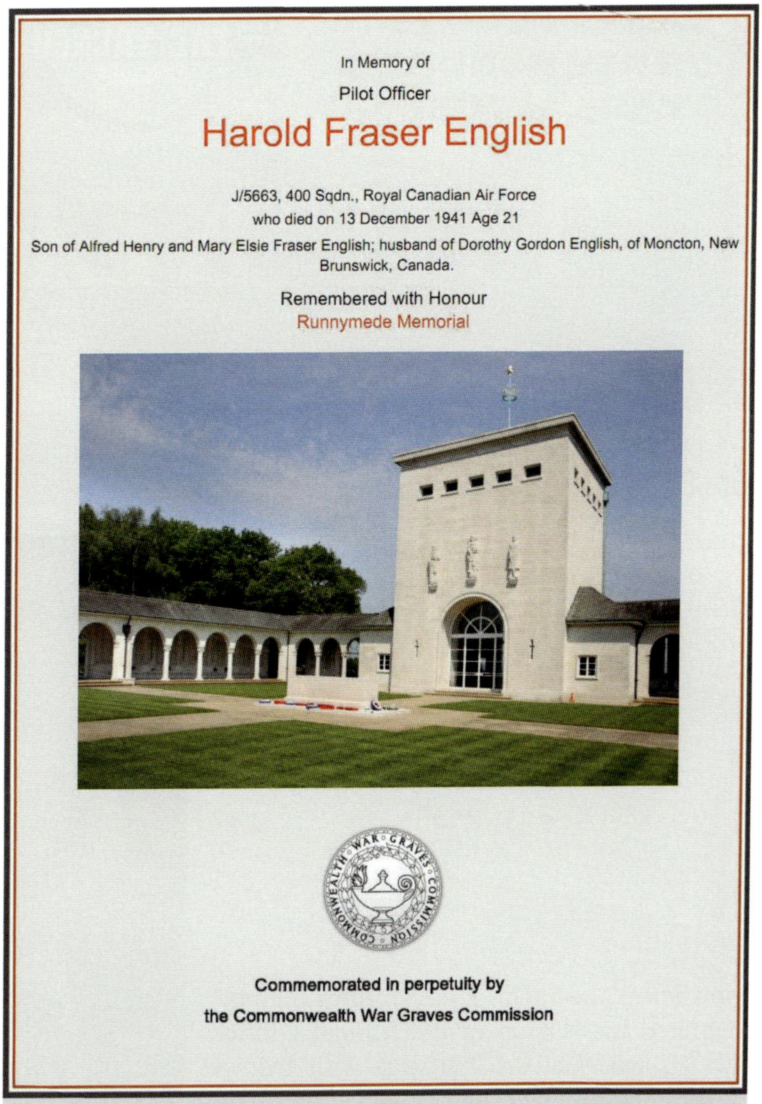

In Memory of
Pilot Officer

Harold Fraser English

J/5663, 400 Sqdn., Royal Canadian Air Force
who died on 13 December 1941 Age 21
Son of Alfred Henry and Mary Elsie Fraser English; husband of Dorothy Gordon English, of Moncton, New Brunswick, Canada.

Remembered with Honour
Runnymede Memorial

Commemorated in perpetuity by
the Commonwealth War Graves Commission

Runnymede memorial

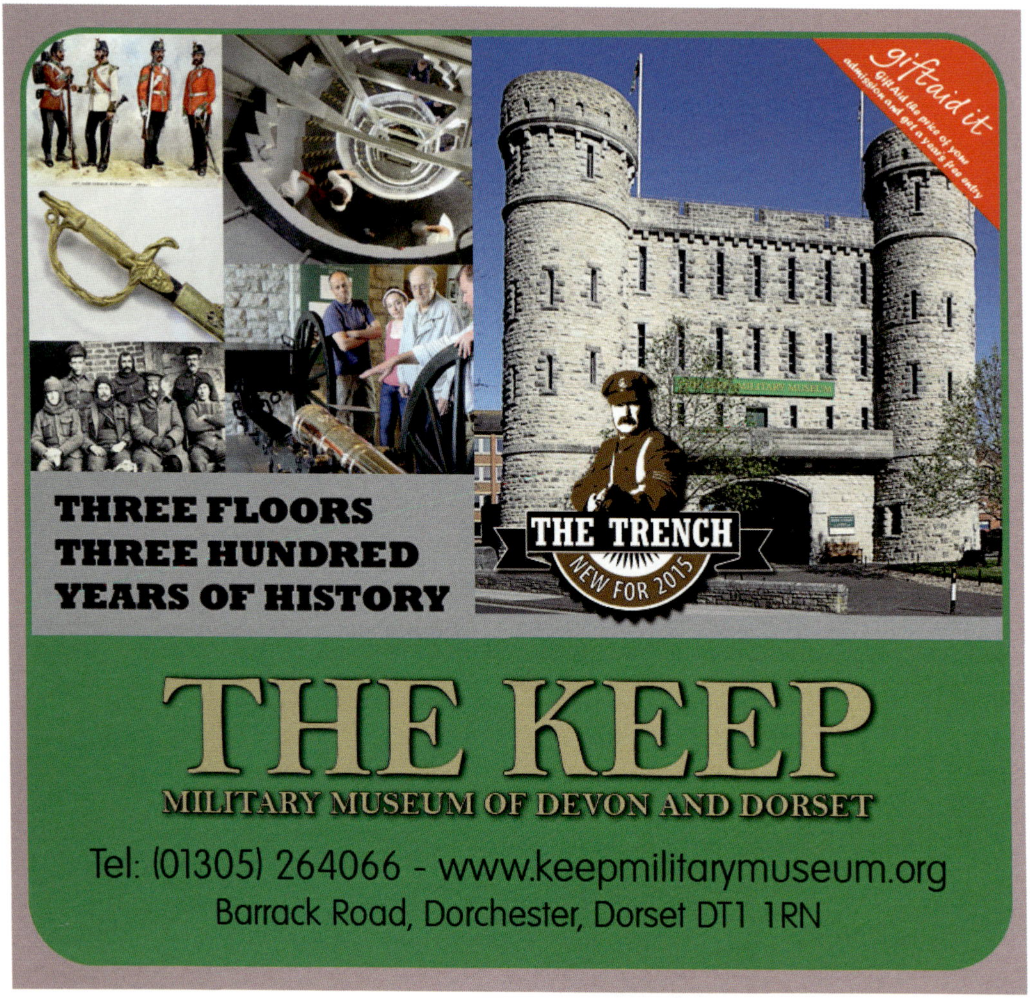
giftaid it
Gift Aid the price of your admission and get a year's free entry
THREE FLOORS
THREE HUNDRED
YEARS OF HISTORY
THE TRENCH
NEW FOR 2015
THE KEEP
MILITARY MUSEUM OF DEVON AND DORSET
Tel: (01305) 264066 - www.keepmilitarymuseum.org
Barrack Road, Dorchester, Dorset DT1 1RN

ORIGINAL WHITE
MOORES
DORSET KNOB
BISCUITS
BADGER

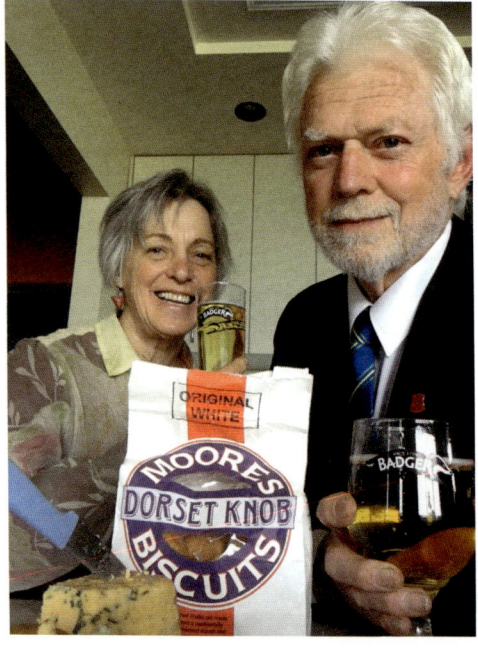

Contributor and SoDM Member John Dennett celebrated his version of the Annual Dinner with his wife Gail in Tasmania with Dorset Knobs, Badger Beer and a substitute Blue Vinny. See Page 31.

Colmer vs Cumulus

by Chris Slade

Don't you threaten me you bank of cloud.
I was here for years before you came;
Topped off with a tuft of trees so proud.
Unlike you, I've even got a name.
Colmer's Hill's the name I proudly bear.
Colmer was the parson hereabouts.
No more than he will I heed thund'rous shouts.
Get on your way, you wet amorphous blob!
Moisten me with rain and I'll not care:
Wrap me in your blanket –I'll not sob.
Even blast with thunder if you dare.
On second thoughts, I'll maybe ask you please,
Don't blow down or lightning strike my trees.

Protect the important things in life...

Home Insurance
Individually tailored to suit your needs.

Arranged by...
DAVID UPSHALL
Insurance Services

Tel: 01305 268883
44 South Street, Dorchester, Dorset DT1 1DQ
Email: d.upshall@gmail.com
www.davidupshall.co.uk

Authorised and regulated by the Financial Conduct Authority

Keep Changing: News from the Military Museum

Christopher Jary

Very recent visitors to the Keep Military Museum have been surprised by some major changes on the ground floor. The first hall remains unchanged. The 25-pounder field gun of the 94th Field Regiment (Dorset Yeomanry) still stands beside the First World War Dorset Yeoman on horseback.

Beyond, the brass barrel of the gun captured by the 54th Regiment at Marabout still reflects the light from the front window and, beside the archway, stands the cross from Wagon Hill remembering the men of the 1st Devonshire Regiment who died near Ladysmith in January 1900. But, as one moves beyond into the corridor, things start to change.

The cell, which once displayed some of the more gruesome aspects of 19th century military punishment, has been transformed. It now forms the centrepiece of a new display about the 300 soldiers shot for desertion during the First World War. Among them were one Devon and two Dorsets, one of whom was actually held in this cell for a short time before being returned to France to face court martial and a firing squad. A hundred years on, the subject of these executions remains one that fuels great emotion and argument. I will not spoil the effect by describing it here. Instead, I will simply say that the remarkable, imaginative display in the cell provides a deeply moving backdrop to the story of the executions, which is presented with historical objectivity, allowing today's visitors to understand the facts and the context and to judge the matter for themselves.

Turn right from the cell and you will realise the extent of the improvements that have been made. The once sparsely furnished education room now houses the Dorset at War Gallery, which displays all sorts of material, concentrating on the human stories of the varied parts played by the people of our County in war.

The First World War section includes the touching story of Horace Collier, who left Cerne Abbas in the first weeks of the war and never returned to his sweetheart, Birdie Amey, and the happier tale of poet and musician Skip Wheller, who came home from the horrors of Mesopotamia with his sense of humour intact. The Second War display includes the Air Raid Precautions' (ARP) Map of the County, showing the location of every bomb dropped on Dorset throughout the war.

An Operations Board from RAF Warmwell records the little-known fighter bomber attacks on enemy targets in France flown

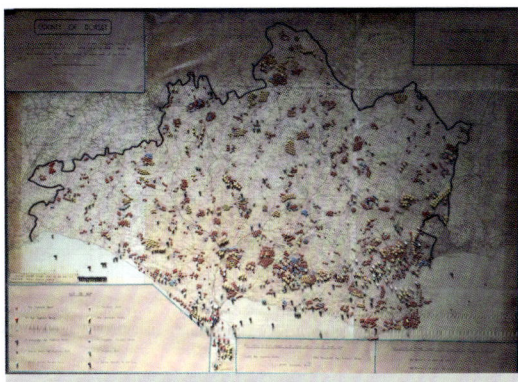
1939-45 Dorset Map of bombs and aircraft crashes

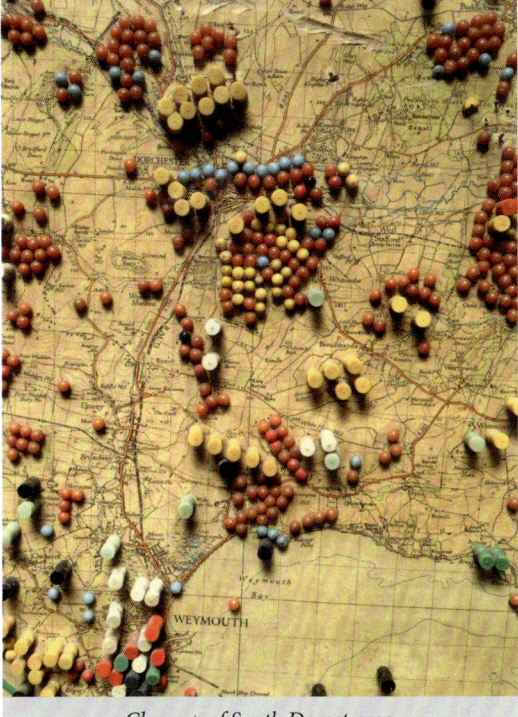
Close up of South Dorset area

The new exhibition was opened in early July by John Young MC JP DL, High Sheriff of Dorset. At the same time the room in which it is housed was renamed The Speakman Room to mark (on his eightieth birthday) the massive contribution to the Keep Museum made over many years by Major Nick Speakman MBE TD. For the Museum the Dorset at War exhibition represents a first step in a new direction. It is not just about the army. It is not necessarily about any of the regiments the Museum proudly represents, but it is about our home County and we hope very much that it will move and be of interest to the community we serve and our many friends and neighbours.

More changes will follow this year. Very recently Dorset County Council has announced that they are generously donating to the Keep the oil painting of the Dorset Yeomanry's charge at Agagia in 1916. This will be prominently displayed as soon as it can be managed. This year we have acquired two Distinguished Conduct Medals – the award just below the VC – won by Warrant Officers during the 2nd Dorsets' successful rearguard stand at Festubert in 1940. We bought one, but the other was the generous gift of RSM Gary Cooper's son. So we now have three of the four DCMs won in this single action. Our plan, therefore, is to revamp our France 1940 display to tell the inspiring story of the bravery of some of the Dorsets in this battle, and of the remarkable withdrawal, led personally by their gallant Colonel, which enabled them to escape from Dunkirk.

by RAF Fighter Command's Westland Whirlwinds based at what is now Crossways. And the Bismarck wall shows the forgotten links between Dorset and the sinking of the German pocket battleship. The torpedo that first damaged Bismarck was manufactured at Portland, the pilot of the Swordfish that dropped it was a Dorset man, and the ship whose torpedo finally sank Bismarck was the cruiser HMS Dorsetshire. The Captain's pennant, flown during the action, forms part of the new display.

In the years ahead the Keep will keep changing so we hope very much that our visitors will keep coming back. When you come, look out for the pop bottle in the Dorset at War exhibition. It's my wife's favourite exhibit.

HMS Vanguard

Greg Schofield

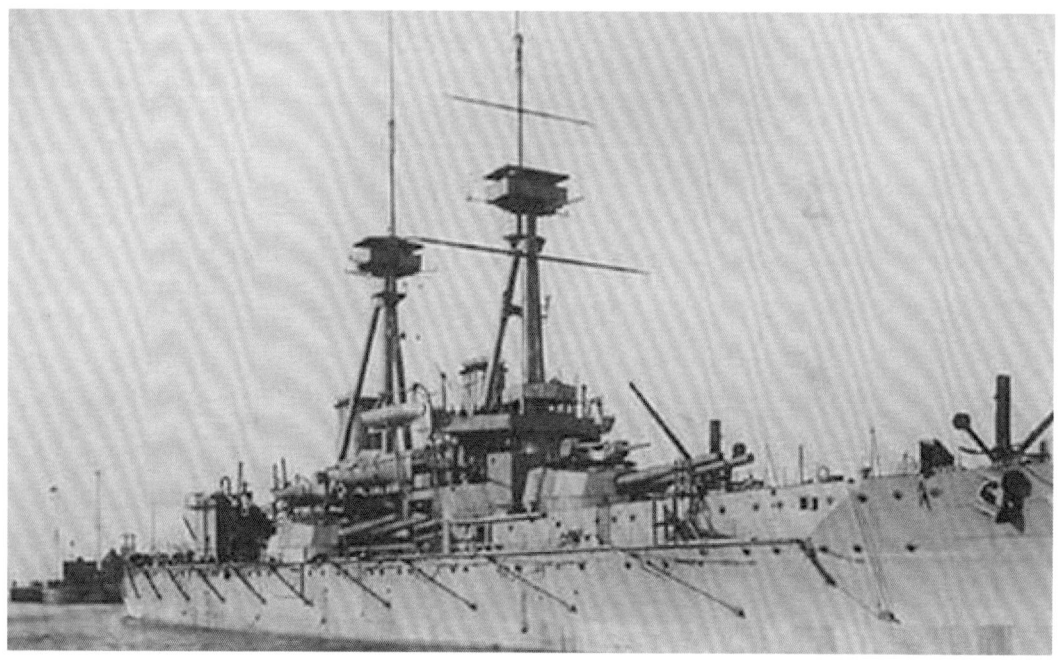

9th July 2017 was the centenary of the sinking of HMS Vanguard at Scapa Flow in the Orkney Islands. A St Vincent class battleship and veteran of the Battle of Jutland, she suddenly blew up just before midnight. A definitive cause for the cordite explosion in one of the two magazines which served the midships turrets 'P' and 'Q', has never been found.

Navy divers have gone down to place a new naval ensign on the wreck to commemorate the over 800 dead, amongst whom were three Weymouth men:-

Walter Hebbern - A Gunner/Corporal in the Royal Marine Artillery.
He lived at 8, East Row, St Leonard's Road, Chapelhay, and left four young children.

Alfred Rowland Herbert Mills - Officer's Steward 2nd Class, aged 33.
He had been in the Navy for 16 years and on HMS Vanguard since 1914; before that he had served on HMS Black Prince. He lived at 52, Cromwell Road, Westham.

Frederick Charles Poore - Officer's Steward 1st Class, aged 39.
He was one of the best known Weymouth men on the ship, and lived at 'Bay View', Augusta Place, Esplanade.

Editor's note I used to drink with Walter's son, affectionately known as 'Ebbo', in the Cove Inn, Weymouth, I played football for the Cove with his grandson Terry and I went to school with his granddaughter Wendy.

I contacted Terry and Wendy, Les "Ebbo" Hebbern's children and Walter Hebbern's grandchildren.

Terry then showed me a few mementoes about his grandfather. Not only did he have a photo of Walter who was a gunner in the Royal Marine Artillery on board HMS Vanguard but he also had the 1914-18 Star, and the Victory and British War Medals given posthumously to his widow, Beatrice Ethel Hebbern.

There was also a piece of wood carved to look like a book with "In Memory of HMS Vangaurd (sic) July 9th 1917" incised on the back of the 'book' This was carved from a piece of wood from HMS Vanguard and this was given to Les when he was working at Whiteheads. A fellow worker had heard that his father Walter had died on HMS Vanguard in Scapa Flow and he said to Les "I was at Scapa and I have something for your mother" and presented the wooden book carving to him.

It came to the Crunch

Albert Douglas Gillen

I can't get out where I got in
Things are looking pretty grim
This "Blue" has fallen for the trap
Whose door just closed with silent snap

That stinking mackerel made me drool
Careless, taken for a fool
Orange now will be my pallor
My blue will change to that bright colour

Soon I'll meet the cooking-team
Enough I've heard, to make me scream
Already I can feel the crunch
Of broken shell before they munch

Lobster in a sea-food place
Where massive bill the diners face
They'll use shell-pliers, me to crack
Crack my claws, crack my back

Crack my legs, probe out the meat
Hope they find me, wholesome, sweet
I'm Thermidor or Lobster Stew
With pride of place on the menu

Underwater photograph of Blue lobster courtesy of Colin Garrett,
orange cooked lobster courtesy of Weyfish Ltd, Weymouth

Breakout

by Jack W. Sweet

On 16th May 1829, twenty five years-old William Ridout was brought to the County Gaol in Dorchester to await his trial at the Dorset July Quarter Sessions on the charge of stealing pewter plates from a shop. Some three weeks later on 5 June, Thomas Francis, aged 35, arrived at the gaol on the charge of stealing fowls, also to await trial at the Quarter Sessions. If found guilty, the least they could expect would be a term of hard labour in the County Gaol.

On 8 June, 19 years-old George Moore was brought in on the serious charge of entering the dwelling house of his grandmother, Mrs Elizabeth Moore, at Longfleet near Poole, and stealing a deal box, watch and articles of clothing 'above the value of Five Pounds'. George Moore would be sent to the Dorset August Assizes and if found guilty would almost certainly be transported to the principal Australian penal colony in Van Diemen's Land, now Tasmania.

The three men found themselves sharing a cell and, no doubt despairing of their future freedom, hatched a plan to escape. Working on the brickwork over the cell door they broke through at about two o'clock on Monday morning 6 July and carrying a rope cut from their blankets crossed the yard, scaled the prison wall and disappeared into the night.

However, their escape was soon discovered and wanted posters offering a reward of five pounds each for their recapture were soon being distributed across the area. Freedom was short-lived and, at about midnight, the three were captured near Parkstone; two hours later they were back in Dorchester Gaol. On 14 July William Ridout and Thomas Francis were found guilty of their crimes at the Quarter Sessions and each sentenced to 12 calendar months hard labour in Dorchester Gaol.

George Moore appeared at the Dorset Assizes on 6 August, was found guilty and sentenced to seven years penal servitude in Van Diemen's Land. He was taken to the Captivity prison hulk in Portsmouth Harbour where he remained until 1 April 1830 when, with 159 other prisoners, he left on the convict ship Sir Charles Forbes, arriving in Van Diemen's Land nearly four months later on 27 July.

Some six months later, the Dorset County Chronicle reported on Thursday, 26 November 1829 that: 'Two persons for trial attempted to effect an escape from our County Gaol on Thursday evening about 6 o'clock; they had got over the fence of their yard into the garden, but being missed, an alarm was given by a fellow prisoner and they were secured before they had time to scale the boundary wall. They had cut up their bedding and made it into a kind of ladder for the purpose of climbing the wall.' The fate of the two unnamed prisoners, both in the prison and at their trials, remains unknown.burglary and horse stealing, was found guilty and sentenced to transportation for life.

Sources: Dorset County Chronicle, 1829 and 1834-36; Sherborne Mercury, 1829 and 1834-36, Dorchester Gaol Records.

Major-General Colin Shortis CB CBE (1934-2017)

Christopher Jary

In the summer of 2012, when I was asked to write the final volume of the history of the Dorset Regiment, I was called to meet Major-General Colin Shortis at his house in Topsham. Bright-eyed, bonhomous and hospitable, his very direct questions, careful listening and piercing way of looking at me made me realise I was being sized up to make sure I was up to the task I had been set. And all the time I could hear my father's voice in the background, saying with approbation: "Proper soldier." During my childhood my father (who at the tender age of twenty had proved himself to be rather a good infantry soldier) often observed that "all good infantry soldiers are slightly nutty". Much less often he would describe someone as a "proper soldier". It was the highest accolade he could award. Like the VC, it was a distinction that took no account of rank. A private soldier could earn it and so could a Field Marshal but, although anyone could earn it, very few did. Over the years I came to recognise the particular qualities that, in his view, constituted that rare animal: "the proper soldier".

No conventional army officer mould could possibly have formed the deeply unconventional Colin Shortis. His mother was Australian, his father was brought up in Darlington, and Colin himself spent his first five years in Burma. His career had an unpromising start when, aged fifteen, he was ill and left Bedford School with no qualifications. Then, in 1951, he enlisted as a private soldier in the Royal Norfolk Regiment. Sent for officer training, he was commissioned into the Royal Fusiliers. In the early 1950s, he was sent with a draft of Fusiliers to be trained by the 1st Battalion of the Dorset Regiment in Hong Kong. The Fusiliers would then join their own Regiment, who were fighting in Korea. The Commanding Officer of the 1st Dorsets at that time was a legend. Knocker White had won a DSO commanding the 2nd Dorsets in Burma. Decidedly eccentric, a thoroughgoing professional soldier and an outstanding battalion commander, he spotted Lieutenant Colin Shortis as a very promising young officer and made him welcome. Months passed and Colin stayed with the Dorsets until one day he asked to see the CO to enquire when he would rejoin the Royal Fusiliers in Korea.

"But you're one of us now, Colin," said White. Colin gently explained that he would like to join the Dorsets but that he did not want to be remembered as the Royal Fusilier who shirked active service. This line of argument convinced Knocker White, who then produced several orders posting Colin to Korea which he had simply ignored. So Colin left for Korea, where he fought as a subaltern, before transferring to the Dorset Regiment, which had become his home. For the rest of his life he remained a consistent Dorset.

Even early in his career he had a way of attracting responsibility and winning respect. Retired officers now in their early eighties still speak with awe of Colin's time as senior subaltern in the 1st Dorsets. His self-disciplined, voraciously enquiring brain made him an accomplished staff officer in appointments in Germany, Aden and Singapore punctuated (after the Dorsets' amalgamation with the Devons) by tours with the 1st Devon and Dorsets. After a spell in MOD, he commanded a company in 1 D&D in Malta, British Honduras and Northern Ireland.

A prodigiously hard-worker with an intuitive understanding of people and an astonishingly open mind, Colin made his professional reputation in Northern Ireland during the Troubles. He carefully studied the history of the Province and listened attentively to the views of junior soldiers and of the people they were protecting. In 1973-74 he led the Northern Ireland Training and Advisory Team, developing new, effective techniques in countering terrorism. As Commanding Officer of the 1st Devon and Dorsets (1974-77) and later as Commander of the 8th Brigade (1978-80), his thoughtful leadership is said to have significantly reduced the number of violent incidents.

Having demonstrated diplomacy and effectiveness in sensitive political situations, he was an obvious choice to command the British Military Advisory and Training Team who helped establish the Zimbabwean National Army. In 1983 he became Director of Infantry before retiring from his final appointment as GOC North-West District in 1989.

Colin retired as a Major-General, having been appointed CBE in 1980 and CB in 1989. He was Colonel Commandant of The Prince of Wales's Division from 1983 until 1988 and Colonel of the Devonshire and Dorset Regiment from 1984 until 1990. He did a great deal to re-establish the Keep Military Museum in Dorchester on solid organisational foundations. He was Commodore of the Army Sailing Association, Chairman of the Army Mountaineering Association and President of the Devonshire and Dorset Regimental Association.

His devotion to his family ran deep and was reciprocated. In 1957 Colin married Sylvia Jenkinson, with whom he had two sons and two daughters. After Sylvia's death, he married Sylvia Rampton in 2009, gaining a stepson and stepdaughter. In his family eulogy at Colin's funeral his son, Dr Tim Shortis, drew a deeply affectionate and carefully-drawn portrait of his father. Brigadier Simon Young and Major Don Jellard then gave amusing and affectionate army perspectives on the soldier with whom they served.

General Colin died, just short of his 83rd birthday, on 8th January 2017. A very distinguished soldier, he was much more than that. He was also a remarkable man: thoughtful, open-minded, enthusiastic, energetic and utterly lacking in pomposity, personal ambition or self-regard. The Dorset Regiment Old Comrades, in whose ranks he marched at his last Minden Dorsets' Reunion in July 2016, had the measure of the man. "Why do they call me Mad Fred?" he once enquired, genuinely puzzled by his nickname. The truth was that, despite any amount of gold braid on his hat, irrespective of his decorations and high rank, he remained one of them, happy in their company and rightly secure in their affection and respect. Mention his name and old soldiers smile. His Old Comrades – and a great many more of us besides – will miss the warmth of Colin's company very much indeed.

Weymouth & Melcombe and the Monmouth Rebellion

Greg Schofield

Preface

In the 1990s I took 'A' level History students on field trips on five occasions to study the Monmouth Rebellion in depth as part of their exam requirements. Each time we were fortunate to have a lecture from Richard Dunning, 'Somerset County Historian'; he had a particular interest in the Rebellion and uncovered much new unpublished evidence which he imparted to us, along with many less obvious aspects which threw a new light on it.

Browsing through some of the local history records in Weymouth Library I came across references to the Monmouth Rebellion, and with a fresh understanding of some of the issues and interpretations involved, those events appeared in a new light, hence this article.

I would like to record my grateful thanks to Maureen Attwool and Chris Pafford for their willing and helpful assistance.

Lyme Regis to Sedgemoor

In June 1685, the illegitimate son of Charles II, the Protestant Duke of Monmouth, who was well known and popular in the South West, landed at Lyme Regis and raised the flag of rebellion against his uncle, the Catholic King James II.

James II

This was a period of strongly held religious views and England being a strongly Protestant country, there appeared to be widespread suspicion of James II's religious intentions. Therefore, it is not surprising that large numbers of Lyme Regis men flocked to his banner, and in the next few days, many more men came in from the surrounding countryside to swell his growing army. After a few days he launched a raid into Bridport to get more recruits and horses, but this developed into a skirmish against Royal troops based in the Bull Hotel, and nothing was gained.

In an attempt to raise the West Country en masse, he went on a line of march from Lyme to Axminster, Chard, Ilminster, Taunton, Wells, the outskirts of Bristol, Bath, Frome, Shepton Mallet and back to Bridgwater. He gained many new recruits, but not as many as had been hoped for.

The English army at this time was very small, but as luck would have it there was locally a force of Dragoons under a brilliant young officer, John Churchill, the future Duke of Marlborough, arguably the greatest military commander this country has ever produced. He had been brought up locally 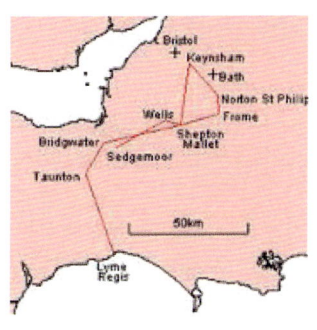 and therefore had a good working knowledge of the local countryside. His force was too small to put down the rebellion, but it was sufficient to constrain it and pose a threat to potential recruits attempting to join the rebels. Churchill was waiting for regular battle-hardened troops freshly returned from fighting in Tangiers to join him. Known as 'Kirk's Lambs' from their Colonel's name and their regimental cap badge, they were anything but!

The rest of the king's armies were raised through the County Militia system by the Lord Lieutenant. They were largely untrained and ill equipped, but then, so were the rebels. The real problem was their loyalty; if they were brought to battle would they actually fight or would they desert en masse to the rebels? Accordingly they were mustered and kept in the general area as a potential threat to the rebels, but not actually brought into battle. Nevertheless, there were deserters from the militia who joined the rebels.

A further blow to Monmouth's recruitment was the failure of any of the major or minor nobility or landowners to commit them to his cause, which would have brought recruits and money. But then they didn't come out in active support of the King either. The only conclusion that can be drawn is that memories of the Civil War still being fresh in the mind and the consequences of backing the wrong side, they were sitting on the fence and waiting to see which way the cards fell before committing themselves.

By the 6th July, Monmouth's army was based in Bridgewater whilst the Royalist army had concentrated at the village of Weston Zoyland about 2 miles away, being camped on the Sedgemoor just outside. Monmouth decided on a night march and surprise attack, but the accidental discharge of a pistol warned the Royalists they were approaching and the Bussex Rhyne (drainage ditch) in front of the camp prevented the attack being pressed home. There were still chances for the rebels to win, but in the dark and confusion they were missed and the better disciplined and trained Royal Army was triumphant. They lost 27 men; the rebel losses are disputed, varying between 727 and 2,700.

Aftermath

History showed that Rebels could expect little or no mercy; the Northern Rising, Peasant's Revolt, Pilgrimage of Grace, Western Rising and Kett Rebellion, for example, had all ended with mass slaughter. What was to follow now was equally brutal.

The rebel survivors were imprisoned in Weston Zoyland church and there they remained, their wounds untreated, whilst Judge Jeffreys was sent for and extensive enquiries made in every parish where the rebellion had occurred for anyone who was absent during that period. The result of that enquiry was that for the first time in British history we have a complete list of all the names of the rebels and where they came from.

Monmouth was quickly found, hiding in a ditch, and taken as a prisoner to London. No trial was necessary as an 'Act of Attainder' had been passed by Parliament, and despite him pleading for mercy, he was summarily beheaded. In a macabre twist, it was realised that despite being of royal blood there was no portrait of him, so the day after he was buried he was disinterred, the head stuck back on and a portrait painted.

Judge Jeffreys was making his way to Salisbury for the first assize, full of vindictiveness and suffering from a painful kidney disease (probably stones). On his way he stopped off at Winchester to condemn to death Alice Lisle, a deeply religious woman who had been caught sheltering two fleeing rebels; there was no evidence that she was aware of their crime, but an example had to be made!

The Bloody Assizes took place at Salisbury, Dorchester, Taunton and Wells. Figures vary, but it appears that over 1,400 cases were heard, of which 1,381 rebels were found guilty and condemned to be hanged, drawn and quartered. The King exercised the prerogative of mercy in some cases and it ended with 320 being executed and the sentence for 800 commuted to transportation. There was a good reason for this; before the final battle had been fought, slave owners at the King's court had petitioned him to buy up to 1,000 rebels to use as slaves on their sugar plantations in the West Indies. The King could make a lot of money out of this and it was not an act of mercy; the brutality and hardship involved is well illustrated in Raphael Sabatini's novel Captain Blood.

In time honoured fashion, once the condemned had been beheaded and their bodies quartered, their heads and quarters were displayed in prominent sites around the area where the rebellion had taken place; the description by travellers of "...a charnel house..." was frequently used. Special treatment was reserved for Lyme Regis where the rebellion had originated; heads and quarters were displayed on the spiked railings around the church, and there they remained until King James was deposed in 1688. Indeed, any attempt to remove any body part, anywhere, would result in severe punishment.

Weymouth & Melcombe Regis

Thanks to the thorough enquiries made to find the names of the rebels, it is known that no one from Weymouth or Melcombe joined the rebel army. But, the rebellion didn't leave the town uninvolved.

Very soon after Monmouth's landing at Lyme Regis, a copy of his Proclamation arrived in Weymouth and Melcombe. What happened next thoroughly alarmed the town authorities. William Wiseman, a 14 year old apprentice barber surgeon read out the proclamation to a crowd which had assembled; from the reaction of the authorities it can only be assumed that he was trying to incite support for the rebellion. They had him arrested and sent to gaol in Dorchester to await trial and punishment.

The authorities' swift and harsh reaction to Wiseman's action is understandable. The Civil War experience will have been within many of their memories and very firmly in their minds. At that time Weymouth had supported the King and Melcombe Parliament; the division within the borough had led to much bitter fighting, 250 dead and considerable destruction of property. (See The Crabchurch Conspiracy) There had been much long term bitterness and the scars had only been healed with the passage of time. The last thing wanted now was for the town to divide along Monmouth/King James lines and violence breaking out again. The prompt and harsh treatment of Wiseman made it clear to local residents that any of them thinking of getting involved and taking sides could expect similar treatment. It would appear that it had the desired result.

Wiseman appeared before Judge Jeffreys at the Dorchester Assize, where he was sentenced to be whipped for having read the Proclamation. The sentence was carried out by the gaoler, who, having concern for Wiseman's youth, administered the whipping as lightly as he thought he could get away with. But a Clergyman called Blanchard took exception and said to the gaoler: '...he would do his business for him with the Lord Chief Justice, for shamming his sentence in not whipping him half enough...' to which the gaoler replied:'... you talk of the cruelties of the popish priests, but commend me to Church of England priest for cruelty...' (1) Clearly Blanchard took his complaint to Jeffreys, who ordered that the boy be whipped again on the following day. This time the whipping was so severe that it was feared the boy would die. That he didn't is clear, for after Jeffreys departed, Wiseman was taken back to Melcombe and whipped through the town, after which his sentence terminated. What happened to him subsequently is unknown, but in later years there was a Dr Wiseman known to be living in Weymouth; given that he was apprenticed as a barber surgeon, it is conceivable that this is the same person. He died in January 1744.

The town was to find out that it had not yet finished with the rebellion. The Dorchester Assize took place in early September, and Jeffreys being in no mood for clemency, handed down death sentences to 251 rebels, although, only 74 of these sentences were actually carried out. On the 14th September the Council received the following: 'By virtue of an order to the Sheriff, W. Lewes, from the Right Hon. George Lord Jeffery, and a Precept from the Sheriff to the Mayor, etc., commanding them to erect within the Borough "a sufficient gallowes for the executing the several persons sentenced and appointed to be executed on Tuesday next within your said Borough." It is ordered that the Gallows be erected on or near Greenhill in the confines of your Borough.' (2)

Although Weymouth and Melcombe Regis had played no part in the rebellion, a major demonstration of the fate that awaited rebels and traitors was to be made locally:

'Twelve persons being executed ... their heads and quarters were disposed of by the Maior according to the Sheriff's pcept ... as followeth.

To	Upwey	4 quarters	1 head
	Sutton Poyntz	2	1
	Osmington	4	1
	Preston	2	
	Weeke	4	
	Winfrith	4	1
	Broadmaine	2	1
	Radipoll	2	
	Winterborne St. Martin	2	
	Puddletowne	4	1
	Bincombe	2	
		32	6
WEYMOUTH.			
	Grand Piere	6	1
	Townend	2	
	Neare the Windmill	4	1
	Waymouth Townhall	2	
	The Bridge	1	2
	Melcombe Townhall	1	2
		16	6
(TOTAL		48	12) (3)

The fate of traitors was to be hanged, cut down whilst still alive, their entrails cut out and burned before their eyes, then beheaded and quartered, their quarters being boiled in pitch to preserve them for as long as possible whilst on display: That these sentences were carried out with all the ritual horror that it entailed is demonstrated by details of payment made to some of those involved;

'14th October.   To Bill of Disbursements for ye Gallows, Burning and boiling ye rebels executed p ordr att this Towne. £15.14.3.' (4)

'20th November.   Paid to Mr. Mayor at the "Beare" ... for setting up the post with the quarters of the rebels at Weymouth towne end.   1s. 6d.' (5)

Many of the rebels whose death sentences had been reduced to transportation sailed from Weymouth on the ships Betty, and ironically, The Happy Return, both being listed as Weymouth ships transporting convicts. In addition to the Dorchester prisoners, between 15th and 17th October, 200 were marched in chains from Wells to Weymouth for shipment, 30 escaping en route. The Betty sailed with 80 convicts and 'one serving maid', arriving at Barbados in January 1686, having buried eight rebels at sea. The Happy Return took all her 91 rebels to Barbados without any deaths. Very few were to return.

Postscript

As a consequence of the rebellion, James II wanted a large standing army in the European style, with Catholic officers. This filled leading Protestants with alarm; there is no evidence that he wanted to use it to force the English to return to Catholicism, but the flight to England of tens of thousands of Huguenots (French Protestants) from persecution, and his plans to grant toleration to English Catholics, only raised suspicion of his intentions. To begin with Protestants were prepared to wait; James was an old man, time wasn't on his side. On his death, his daughter Mary would inherit the throne and she was Protestant. His wife, Mary of Modena, was thought to be too old to have any more children, but in June 1688, in suspicious circumstances, she gave birth to a son; a Catholic succession seemed assured. Now desperate, leading Protestants invited James' daughter Mary and her husband William of Orange to take the throne. On 5th November, 1688 they landed at Brixham and marched on London; support for James melted away and he fled the country.

The Glorious Revolution followed and with it pardons for the Monmouth rebels. At last the grisly relics of the executions could be removed. In the West Indies transported rebels were freed from slavery, but no arrangements were made to bring them home and few were able to afford the trip, so very few returned, indeed many may not have wanted to. There is some evidence to show that many rebuilt their lives in the Caribbean whilst others emigrated to the British Colonies in North America.

Footnotes:
1. G.R. Ellis, *History and Antiques of Weymouth and Melcombe Regis*, Benson, 1829, p.120
2. H. J. Moule M.A., *Descriptive Catalogue of the Charters, Minute Books and Other Documents of the Borough of Weymouth and Melcombe Regis, A.D. 1252 to 1800*, Sherren & Sons, 1883, III. 139, p.85
3. ibid p.85
4. ibid p.85
5. op cit V. 64, p.146

JURASSIC STORM

Kay Ennals MBE

Grey skies with heavy darkened clouds
hung over our jurassic land,
beaches went quiet - there was no sound
except for sea-gulls winging around.

suddenly a strong wind blew —
the sky now held a blackened hue —
not quite sure what was to ensue
crowds left the shore as concerns grew.

the clouds hurled defiance! fighting they clashed —
until at last fork lightening flashed -—
jarring and grumbling as if in pain -—
the darkest clouds unleashed their rain.

the wind blew cold - rain turned to hail
which hit the ground hard and bounced up again,
sea-gulls crouched in their craggy cover —
people stayed close to one another.

but then a challenge from warm rays of sun
cleared the clouds — then the storm had gone!!
water puddles reflected like glass -—
illuminating the wind-blown task!

trees straightened up - plants survived —
people tracked back to the brighter seaside,
music came from a busking band —
children once more were playing with sand.

it was back to a landscape washed and clean
back to the happy holiday scene -—
back to the beaches people love most -
back to the super Jurassic coast.

The Dorchester Company and the Vision of the Reverend John White

David Cuckson

At the back of the Dorset County Museum, in Colliton Street, Dorchester, there stands an old building, forlorn now but still standing as a memorial to the person who led the transformation of the town in his own time and, even more significantly, played a key role in the early colonisation of what was to become the United States of America. The only indication that this is an important historical site is given by a plaque on the wall erected by the Dorchester Heritage Committee. This records that this was the residence of John White, where he lived from 1575 to 1648, that he was Rector of Holy Trinity and St Peter's, Dorchester, and that he is buried in the porch of St Peter's, before setting out a brief outline of his life.

John White's Rectory, Colliton Street, Dorchester, in 2017

In Dorchester John White rallied the folk of the town after the disastrous fire of 1613, inspiring them so to reform the government of the town and the conduct of individuals that it became a model 'commonwealth' after the Puritan ideal which he espoused. In addition to good order, a regime of social welfare was established, with systems of care put in place for the education of the young, the relief of the poor and almshouses for those no longer able to look after themselves (the last still continuing in the charitable trust to this day and with one original building surviving in Napper's Mite in South Street). He also encouraged the people to give money to help those outside their own community, including towns affected by the plague or other disaster, and the people of the Palatinate (in modern Germany) suffering from the effects of war. It was this kind of wider vision that turned his thoughts across the Atlantic to the New World.

Napper's Mite

Over the previous century the English sailors had become used to crossing the Atlantic and exploring the coasts of North America. The fishing was especially good in the seas to the south of Newfoundland and English ships went there on a regular basis. At the beginning of the seventeenth century thoughts turned to establishing colonies on the mainland. The first of these was in Virginia, and in 1620 New England saw the arrival of the Pilgrim Fathers in the Mayflower. John White would have been aware of, and no doubt taken a keen interest in, all this. Merchants in Dorchester were trading through the harbour at Weymouth, and many of the fishermen based there carried out long voyages to catch cod etc, and perhaps also to do some trade in furs with the indigenous people. John White, however, would not have wanted to link up with the first colonists. Those in Virginia tended to belong to the High Church wing of the Church of England and were unlikely to be sympathetically inclined to the kind of Puritanism practised in Dorchester. The Pilgrim settlement at New Plymouth, on the other hand, was largely made up of Separatists, people who could not put up with the Church of England at all, even the kind of moderate Puritanism preached by John White, and who had left England altogether, first for the Netherlands and now for the New World, in order to 'do their own thing' free from persecution.

John White pondered over the life of the Weymouth fishermen sailing on a regular basis to the New World. 'Being usually upon their voyages nine or ten months in the year they were left all the while without any means of instruction', by which he meant guidance in matters of religion. Furthermore, the ships were 'double-manned'; more men were needed than were required to sail the ships across the Atlantic and back again, to fish the American waters and salt the catch down for the journey back to Europe. What if a settlement was established on the coast of New England, where the spare men could be left behind to form the nucleus of a colony? They would be on the spot for the next year's season, and in the meantime they could grow crops, tend cattle and find other food locally to feed themselves and the sailors returning in the spring, as well as making salt from seawater and keeping the fishing gear in repair. A minister could also be appointed to have pastoral oversight of this little community which could grow into the kind of godly commonwealth being experienced in Dorchester. This was the vision. One might perhaps want to criticise White for being naïve, in thinking that men recruited as fishermen could turn their hands equally to farming, and in beginning the enterprise with an inadequate financial base, but equally he must be praised for pushing ahead while the majority merely talked, and for persisting until success was achieved.

The Council of New England had put in place a procedure to be followed for the establishment of new settlements by English groups. An initial authority could be granted for the occupation of land as long as it was at least 10 miles from the nearest English settlement, or separated by a river. It was also possible to obtain a licence to allow a wider area to be assessed to identify a suitable location. If the initial occupation proved successful within a period of seven years, then the original indenture could be exchanged for letters or grants of incorporation, which gave a formal constitution to the new community, with some powers of local government. Up until 1622 you had to be a member of the Council to apply, but then there was a change, so that others could also be considered, 'provided they be persons of honour or gentlemen of blood, except six Western Merchants'. This gave John White the opening he needed. He already knew some merchants who would qualify and it was not difficult to find some 'gentlemen of blood', who together would form the nucleus to promote his chosen project.

One of the 'Western Merchants' was Richard Bushrod. He was based in Dorchester and he agreed to front the application for a licence, as the first step to founding a colony in New England. Then Sir Walter Erle, of Charborough in Dorset, took over the leading role and chaired a formal meeting to promote the scheme locally. There the great prospects for investors were outlined: the possibilities for the grant of land in the new colony, opportunities for local unemployed, especially the young, to find work, a potential market for clothes etc, and access to commodities such as timber, flax, hemp and dye-stuffs. Finally there was a call to Christian mission, 'how to settle the Christian faith in these heathenish and desert parts of the world'. The initial response was sufficiently positive for a subsequent meeting to choose a committee to oversee the new enterprise with Sir Walter Erle named as Governor and John Humphrey of Chaldon, near Dorchester, as Treasurer. Before long about 120 people had subscribed to the Dorchester Company, including 50 Dorset gentry, 30 merchants, mostly from Dorchester, and 20 clergymen. Over £30,000 was raised, which was judged sufficient to launch the project.

The first major expenditure was the acquisition of a small ship, of about 50 tons, The Fellowship, which was equipped and sent out with a full crew, plus the extra men who could be left to over-winter in New England. Unfortunately, by the time everything was ready, they were running about six weeks late in the season and they missed the best of the fishing. Nevertheless they carried on with the original scheme and left 14 men at Cape Ann, at the northern limit of Massachusetts Bay (now Gloucester) before sailing to Spain to sell their cargo of salt cod, albeit at a poor price. The next year they bought a second ship, a Flemish fly-boat of about 140 tons, which they tried to adapt to their purposes by the addition of a second deck. This was something of a disaster, because the alterations made the ship top heavy and further refinements had to be made before the ship was safe to sail across the Atlantic. So again the best of the fishing was missed, with the inevitable impact on profitability, but this time 32 men were left at Cape Ann, together with cattle, food and equipment to help them through the winter. For the third season they added an extra ship but once more they were hit by bad luck. One of the ships sprang a leak on the ocean crossing and had to return to Weymouth and the market for fish in Spain collapsed because of war between the two countries.

John White, a modern drawing by Jo Duncan, based on an old woodcut

The Company was now running out of money, and there was no immediate prospect of it making any kind of profit in the short term. John White himself acknowledged fundamental weaknesses in his original concept. 'The very project itself of planting by the help of a fishing voyage can never answer the success that it seems to promise.' They had not so far identified a location that provided both a good base for the fishermen and suitable land for agriculture; Cape Ann was acceptable to the fishermen but it offered poor conditions for those who were expected to live there year round. Then there proved to be a skills issue as well. The settlers had been chosen primarily because they were fishermen and thus able to provide the extra help needed during the fishing season. But they were not farmers and they found it difficult to adapt to a life devoted to the care of crops and animals. It came down to the fact that the Company had been trying to achieve its aim of establishing a settlement 'on the cheap'. To be successful a settlement had to be made up of all the elements of a rural community, with fishing just one element among many. That was more than the Company could afford on the basis of the money raised so far.

However, not everyone currently at Cape Ann wanted to give up and come home. The numbers had been added to by some folk who had started out with the Pilgrim Fathers at Plymouth but who had not settled under their stricter form of Puritan life and had either left of their own volition or been told to leave. They had travelled up the coast where they came into contact with the Cape Ann settlement. Roger Conant was described as 'a religious, sober and prudent gentleman', and he also happened to be the brother of John Conant who was well known to John White. His reputation and relationship were sufficient for John White to identify him as a potential leader for the settlement and he resolved to 'commit to him the charge of all their affairs, as well fishing as planting'. Another in this group was the Reverend John Lyford, who was invited to be their minister. Both, no doubt, fell into the category of what John White described as 'a few of the most honest and industrious' who decided to 'stay behind and take charge of the cattle sent over the year before, which they performed accordingly'. Roger Conant, in particular, did not want to leave New England, but did not feel that Cape Ann was the best place to develop and he suggested to John White a move to what he considered to be a more promising location, at a place called Naumkeag, which in due course would be renamed Salem.

The new site was on a neck of land, with the sea on both sides, either of which would provide anchorage for visiting ships. The area where they built their first houses was rocky, but there was land nearby with good enough soil to grow crops and pasture the cattle, with woods for timber and where pigs could forage when they were not eating clams from the shore. They began to establish a settlement, and most of the group were hopeful of making a home here. A few, however, were not so sure, including Mr Lyford, their minister, who decided to move south to Virginia. Roger Conant later claimed, probably correctly, to have been primarily responsible for keeping a small community together there. As he put it, 'When in the infancy thereof it was in great hazard of being deserted I was the means, through grace assisting me, to stop the flight of those few that then were here with me, and that by my utter denial to go away with them, who would have gone either for England or mostly for Virginia but hereupon stayed to the hazard of our lives'.

Back in England, with the Dorchester Company in the process of being wound up, it fell to a smaller group to maintain some level of support for the settlers. John White was one, Roger

Conant's brother John another, and Richard Bushrod and a few other Dorchester merchants supplied the financial muscle. A ship was dispatched in the spring with more cattle as well as, presumably, further men and equipment, and they found that the community had weathered the winter well enough. They welcomed the new arrivals and supplies but were disappointed at the lack of positive news about their future. They had hoped to be given formal authority to occupy their new site, without which it could have been open to others back in England to apply in their stead and force them to leave. Accordingly they sent one of their number, John Woodbury, with the ship on its return journey to England to plead that something be done urgently to make their position secure.

There were then about 20 people at Naumkeag/ Salem, and they busied themselves building houses (mostly based on wooden frames brought over from England) and developing the farm land as best they could, in the hope that by the following spring John Woodbury would return with better news. One or two of them, including Roger Conant, had their wives with them, and the Conants saw the birth of the first English child there, perhaps a sign for a happier future. In his old age Roger Conant recalled writing at this time to his friends back in England, recommending New England as a potential haven for religious refugees. This positive outlook was just the encouragement that John White needed.

John White was not about to give up on his hopes for establishing a model godly community in New England. The initial efforts had suffered from the effects of a degree of over-optimism and naivety, especially in sending out the first voyage part way into the season and in the ill-thought out conversion of their second ship the following year, but also from bad luck, especially in the collapse of the market for fish in Spain. For many of the investors in the Dorchester Company enough was enough and they wanted to extract themselves from the venture as cheaply as possible. However, something had to be done about the small group of settlers remaining at Naumkeag/ Salem under the leadership of Roger Conant, either to bring them back to England or transfer them to another group of investors. John White thought of a third alternative, namely to bring in new investors to add to those Dorset folk who were prepared to carry on. So those who remained loyal to the enterprise approached their friends and acquaintances and John White busied himself 'conferring casually with some gentlemen of London'. According to his own account later he encountered a mixed response but out of all the conversations sufficient funds were forthcoming from new investors to send out a ship with further supplies immediately to support the existing settlement and to plan a significant new initiative.

The promise of new investment was conditional on further volunteers being identified to emigrate to New England, together with a suitable leader for them. Somebody mentioned the name of John Endecott, 'a man well known to persons of good note'. There are different accounts of his background, but he seems of have the qualities they were looking for at the time. He was enthusiastic about the project and ready to take the necessary responsibility. As it subsequently turned out he was a man of strong opinions and inclined to be hot-tempered. His views on matters of religion were more radical than John White's and he later risked upsetting the uneasy relationship between the settlers and King Charles' Government in England by ripping the cross out of an English flag when Royal Navy ships were visiting Boston harbour, on the grounds that displaying a cross in this way was 'Papist'. For the moment, however, he seemed to be the best person to found a new colony on the old foundation. He was also able to put forward his own stake for the project and was listed as one of those to whom an indenture was granted for the formal establishment of a colony in New England. This grant covered all the territory between a line three miles north of the Merrimack River and another three miles south of the Charles River; these lines were then extended west all the way across the continent from the Atlantic to the Pacific Ocean. This area included the existing small settlement at Naumkeag/ Salem, and so it was confirmed that the new company, now (in 1628) known as the New England Company, would succeed to all the remaining interests of the Dorchester Company. With the grant of a royal charter the following year the company would be referred to as 'the Company of the Massachusetts Bay in New England'.

John Woodbury returned to New England with the extra supplies arranged by John White, this time accompanied by his son. He came with a message of hope for the small group who had struggled through another winter. Their hold on the territory was to be made secure as part of the grant to the new Company, and the resources available to them by way of manpower and financial support was going to increase dramatically with the involvement of a significant number of wealthy London merchants. They waited eagerly, therefore, for the next ship to arrive. During the summer the Abigail sailed from Weymouth with

Roger Conant's house, Salem, Mass

John Endecott and his wife with further pioneers. Many of these new settlers were people employed by the Company to help generate more income and profits for the Company from the natural resources in the colony in terms of fish, crops, timber, furs etc. The ship's cargo included 2 pipes of Madeira wine (in total about 252 wine gallons), perhaps destined for the new Governor's table, as well as more practical supplies such as lead, nails, food including quantities of butter, clothing including three dozen hats, and munitions including gunpowder and 20 muskets.

According to John Woodbury's son, Humphry, writing later, John Endecott quickly indicated that as far as he was concerned his arrival was not a mere continuation of what had gone on before. He announced that the new Company had purchased the 'houses, boats and servants' from the Dorchester Company and he also identified a desirable house left at Cape Ann which he ordered to be dismantled and transferred to the new settlement. He also charged a premium on goods brought over and put only a very low valuation on beaver skins, for example, offered by way of exchange, i.e. allowing for an increased profit to the Company. He also tried to limit the scope of what kind of work the settlers could do, which brought the original band to the point of mutiny. Some of them, of course, had come from other New World settlements and regarded themselves as freelance pioneers rather than servants of any company, whether the Dorchester or the Massachusetts Bay. They were on the point of leaving to join a group elsewhere when John Endecott realised that he had to give some ground, and made just enough concessions to enable Roger Conant to persuade his followers to stay and make the best of the new regime.

Those in England trying to manage this new enterprise at a distance were dependent on news being brought by returning ships. This would have included formal reports and also letters from the settlers, supplemented no doubt by comments by the ship's captain and others. John Endecott's message was extremely positive; the location was good and the prospects excellent in terms of scope for a greatly enlarged community. Roger Conant, on the other hand, wrote more cautiously, reflecting the tensions between the old planters and the new arrivals. The Company as a whole was happy to progress plans for further development and looked to send out many more emigrants. John White supported this, but had some reservations as to the aims and objectives of the undertaking. Some of the backers seemed to be more interested in the 'bottom line', i.e. the profit that they could make, rather than the welfare of the emigrants, to the point where they were losing sight of the religious vision which was John White's starting point (and as stated as the Company's principal object). There was also a concern that some of the new pioneers coming forward were turning out to have more radical 'Separatist' views than John White was comfortable with.

New interest in the venture was coming from Lincolnshire and East Anglia, both of which areas would produce people who would have a major influence on the way in which the Massachusetts Bay colony would develop. John Cotton was already an established minister in Boston, in Lincolnshire – a Puritan, but still for the moment able to remain within the Church of England. Like John White he encouraged others to emigrate to New England, but unlike him in the end decided to emigrate himself rather than suffer under the reforms of William Laud. East Anglia produced the man who was to turn out to be the greatest leader in the early years of the new colony, John Winthrop. At this time he was practising as a lawyer in London and he comes on the scene first as an interested onlooker but very quickly he came to be central to the new initiatives.

As a first response to John Endecott's report he was told to expect between two and three hundred new emigrants, with a hundred cattle and other supplies, all to arrive in the following spring (1629). He was also informed that the party would include two ministers, who 'shall be by the approbation of Mr White of Dorchester and Mr Davenport'. Five ships set sail, including the Talbot, the George, the Four Sisters, and the Mayflower. The fifth ship, the Lyon's Whelp, was of particular interest to John White because it carried about 40 emigrants whom he had assembled from Dorset and Somerset and 'specially from Dorchester and other places thereabouts'. These included the Sprague family of Fordington and of Upwey, who were personal friends of his. There were now enough people overall to split into two communities, with the larger part remaining in Salem and the others moving a short distance away to found a new settlement at Charlestown.

John White continued to be involved, albeit still from a distance, in the development of the colony in Massachusetts Bay. In 1630, while John Winthrop led a small fleet of ships on behalf of the Company generally, John White organised another ship, the Mary and John, to set off separately, in advance of the rest, with folk he had gathered from Dorset and neighbouring counties. And so the story continued, with the founding of a new settlement given the name Dorchester (now a suburb of Boston), and then, a few years later, with a group of these settlers, including some Dorset folk, moving on into Connecticut to found another Dorchester, although this one was later renamed Windsor.

The Dorset County Museum now wants to incorporate John White's old rectory into the main body of the museum as part of its current development plans. This is a great opportunity to include a fitting tribute to John White's life and work, for the benefit of both those people now living in Dorset and, perhaps even more, those visitors from 'across the pond' who would welcome something tangible in his adopted home town of the one who has been called 'Father of Massachusetts'.

Cut-away model of the Mary and John - courtesy of Dorset County Museum

This article is largely taken from David Cuckson's book, Dorchester's New World: The Vision of John White, 'Founder of Massachusetts', published by YouCaxton.co.uk.

Unveiling a Commemorative Stone in memory of the Wrackleford Auxiliary Unit G.H.Q. Reserve Battalion 1940 - 1944 [Churchill's Secret Army]

By David Downton

The Wrackleford Auxiliary Unit was part of a secret army formed in 1940 under the direction of Winston Churchill, which was incorporated in one of three Reserve Battalions. They were to provide under-cover resistance behind enemy lines in the event of a German invasion. The Unit operated from a local, concealed and camouflaged underground bunker, located in a copse called "The Rookery", opposite Wrackleford House. Personnel were local men who knew the area well and were trained in guerrilla tactics, including demolition, sabotage and assassination.

These men were well able to live off the land if necessary. They were usually better armed than the regular army with Thompson sub-machine guns [the Tommy Gun], Smith and Wesson revolvers, Sten Guns and the Fairbairn Sykes commando dagger. According to records, Churchill also reached a secret agreement with the Americans to arm these partisans with Colt 45 revolvers, seized from gangsters by the FBI! The Auxiliers, as they were called, were ostensibly members of their local Home Guard platoon .Their existence was so secret not even their family knew about them. At the conclusion of hostilities they were given no recognition, except a small lapel badge which is illustrated. However, in the early nineties they became eligible for the Defence Medal which, after the War, had been awarded to former members of The Home Guard. It was not until 2013 that remaining veterans from the 640 wartime patrols were included in the Remembrance Sunday parade past the Cenotaph, able to lay a wreath to honour their former comrades.

Early in 2015 I was writing an article on the life of my Uncle Lewis who lived at Stratton, a village just outside Dorchester. He had worked on the Wrackleford Estate for the Pope family, in later years as their much valued farm foreman. My cousin Heather had been Lewis's executor and I approached her to seek photographs for inclusion in the article. When doing this, she mentioned a small lapel badge passed on to another cousin, interested in military history. A quick telephone call established the badge had indeed, been awarded to members of Churchill's Secret Army. Uncle Lewis had been one of them. Subsequently she discovered a faded typewritten letter marked "most secret". This document should have been destroyed as it contained operational details had the unit been activated. Maybe this was Lewis's way of telling relations eventually, of his wartime role, for he kept the secret from family and friends throughout his life.

When we visited the excellent website of The Coleshill Auxiliary Research Team, we found a list of personnel from the Wrackleford Unit and discovered many familiar names. Heather had grown up in Stratton so knew most of them. I was pleased to recognise Percy

Jack Northover

Fost, whose son Lewis was one of my friends and had died, sadly, a few months before the Dedication. Lewis knew nothing of father's involvement as an Auxiliary and believed he had been in the Home Guard throughout the War. We also became aware of Auxilier Jack Northover, a former Unit member who, hale and hearty at 89, was living locally. What luck!

We arranged an interview with Jack who was able to validate the training received, range of weapons [he included knuckledusters!], and operational orders including assassinating potential informers and local collaborators. Jack had already shown the Coleshill Research Team the Unit's secret underground bunker in Wrackleford, enhancing their archives. Being a big strong lad, the Home Guard had accepted him unofficially at only fifteen. He became an Auxiliary at seventeen, replacing elder brother George, who joined the RAF as a sergeant gunner in Lancaster bombers. George at just twenty two was tragically killed in action over Germany, and this strengthened Jack's resolve to play a role in The British Resistance Movement. He was an apprentice at the Dorchester firm of Lott and Walne and we marvelled how such a young man was able to keep his secret, not only from family, but from friends and work colleagues.

Jack's family played a major role in the Wrackleford Unit. His father, a veteran of the Great War, was platoon sergeant and his brother was a member until joining the RAF. Percy Fost became gamekeeper for the Wrackleford Estate and led the Unit after Sergeant Northover's early death at the age of 53. Harry Atkins had long service with the Unit and served from July 1940 until they were stood down in 1944. .He worked as a tractor driver for Harry Christopher who farmed at Wrackleford and commanded the local Home Guard. Interestingly, I taught Harry Atkins daughter Margaret, during my early days in teaching and when we later met, she told me her family knew nothing of father's involvement until recent years.

Harry Atkins member of the unit from 1940-1944

Lewis Downton worked on the Pope Family farm at Stratton and lived in Dairy Cottage of which I have many happy memories as a young boy. His house and garden are incorporated in the site of the new Village Hall and Village Green. Lewis became their farm foreman sometime after the War. William Steer was farm foreman during the War but we were unable to trace his relatives.

The oldest member, James Hounslow, was born in 1885 and from the records was 57 when he enlisted. This seems rather old for a combat soldier but as Gamekeeper for Mr Middleton, who farmed at Bradford Peverill, his lifestyle would have kept him very fit. We were unable to trace any of James relatives. My cousin and I decided the brave men of the Wrackleford Patrol should have a permanent memorial as they were given no acknowledgement, as others were, at the cessation of hostilities. Indeed, it seemed the Authorities wanted their very existence expunged from wartime events. We wrote a comprehensive letter to relatives of Patrol members and other people who we thought might support our project, then sought permission from Stratton Parish Council to site the Memorial on The Village Green, part of which had been Uncle Lewis's large garden. The Parish Council was very supportive and readily gave permission. We were pleased to hear that planning permission was unnecessary, as this would have prolonged the time for the stone to be erected. Dr Will Ward, Dorset Organiser for the Coleshill Auxiliaries Research Team, gave a talk to Stratton History Society about the Auxiliary movement and its role in the British Resistance, where I was given an opportunity to outline what we hoped to achieve. I gave talks to other organisations and this led to four sponsors pledging valuable financial support. We secured the services of Valentine Quinn, a stonemason from Langton Matravers; to hand carve the tablet in Purbeck stone. Peter Hallett, local builder, and formerly a farm worker colleague of Lewis, generously volunteered to erect the memorial free of charge. This was a satisfying start but there was much yet to be done.

It took eighteen months to bring the project to fruition, with further financial support from families, relatives and friends of the Unit. Finally the Dedication took place on May 20th 2017 on Stratton Village Green. Mr Andrew Aylott, Chair of Stratton Parish Council, welcomed dignitaries, relations, invited guests and villagers, then introduced Major-general Tony Jeapes whose distinguished Army career included commanding 22 SAS for several years. I was particularly keen to invite Tony Jeapes to play a leading part in the ceremony and we were all delighted he was able to accept, as several Auxiliers countrywide went on to join the SAS when their units were stood down. He reminded those present what life was like in wartime Britain. "Back in the 1940s we were a tough nation and we had to be.......we had the enemy sat the other side of the Channel waiting to come over." "He said the men of The Auxiliary Units "were the spirit of resistance. We were pleased also, to welcome Mrs Jenny Jeapes, whose father Lieutenant colonel White had commanded the 2nd Battalion Dorset Regiment at the battle of the Governors tennis court in Kohima, Burma, during bitter fighting against the

Jack Northover speaks at the ceremony

Japanese in World War 2. It was poignant that Mark Downton, playing the Last Post and Reveille during the ceremony, was the grandson of Company Sergeant Major, Herbert Downton, killed fighting there under Lieutenant-colonel White's command.

Major-general Jeapes introduced Jack Northover, a member of the Wrackleford Unit; at 90 one of very few surviving Auxiliers in the country. Jack told how it seemed like a great adventure at the time, but later they realised how important it was. "Thankfully we were never put to use, but we would have done our best." He said he was proud of the memorial to the unit and honoured to be remembered along with all those he had served with. Her Majesty's Lord Lieutenant, Mr Angus Campbell, unveiled the memorial stone and said that the country should be pleased and proud that it had "people of such strength of will", and laid a wreath in their memory.

British Legion Standard Bearers and Parade Marshall

The Rev. Dr John Travell, who gave great support and encouragement during the course of the project, led the dedication and took the Service of Remembrance, where he included tributes and prayers for all the men and women of Stratton serving their country during the War, who were also remembered on the memorial stone.

Heather and I, commissioned Devina Symes, author and poet, to write a special poem in Dorset dialect, entitled "The Wrackleford Zev'n." Devina attended the ceremony to read her poem, a delightful potted history of the Unit and much appreciated by those present. It was fitting there should be a tribute from the Pope family of the Wrackleford Estate and Stratton Farms who had been employers and friends for successive generations to many of the men. Baroness Kate Pope, who regularly returns to the village where she grew up, spoke of support, wisdom and advice she had received from some of the men and their families as a young girl ... "Percy Fost knew every ditch, every hole in the hedge, every rabbit warren - as well as the best place to build camps. There was always a cup of very sweet tea from Lewis and Mabel or a wise piece of advice about where to pick the best blackberries. Their home was always welcoming. Mr Downton used to say "keep your mouth shut and your ears and eyes open." Childhood memories which perceived some qualities of men prepared to fight to the end for the Land they loved.

Percy Fost receiving a medal for Services to Gamekeeping from Prince Charles

Several close family relatives of the Wrackleford Unit and Mr David Forrester, a representative of the Society of Dorset Men, then laid floral tributes. The Royal British Legion County Standard Bearers, Yvonne Thrumble (Wimborne) and John Ridout (Puddletown), were under the direction of Parade Marshall Spencer Hare when Mark Downton, former bandsman of 13/18th Hussars, played The Last Post and Reveille to conclude the Ceremony. Relatives, guests and visitors enjoyed a buffet in the Village Hall and saw an exhibition about the Patrol and Auxiliary Units around the country, staged by members of The Coleshill Auxiliary Research Team, some of whom had travelled long distances to support us.

Their efforts, an integral part of the day, were much appreciated, especially as most people had little or no knowledge of these secret units. The exhibition included photographs, documents, kit and weapons used by the patrols, many of them original.

Display of artefacts

Information board

When Colonel F.W.R. Douglas, Commander of the Auxiliary Units stood down his men in November 1944 he wrote to them "You were invited to do a job requiring more skill and coolness, more hard work and greater danger than any other voluntary organisation. In view of the fact that your lives depended on secrecy, no public recognition will be possible."

We are proud to have achieved recognition for men who would have fought to the end for their Country ...."We will remember them."

Memorial Stone

The Wrackleford Zev'n.

by Devina Symes

> The last real zecret ov World War Two
> 'Ave recently bin disclosed,
> 'Tis about zev'n men vrom Wrackleford;
> An' 'ere be the names of those.

Jack and Horace Northover, an' Percy Fost,
Lewis Downton, an' William Steer
James Hounslow, an' Harry Atkins,
Sich brave men, who zhowed noo vear.

> They were part o' Churchill's zecret army,
> Z'posedly in the Hwome Guard's patrol,
> But really trainin' in guerrilla warvare;
> 'Ad to pledge not to tell a zoul.

The Auxiliary Unit was 'stablished
Cos they Germans were really tryin'
To invade old England, wi' an operation
Be the codename ov Zea Lion.

> They were armed wi' Colt vorty vives,
> Which 'ad bin conviscated by Americy,
> An' in a copse near the measter's 'ouse
> Was their zecret bunker, in the Rookery.

They 'ad to zign the 'fficial zecret act,
An' were loyal to thik vow an' each other,
'Twas jist two year's agoo that Jack did zhow
Where they did goo under cover.

> Course, all o' 'em were a crack zhot,
> An' 'ad in depth knowledge ov the land,
> They weren't aveared by what they heard,
> To teake the job in 'and.

Specially trained for the dangerous task,
To protect their King an' their Country,
They men were willin' to goo a killin'
To lose their lives, wi' no zelf pity.

> Cos if they Germans 'ad invaded,
> They all 'ad to reach vor their gun,

To 'ssassinate local 'fficials,
Stop 'em collaborating wi' the Hun.

Vour years they carried thik zecret,
An' when war ended, they didn't tell,
No glory or recognition vor 'em,
Jist a zmall badge vor their lapel.

Well, ader Lewis Downton passed away,
Vindin' 'is badge were a vital clue,
Interviews an' research vollered,
An' thass how we'm 'ere today, you!

When word got out ov what 'twas about
Volk wanted to honour the zev'n,
By gettin' a stwone memorial 'rected,
To enzure we'll never vorget 'em.

Devina Symes reading her poem at the ceremony

The Wrackleford Seven were members of the Wartime British Resistance Organisation, known as Auxiliaries and often named "Churchill's Secret Army".

Bridport's First Firework Demonstration

by Jack W. Sweet

Wednesday evening the 5th of November 1884 was to be the - 'first Firework's Demonstration which has been worthy of the name to celebrate the anniversary of the Gunpowder Plot', and on the summit of Allington Hill, a large bonfire awaited ignition. This however, was not to be, at least not on the fifth, as with its usual capacity to foil the best of intentions, the British weather decided the issue - the rain poured down in torrents.

By 1884 many residents of Bridport had become wearied of - 'the disorderly and dangerous scenes which have in passed years disgraced the streets of the town on the 5th of November', and in October of that year the Mayor convened a public meeting in the Town Hall with the aim of - 'Having an organised demonstration to counteract the uproar which annually prevailed in the streets.'

The result was the classic way forward, a committee of 22 enthusiastic townsmen was formed to report on the possibility of promoting such an event and at its first meeting on 8th October, another 18 were co-opted. A week later another public meeting was called and the committee presented its report outlining the arrangements. There would be a procession led by an 'efficient band' which would march through the town in 'grotesque costumes' carrying flaming torches and coloured lights. Roman Candles and 'Chinese Fires' would be discharged along the route and a number of 'captains' would lead companies of revellers and supervise the proceedings. A large bonfire would be placed on the summit of Allington Hill and 'a war dance would be executed by the various tribes around it'. The demonstration would end with a grand fireworks display on the Hill. It was also recommended that the town be divided into four districts for fund raising.

The recommendations were adopted and during the days leading up to the Fifth, there was no shortage of enthusiasm in Bridport. By the great day everything was ready - but as we have read, the weather intervened. Could all that hard work and enthusiasm be for nothing? - Definitely not! The committee decided to postpone the demonstration until the following evening as there were signs that the weather would improve.

And so it did.

At 6.45pm on the sixth, the grand procession began to assemble in East Street near the White Bull Inn, to be led by the Grand High Marshall, Mr C Edmunds with his four attendants resplendent in their elegant flaxen wigs made by Miss Foot, hairdresser and perruquier of East Street, and guarded by two companies of soldiers and sailors. Next in line was the Band of the '999th Highlanders'+ conducted by the HRH the King of Prussia, then the carriage of the Bridport Fire Brigade manned by ten firemen in their new uniforms. The procession numbering some 300 marchers formed up into 18 companies and was described by the Bridport News as a 'Heterogeneous Mass of Conglomerate Humanity as the Americans would call it.'

A bugle called and at half-past seven the companies fell into two lines, the torches were lit and to the sound of the '999th Highlanders', the procession moved off.

Before going further this might be an opportune moment to describe some of the participants in the only contemporary description that has come down to us via the columns of the Bridport News of 7th November 1884. There were: 'Soldiers, sailors, clowns, clerics, policemen, courtiers, jesters, Chinese, "Ladies of the period", and "young men of the day", Zulus, Guy Fawkes, an executioner, Saxon Prince, military costumes of a great variety, hideous impersonations of His Satanic Majesty, Mephistopheles, a servant girl with perambulator of infants, all jaded together and formed a truly motley assemblage.'

The procession marched down South Street, wheeled about outside the Gas Works and returning to the Town Hall, turned left along West Street to Allington and then up North Allington to the top of the Hill. The route through streets was crowded on both sides along which the company captains lit coloured lights and let off fireworks. Once again the News described the scene in its expressive 19th century commentary:

'Shouts of applause and shrieks of laughter greeted the saturnalia as it proceeded on its way, and the greatest satisfaction and delight were manifest in an unmistakable manner on all sides.'

Followed by hundreds of spectators, the torch-lit procession wound its way up Allington Hill and formed a circle around the bonfire on the summit. The bonfire was then lit, the torches were thrown onto the blaze and the fireworks' show commenced, all to the accompaniment of the band of the local company of the Dorset Rifle Volunteers 'stationed in a hollow and who suitably enlivened the occasion with excellent music'. However, there were no reports of tribal war dancing around the bonfire.

At ten o'clock when the bonfire had died down, all the fireworks let off, the band played the National Anthem, three cheers were given for Grand High Marshal and the committee, and the gathering slowly dispersed down the Hill.

On 7th November the Bridport News could report that: 'Everything passed off without the slightest hitch, nor was there any accident whatsoever to mar the evening's pleasure. This of course, is highly gratifying and creditable to all concerned.'

Also, there appears to have been no Fifth of November related cases brought before the town magistrates during the next few weeks.

Sources: Bridport News 1884

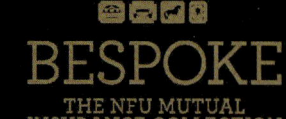

We insure it.
You enjoy it.

For more information on our Bespoke Insurance Collection, please pop into our Sturminster Newton branch or call us now on 01258 473299 and we'll put you in contact with your personal NFU Mutual Agent.

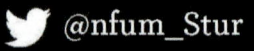
@nfum_Stur

Our Agents are appointed representatives of The National Farmers Union Mutual Insurance Society Limited (No. 111982). Registered in England. Registered Office: Tiddington Road, Stratford upon Avon, Warwickshire, CV37 7BJ. Authorised by the Prudential Regulation Authority and regulated by the Financial Conduct Authority and the Prudential Regulation Authority. A member of the Association of British Insurers.
For security and training purposes, telephone calls may be recorded and monitored.

Two Moonfleet Churches – and a Mystery

Michael Ward, 2017

The Church of the Holy Trinity, Fleet   Michèle Ireland

In his bestselling 1970 book 'Future Shock', the late Alvin Toffler predicted that too much change in too short a time would become highly stressful for many people. Toffler viewed history as following three distinct stages: an agrarian one where most people worked on the land, an industrial one where most people worked in factories and a post-industrial one. The post-industrial one, Toffler's 'third wave', is our present age, where information processing increasingly characterises the worlds of work and leisure. Goods, services, industries and skills become obsolete frighteningly quickly. People frequently change careers, locations and lifestyles. Always we are exposed to more and more information. (Toffler popularised the term 'information overload'.) I once read that apparently we are exposed to more information in a single day than many 18th century people were in their entire lifetimes. The acceleration of information is relentless. We weren't biologically designed for our present age of acute uncertainty. We certainly weren't biologically designed to be texting, emailing, viewing screens and phoning on a potentially 24/7 basis! The result? Insidiously rising levels of stress, often bringing health problems.

Places of Peace

One preventive tactic is to deliberately seek out places of peace. A place of peace may be psychological – sitting in a favourite chair, quietly relaxing (crucially with phones, computers and televisions switched off!) It may also be physical. A classic example is London parks. People have always visited them at lunchtime. But next time you're in London, just observe. It's as though people are fleeing to these parks for an all too brief refuge from their frenetic work lives.

Churches are also places of peace. It's not necessary to be a churchgoer (I'm not) or indeed to have any religious or spiritual beliefs. But if you go into practically any church of any denomination and sit for a few quiet minutes, I guarantee that you'll feel markedly more at peace. Of course it's necessary to find a church which is open but don't worry: the two which I'm going to tell you about are open most of the day, courtesy of kind and caring neighbours.

Moonfleet

John Meade Falkner's classic 1898 book Moonfleet is based on the small, scattered village of Fleet, by our world-famous Chesil Beach. (The name 'Fleet' is said to come from fleot, an Old English word for an inlet or estuary.) If you should happen to be in the area, it's well worth taking the turnoff to Fleet, at a prominent roundabout just outside Chickerell

Fleet Old Church - Michèle Ireland

on the Weymouth to Bridport road. A short drive along a pleasantly leafy lane will bring you to a prominent church on the right-hand side. This is the church of the Holy Trinity. It's best to park carefully near here and take a short walk back along the road. You will find the intriguingly named Butter Street on what is now your right-hand side. Just past the end of Butter Street, in a quiet, tree-lined glade, is Fleet Old Church.

To enter the chancel, all that remains of Fleet Old Church, is to encounter more than a thousand years of history. A simple plaque notes, 'This community is recorded in the Domesday Book 1086'. A sign tells us that, 'The villagers of Fleet have welcomed visitors to this church since medieval times, when Benedictine monks paused here for refreshment of body and spirit and gave alms to the church on their journeys between St Peter's monastery at Abbotsbury and Holy Trinity at Christchurch.' Another plaque is in memory of John Meade Falkner who popularised the area. A second sign informs us that the activities practised in Moonfleet were no passing flight of fancy. 'During the old smuggling days, this vault is said to have been used by smugglers for the storage of wines, spirits and other contraband. A secret underground passage runs from this vault, which is supposed to have communicated with the Fleet Water.'

The Visitor's Book is filled with appreciative notes from people from all over the world. One such comment from October 10th 2016 observes, 'What a beautiful church. Very peaceful and tranquil.' Another from July 9th 2017 expresses almost exactly the same sentiments, "What a beautiful place to visit. So tranquil." For both these visitors and doubtless for many more, Fleet Old Church was truly a place of peace.

The Great Storm of 1824

But it wasn't always a place of peace. A copy of an 1824 document written by the Rev. George Chamberlaine, Rector of Wyke Regis, records, 'a dreadful catastrophe which caused such destruction along the whole Western coast of the Kingdom… The village of Chisel was nearly destroyed, 28 of the inhabitants were drowned and upwards of 80 houses damaged or washed down by a tremendous surf which broke over Chisel Bank and tore everything away with irresistible violence before it.'

A combination of a heavy gale with a spring tide became, 'a most dreadful hurricane such as had never been known before in the memory of man… The sea ran down the street of Chisel with sufficient depth of water to float a vessel of 100 tons burden and the wrecks of the houses with the furniture of the poor inhabitants was everywhere strewed on the shore. The boats of the poor fishermen of Wyke as well as those of Portland were almost totally destroyed. Three fourths of the Esplanade at Melcombe Regis were entirely thrown down and demolished. In short, a scene of greater distress and misery can hardly be conceived than was occasioned by this storm. The same storm destroyed the church at Fleet and threw down several houses but fortunately no lives were lost.'

The Old Church, as we see it, is only a small part of what once stood. After the great storm of 1824, collections were made at other churches and funds were raised to build a replacement farther inland. This is the church of the Holy Trinity, to which we now return. Both inside and out, the new church is an absolutely splendid example of its type. In the entrance, we see a simple yet very moving wooden cross to commemorate a Major

H. C. Cavendish, R.F.A., killed in action on August 1st 1916. To the left of the chancel hangs an American flag, 'In memory of U.S. troops stationed at Fleet, 1944.' It's sobering to reflect upon those legions of young Americans who gave their lives on the Normandy beaches for a liberty which we so easily take for granted today.

Church of the Holy Trinity, Interior   Michèle Ireland

Outside the church are a few rows of headstones. If I remember correctly, one of these used to have an inscription to two sisters named Pandora and Xanthippe. I've always loved Pandora as a name. But Xanthippe? The most famous Xanthippe in history was the wife of Socrates. Allegedly she was several decades younger than the great philosopher and of distinctly troublesome spirit. Indeed Socrates insisted that he chose her for exactly this attribute, on the basis that if he could get along with her he could get along with well-nigh anyone! It is claimed that on one occasion Xanthippe was so exasperated with her husband that she emptied a chamber pot over his head. The poor fellow is supposed to have endured the unexpected downpour with equanimity and merely remarked, "After thunder comes the rain."

An Unfair Verdict of History?

One consequence of this Socratic marital strife is that the name Xanthippe has connotations of a nagging, troublesome shrew. So who on earth can have so named the Xanthippe of the graveyard at Holy Trinity? I certainly can't imagine it was her mother – or any other female for that matter. In Greek mythology Pandora was the first mortal woman. Zeus gave her a large jar containing all the possible troubles of mankind; naturally she opened it. I suspect their father was a doughty classicist with a dry sense of humour, naming his daughters as a matched pair.

However let's not forget that until very recently almost all of history was written by men. Certainly throughout the ages there has been no shortage of men who have opened Pandora's boxes with calamitous results for all concerned. And Socrates? Undoubtedly he was one of the wisest people who have ever lived. However his inability to deal with such practical matters as earning a living would have driven practically any spouse to exasperation. So I rather suspect history has been somewhat unfair to Pandora and decidedly unfair to Xanthippe. And I hope that Pandora and Xanthippe of Fleet lived happy and productive lives. On a recent visit to the Holy Trinity I was surprised to see that their headstone had disappeared. Undoubtedly there will be readers of The Dorset Year Book who know far more about these churches than I can ever hope to do. And perhaps someone may enlighten us about Pandora and Xanthippe.

So there you have it – two churches and a mystery. It's well worth driving a little further, going for a wander along the Fleet and perhaps having a coffee at the aptly named Moonfleet Manor. Although easily accessible, the whole area feels charmingly remote. I'm sure Alvin Toffler would have enjoyed this welcome respite from our frenetic world. I very much hope that you will too.

Moreton Church

Fran Gardner

A church like
none I've seen before.
Clear windows -
suffusing the space
with light and peace.
The glass -
etched to perfection.
With scenes of
country life, and
natures' bounty.
What better for
the house of God.
Than the beauty of
His creation !!

From the Year Book 100 Years Ago

Rev. Dr. John Travell

Once again, the Year Book's opening contributions are from the Society's two first Presidents, with a short poem by Thomas Hardy, 'Birds at Winter Nightfall' and a long article by Sir Frederick Treves, 'A Draft of the Dorsets', in which Treves describes watching a draft of new recruits marching off to war. He was staying in a seaside hotel and heard early in the morning on Christmas Eve, the sound of the marching band as the small group of twenty men set of for the Front. He watched them from his window laden with their equipment and packs and wonders for how many of them this would be their last sight of their home land, which lie contrasts with the 'hideous riot of murder and death, deafened by the crash of artillery and the roar of shells' and 'the scene of violence and destruction' they would be entering so soon after Christmas Day.

The Year Book, published after the end of the war in November, 1918, is clearly a peace-time publication, referring to the war's end but presumably going to print too soon to include any accounts of the November Armistice or the celebrations which took place at the end of hostilities. M.E. Francis provides a story 'How Grandma Celebrated' about an elderly couple's response when news of the war's end arrives in their village, and in a poem, 'The Heath'. Harold Wimbury describes how the end of the war brings relief and sadness which is reflected in the countryside.

In a long article, 'My Years of Sport in Dorset', Major C.F. Radclyffe makes no mention of the war but gives an account - with photos - of the hunting, shooting, fishing and falconry outings he enjoyed in the latter half of the nineteenth century. Providing a picture of himself in native dress, worn by him in Siberia in 1906, he writes 'Without doubt there is no better all-round sporting district throughout the length and breadth of England than that which is to be found in the Wessex region immortalised by Thomas Hardy. Fortunate indeed is he who, being imbued with the sporting instinct, was born and bred... in this sportsman's paradise...In the days of my youth it was part of the family creed that the male members of it should be able to ride straight, shoot straight, cast a straight line with a rod, and be able to hit straight with his hands in the noble art of self-defence. All of which things in those days were considered as part of a gentleman's education; Radclyffe's grandfather had been master of the hunt and started a pack of hounds in 1858. As a small boy Radclyffe had been taken to meets in the 1870s in an old London hansom cab. He delighted in shooting 'the variety of game...along the valley of the River Frome, and in the neighbouring valley of the River Piddle...Probably the day which gave me the greatest pleasure with a gun in Dorset was that on which, when still a boy, I bagged 49 snipe in a day with a sixteen-bore gun, Perhaps the proudest day of my life was when, at the age of ten, my father presented me with a single barrel muzzle-loading gun by the celebrated maker, Joe Manton...Looking back over old records, I see that in 1894 1 fired no less than 2 1,000 cartridges at various kinds of game!' Turning to the 'gentle art' of fishing, he describes the Frome and the Piddle as teeming with all kinds of fish, from salmon and trout to grayling, pike, roach and dace.' With a photo to prove it, he tells the tale of his attempts to catch, with an elephant gun, rod, and grappling tackle, in the Frome at Bindon Abbey, what turned out to be a 203 lb sturgeon, 'the largest fish ever caught in fresh water in England. He also maintained at his home the 'largest establishment in Europe of trained hawks.'

The Society's immediate Past-President, Sir Stephen Collins, writes about 'The Swanage of My Youth' describing the buildings and people he remembers: the old church 'now demolished', the dame's school, the bakehouse where 'when kitchen ranges were a rarity, the good folk carried their dinners to be baked in a large oven'. The millpond, from which people obtained their water, the Gunhouse (Or fort) which stood at Peveril Point and small boys watching the coastguards at their drill. 'The memorial to the defeat of the Danes by Alfred the Great, and the painting in the House of Commons which depicts 'England's first great naval battle by which Swanage first became famous over one thousand years ago!' The fire which destroyed the thatched brewery and the new young minster of the Congregational Church (which Collins attended) who organised a line of men passing buckets from the stream 'to little avail.' This minster 'started two institutions quite dear to Swanage' the Tonic Sol Pa Class and the Band of Hope. He remembers sitting in the 'singing gallery' with his father, when the Congregational Church had 'a splendid choir' before organs were introduced and the singing was accompanied by various instruments. Charles G. Harper, in 'A Tour of the Dorset Coast' says 'I declare… that the coast of Dorset is at once the most picturesque and the most unspoiled by modern seashore exploitation in the way of "holiday resorts" of all the shores of England…Of course, the chief obstacle to any development of the Dorset Coast has been the lack of coastwise roads…roads running in any degree parallel with these shores are an impossibility.' Harper also reminisces about old Swanage 'Well do I remember Swanage when it was a little seaport which did nothing but export Purbeck stone'. Then with the building of the railway the town grew and changed, 'but there are many quaint things yet about the place - including the little stone lock-up behind the Town Hall, with iron-plated door and inscription saying that it was "Erected for the Prevention of Wickedness and Vice by the Friends of Religion and Good Order." He says that 'The Town Hall itself is an amazing place, because the frontage of it is…the original elevation of Mercers' Hall, Cheapside, in the City of London, designed by Sir Christopher Wren.' This, along with old lamp-posts from the City and Westminster, and the Gothic clock tower, which 'was originally one of the memorials to the great Duke of Wellington' and had been set up on London Bridge' were 'among the perquisites of Messrs Mowlem and Burt, the contractors' who were natives of Swanage.

The distinguished Editor, Newman Flower, in an Editorial Note on the contents of the Year Book, explains that 'For the first time we have introduced advertisements into the Annual…War has driven up the cost of production.' This Year Book is remarkable in having received contributions from two of the most famous authors of the day; H. G. Wells and Sir H. Rider Haggard. Newman Flower proudly writes 'We are extremely fortunate in having persuaded Mr. H. G. Wells to contribute this year. Sir Rider Haggard writes of agriculture, since agriculture is the industry of our land.' Flower, who was a considerable writer himself, was one of London's leading publishers, and his firm, Cassells, published Wells himself, and several other well-known and successful authors such as G. K. Chesterton and Arnold Bennett. For the Year Book Wells provided a short story, 'The Presence of Fire', about a newly widowed and grief stricken man who is convinced that, weeks after she had died, he had not only felt the presence of his wife but seen her with him by the light of the fire where he was sitting. Flower made his own contribution to the Year Book with a story, 'Man O' Dorset', about two boys ferreting together and then, grown up, meeting again in the trenches in France during the war, before one of them is killed.

Rider Haggard, the famous author of 'King Solomon's Mine' writes 'What we Owe to the Land', in which he argues that the importance of the agricultural industry in producing the nation's food is largely misunderstood and under appreciated, but that the recent war made clear its vital importance to the nation's survival. He says that agricultural land should be protected for that purpose and farm workers better rewarded, and men returning from the war who settle on the land should be able to make a decent living.
Harry Pouncy continues his accounts of 'Dorset in the Great War' with 'More Derring-do, Distinctions and Gallant Deaths.' He begins with The Return of the War-faring Native; "Private Bolt, of Netherhay, Broadwindsor, is home on leave from France at last, after four years service. He has fought in some of the most famous actions including Hill 60 and Beaumont Hamel, and been wounded three times. He has the Mons Star." So ran the modest paragraph in a Dorset newspaper of August 1918; Pouncy says 'I deliberately give pride of place to the humble Dorset private, whose case is typical of hundreds like him...He stands in my eye as representative of that "bold peasantry, then- county's pride," who in the autumn of 1914...changed their corduroys into khaki and left for all the uncertainties, hardships and hazards of the trail of war; Pouncy says that 'war-policy as yet bans the publication of a...continuous narration of...any Dorset unit in the twelve months under review' so he can only give accounts of 'individual cases of prowess and the honours won thereby; He begins with 'Distinctions to Well-known Officers' starting with the appointment as Chief of the General Staff of Major-General Louis Bols, who had 'commanded the 1"' Dorsets from Mons to La Bassee,' who had been knighted by the King for his services in the military operations culminating in the capture of Jerusalem. Pouncy lists a great many awards of medals and honours to officers from Dorset and gives brief details of their citations and service careers. Among 'More V.C.s for Dorset Valour' he includes Second-Lieutenant Reginald Haine and Petty-Officer Ernest Pitcher whose stories he had told in the previous Year Book, and describes the award to Jack Counter and the civic reception he received when he returned home to Blandford. A new V.C. had been awarded in July to Lt. Col. Charles Hudson, serving in the Notts and Derby Regiment, who had been educated at Sherborne School. This was the third VC. won by former pupils of Sherborne; the first had been awarded to Admiral Raby in the Crimean War, and the second to General Sir A.G. Hammond, in the Afghan War in 1879, (who, Pouncy says, 'is happily still with us') he adds that there had been eight VC.s among the Australians at the Convalescent Camp at Westham in Weymouth. Writing, 'Heavy has been the toll levied by the war this last twelve months on the young manhood of Dorset' Pouncy provides a long list of those killed in action, giving personal details describing their awards and war stories, and also for many of them, their family backgrounds. Such was the nature of the war that the casualty rate among young officers was very high, and there are many on the list, and some well-known Dorset names are included. As Pouncy says, "All the old county families of Dorset are well-represented in the war." Two members of the Budge family from Poole, both Lt. Colonels, had been killed, both well-known local sportsmen and educated at Weymouth College, and also Lt. Colonel Alan Haig-Brown, the son-in-law of Alfred Pope of Wrackleford. Pouncy gives due credit to the lower ranks; under the heading 'Samples of Dorset Valour' he reports that 'Lance-Corporal Anthony...

took charge of a party of his battalion and successfully stormed a "pill-box" under very hot fire and did not retire until badly wounded. Another Dorset "Lance-Jack", J.E. Carver, established communication by visual signalling, and kept it up, without cover and with no rations, for three days until wounded. Corporal F. C. Dance...captured an enemy bombing-post and held up two counter-attacks with captured German bombs until his men secured the post. Each of these brave fellows was awarded the Military Medal; Company Sergeant-Major Lovegrove had been awarded the DCM, "for rushing two machine gun posts and capturing them and five prisoners". Another Company Sergeant-Major, E. England, "was in November 1918 awarded the DCM for his fighting spirit". During a raid by his battalion he took a Lewis gun down the slope of a ravine and killed a number of the enemy coming out of their dug-outs. Later, although unarmed, he attacked one of the enemy and killed him with his fists!' Major Corbett Smith in an article, 'A Gallant Gentleman of Dorset A true story of the Marne' gives an account of an action near Givenchy, in which a strongly reinforced German army mounted a counter-attack driving back the Bedfords and attacking the exposed flank of the Dorsets. An un-named subaltern was wounded but succeeded in putting an enemy gun out of action, although 400 men were lost from the Dorset Battalion.

The Society marked Dorset Day in London on May 6 with a concert at the Holborn Restaurant. The President, Swinburne-Hanham, explained that this was in place of a dinner which was not possible that year. More than 300 attended. 'The outstanding feature of the gathering was the great preponderance of ladies; Most of the men present were middle aged or in khaki. The main object of the event was to raise money for the comfort fund and to buy a band for the regiment, known as the 'Green Linnets'. Sadly, he had to report that the commander of regiment, Col. Bullock, who had would have been there, had just been killed. The notices for the concert had been sent out in Dorset dialect written by Charles Rogers, known as 'Wold Charl'. These are given in full in the Year Book, which says 'The Society is always anxious to do what it can to promote the dialect and its use.' Paying tribute to Rogers, the Society's Secretary, William Watkins said that "These circulars...had gone all over the world. He had had letters...asking for further copies, so that they could be sent to brothers and friends who are fighting, and also to friends in the colonies.'

'Wold Charl' also contributed a dialect account of the activities of the Society 'To Darset Men Athirt th' Zeas; He begins: Th' Committee o' th' Society o' Darset Men in Lon'on have a-ask'd I to write to our kin-vo'k athirt th' Blue an' down whome to let 'em know a bit o' our doens in the year that have blown away since th' issue o' our last book, an' marvel glad be I zoo to do. We've had noo junketens or merriment t' speak o' d'year, vor th' times wer' out o' joint, but wurk o' th' quiet sort we've a-done in plenty, 'specially vor our vighten heroes at th' warr an' the' batter'd oones at whome.'

The New South Wales branch of the Society contributed its sixth annual report from its AGM held on 20 August in Sydney. A donation was to be sent to the Parent Society towards defraying the expenses of publishing 'the most beautiful Year Book which the members so dearly loved to receive; Subscriptions to the Comfort Fund had been forwarded direct to London, "the winter will soon be on, and comforts will be badly wanted for those 370 emaciated prisoners of war that surrendered at Kut-el-Amara.' There had been a large increase in membership. 'We now have over 125 members affiliated and 55 unaffiliated;

46 members had enlisted for active service and 'seven have made the supreme sacrifice.' The Hon. Secretary, Captain Caines, had been invalided home after active service in Egypt and Palestine, 'For our Commercial Side' Mr. H. S. Henley had recently imported some Dorset Horn Sheep 'that will add to the improvement in the breeds for Australasia, and make our wool even more famous.'

Under the heading 'Dorset's Pioneering Seven' H. Clench writes about A Family Among the First "Free Settlers" of Australia. These were Clench's great uncle, Thomas Rose, a farmer from Sturminster Newton, who with his family had embarked on the 8th August 1792, arriving in Sydney Cove on 15 January, 1793. The ship was overloaded and lost most of its cargo in heavy weather. Rose was granted 120 acres of land, as also were six other settlers, and these grants were now "Strathfield" one of the best suburbs of the City of Sydney; A son was born to Thomas and his wife Jane, on 15'" January, 1794, and this was the first child born to English settlers in Australia. Clench says that the Rose Clench families 'date back to the year 1200' in Dorset, and that the Bridport Archives have many deeds, wills and charters of these families including a will of John Clench dated 1313.

The New Zealand Branch had submitted their seventh annual report and balance sheet, saying 'You will note that part of our funds have been invested in war certificates; and subscriptions to the Creature Comfort Fund had been forwarded to London. An improved train service had enabled them to hold their annual gathering on Dorset Day. The report is full of references to individuals and families from Dorset who had settled in New Zealand, so the Year Book provides more valuable information for those researching their family histories. As well as those serving in the war the report's list of obituaries includes their Vice-President, H. Martin who had come from Weymouth and settled in the Solomon Islands, Mr. William Spicer, born in Upwey, had sailed for New Zealand in April 1861, and lived in Pangatotara where he died aged 79, also Percival Cake, aged 76 from Bincombe and H. Willen, aged 84 from Blandford.

An article from The Times headed 'Newfoundland's Zeal' reported on a speech on the war given by Lord Northcliffe to 'the officers and men of the Newfoundland Forestry Companies engaged in wood-cutting and other timber operations in Scotland; Northcliffe said, The Newfoundland friends round me are mostly the sons of men whose forbears came from Thomas Hardy's Wessex. They sailed from Poole Harbour and from Bristol and their descendants today will find their character accurately described by Mr. Hardy in his books, "The Woodlanders", "Far From the Madding Crowd"' and "Under the Greenwood Tree", and the great array of works of genius in which Mr. Hardy has enshrined the people of the chief state of the ancient heptarchy.'

Another article includes a number of letters the Society's Secretary, William Watkins, had received from overseas, A long letter from A. Brickell, sent from Durban, Natal, replying to a request from Watkins for information about Dorset men, tells of Dorset service men he has met in the Beach Hospital and different convalescent camps in South Africa and men on leave from Mesopotamia. He also meets ships arriving at Cape Town: 'I asked a sailor if any Dorset men were on his boat, and he replied "There is Bridport lad on every boat." Other letters from Bangkok, South Africa and Pietermaritzburg thank the Secretary for sending the Year Book, and say how much it means to them to receive it; "I think it excellent and to me almost every word is precious; it really is a treasure worth possessing." "I have read it from end to end with the deepest interest, and it has quickened a deep desire to return home and visit the old country and old friends."

The Year Book includes a complete list of members and "Dorset Men Beyond the Seas' with 29 in the USA, 5 in South America, and a long list of several pages from New South Wales, Victoria and other parts of Australia, and several pages more from New Zealand and from every part of the world, including China, and a large number in India. It ends with an 'In Memoriam' for members who have died, The Roll of Honour (fifth list) of those serving in the war, and The Scroll of Fame often members killed in action, and a photo of 5 repatriated prisoners from Turkey.

Wildlife in Fortuneswell

Chris Preece

The other day I passed a hedgehog, heading down Hambro Road.
I thought there's nothing for him down there,
maybe he's lost, I turned back but he must have been running.
So if I were asked is there any wildlife in Fortuneswell
I should have to answer,
            Well, yes.

A fox walked by the Britannia Inn, on the pavement. A disco night, lights flashing,
dancing, people singing along to Amarillo.
The fox looked up at the window, I'm sure he shook his head, then
walked on past toward the bus stop. A neighbour had a summer evening visit,
a fox stood on his doorstep and looked around.
            It didn't go in.

There are also a few sparrows in my yard, not many, despite the feast I leave them.
They nest in the wall of the house behind, holes between the stones,
         Passerine caves.

A cock bird often standing at the entrance, spring sunlight reflecting from golden brown
and black breast feathers, for all the world like an eagle on his eyrie, surveying the forests
             below him.

Most pleasing though, on stormy days, from my front window.
Seagulls, above the rooftops, above the cliffs,
Soaring,
            Wheeling and dipping,
                      Dancing with the wind.

THE COLLITON CLUB - DORCHESTER

The Colliton Club is located within Colliton House, a listed 16th Century building, and has been in existence for over 60 years. It is a registered private company limited by guarantee, and operates as a members' social club. Applications for membership are always welcome, and Social membership is only £10 per annum.

The club caters for breakfast, lunches and evening meals, using locally sourced food wherever possible. There is a range of Real Ales always available, and CAMRA members are welcome.

There are 2 skittle alleys, dart boards, snooker and pool tables, and a table tennis room. There is also a club golf society. Rooms are available to hire in the evening, for private functions such as birthdays, anniversaries and weddings.

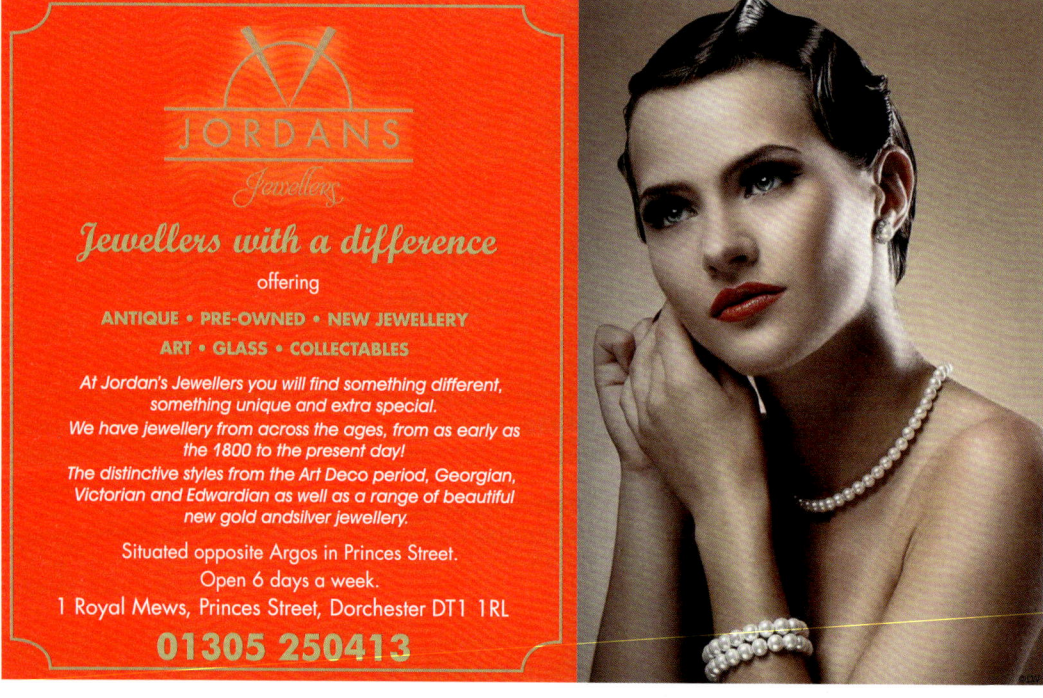

The Christmas Eve Service at Whitcombe Church

Marion Tait

The Christmas Service of Lessons and Carols with Poems by William Barnes
To celebrate the enduring nature of William Barnes and his works.
Hosted by Minette and Alec Walters and presented by William Barnes Society.
Service conducted by Rev Richard Betts

Whitcombe Church stands in a field within an impressive setting. The adjacent hamlet consists of the Manor House, cottages and thatched barns which are arranged round a green. In 1973 the church was vested in the care of the Church Conservation Trust.

On Christmas Eve 2016 Whitcombe Church was transformed into a magical setting.

As the guests arrived the candles from within the church shone brightly offering a welcoming glow and guided one hundred and thirty invited guests across a field, along a track, through a gate and up a path which lead to the south door of the 12th century church.

On entering the church it took a few minutes for our eyes to become accustomed to the candle light and oil lamps. As we became aware of our surroundings we beheld an amazing scene which captured the essence of the night.

The sweet, musty aroma from the straw, the burning scent of wax from the candles and the tangy smell of oil from the hanging lamps permeated the air and the soft warm colours and the hazy veil created a warm and inviting atmosphere. The church was packed to capacity to witness this very special service.

The musicians were seated in the chancel and in the nave seating arrangements consisted of dozens of straw bales for the congregation. On the north wall was a medieval painting depicting St Christopher with the Christ Child sat pick-a-back on his shoulder. St Christopher holds an Orb in his left hand and blesses with his right. He is crossing a stream which clearly contains fish, a crab and a mermaid.

The service began with 'Once in Royal David's City' which is a favourite that most churches use every year. The first verse was sung delightfully by Zoe and Eva Staddon. Further carols included 'Silent Night', 'Away in a Manger' and 'O Little Town of Bethlehem' which were sung by the congregation with great enthusiasm.

The music was provided by the brilliant New Hardy Players and evoked the style of West Gallery Bands. Alastair Simpson trombone, Juliet Braidwood flute, Harriet Still violin, Mike Staddon violin, Catherine Oakley cello, Fiona Staddon bass clarinet, Angela Laycock tenor recorder with Tim Laycock on concertina and as band leader.
The service continued with carols and lessons interspersed with poetry throughout. The Lessons were read by Roger Holehouse: Isaiah The Birth is Foretold, Alec Walters: St Luke The Birth, and Richard Illingworth: St John The Word. The chosen readings really set the scene and told of the wonders of the birth of Christ.

Tim Laycock read 'The Shep'erd Bwoy' verse 3
Poems in the Dorset Dialect by William Barnes. First Collection 1879

> When the cwold winter win' do blow over the hill,
> An' the hore-vrost do whiten the grass,
> An' the breath o' the no'th is so cwold, as to chill
> The warm blood of woone's heart as do pass;
> When the ice o' the pond is so slipp'ry as glass,
> There, a-zingen a zong,
> Or a-whislen among
> The sheep, the poor shep'erd do bide all day long.

Brian Caddy read 'I'm Out O' Door' verse 1
Poems in the Dorset Dialect by William Barnes. Third Collection

> I'm Out O' Door
> I'm out, when, in the Winter's blast,
> The zun, a-runnen lowly round,
> Do mark the sheades the hedge do cast
> At noon, in hoarvrost, on the ground.
> I'm out when snow's a-lyen white
> In keen-air'd vields that I do pass,
> An' moonbeams, vrom, above, do smite
> On ice an' sleeper's window-glass.
> I'm out o'door,
> When win' do zweep,
> by hangen steep,
> Or hollow deep,
> At Lindenore.

Both these verses refer to the frost which had recently decorated Barnes' country side that he loved so dearly.

Alan Chedzoy read 'Zummer Thoughts in Winter Time' verse 1
Poems in the Dorset Dialect by William Barnes. Third Collection

> Well, aya, last evenen, as I shook
> My locks ov hay by leecombe brook,
> The yollow zun did weakly glance
> Apon the winter mead askance,
> A-casten out my narrow sheade
> Athirt the brook, an' on the mead,
> The while agean my lwonesome ears
> Did rustle weatherbeaten spears,
> Below the withy's leafless head
> That over hung the river's bed;
> I there did think o' days that dried
> The new-mow'd grass o' zummer-tide,
> When white-sleeve'd mowers' whetted bleades
> Rung sh'ill along the green-bough'd gleades,
> An' maidens gay, we' playsome chaps,
> A-zot wi' dinners in their laps,
> Did talk we' merry words that rung
> Around the ring, vrom tongue to tongue;
> An' welcome, when the leaves ha' died,
> Be zummer thoughts in winter-tide.

The last carol, 'O Come All Ye, was followed by the Blessing, and Happy Birthday was sung whole heartedly to those who celebrated birthdays on that special day: Marion Tait, Brian Caddy, Dave Burbidge and Juliet Braidwood.

The service ended with the resounding sound of 'Linden Lea' being sung enthusiastically by all. Although many people know the music was composed by Vaughan Williams many are unaware that the words were written by William Barnes.

A retiring collection of £500 was raised in aid of Julia's House and The Churches Conservation Trust. Thank you to all who gave so generously.

It had been a very poignant service for it was at this church Reverend William Barnes had given his last service on 15th February 1885, the same place as he began as a curate many years before in spring 1847. On fine Sundays his wife, Julia would accompany him over the Whitcombe hills where the bell was heard when he appeared in sight.
(Laura's Reflections of her father) William Barnes Collection.

Following the Christmas Service, our charming hosts Minette and Alec Walters very kindly welcomed us to their home and we were lead the way we had come, through the south door, down the path through the gate, along the track and on to the Manor House.

The tables were laden with a magnificent, mouth-watering spread consisting of such a wide choice of delicious delicacies to suit all palettes. The buffet was beautifully presented and included sweet and savoury canapes, delicate triangular sandwiches with such fillings as cream cheese and smoked salmon, platters of assorted meat and pies, fresh sea food and scrumptious cake including Dorset apple cake. The Christmas cake was iced and decorated artistically with iced holly leaves and a red ribbon. The buffet was exquisitely executed, with wine and soft drinks to compliment.

Our hosts were presented with a bouquet of flowers and chocolates for their kindness in hosting the splendid event and opening their home to us all. It had been a truly magical, memorable evening; one of which William Barnes would have been proud.

The churches connected with William Barnes are owned and managed by the Church Conservation Trust which looks after 350 churches throughout the country. Whitcombe and Winterborne Came are open 365 days a year from morning to dusk and the Trust always welcomes visitors and volunteers.

The Family View

by Chris Slade

I stand beside the Church at Came;
Have done so for five hundred years.
My trunk was felled a while ago
But scores of saplings spring anew.

A child stands closer to the gate
As tall as me and bearing fruit
Unmolested by the saw
That harmed me so close to the root.

A grandchild stands beside the door,
She's more a shrub but doing well
Over shaded by the tower
And a nearby sycamore.

Around the place are family graves
With stones displaying names and dates.
The people didn't live as long
or grow as tall as our Family Yew!

The Dorset Regiment's Bugle

Brian C. Moore

Percy Matthews with Silver Bugle in 2008

Sometime during the year 1861 the ladies of Dorchester and surrounding villages presented a silver bugle to the 3rd Dorset Volunteer Rifle Corps. Eighty three years later, on the morning of D Day plus 15, that same bugle was rescued from a sea of mud outside the village of Arromanches in Normandy by the late Sergeant Percy Matthews of Blandford Forum, a serving soldier in the Dorset Regiment. On 31 January 2008 in an interview with the writer, the then frail 88 year old Normandy Veteran told his story.

'I was serving with the 4th Battalion Dorset Regiment and following intensive training we embarked on 16 June 1944, D Day plus 10. Our designated landing point was Gold Beach on the Normandy coast and along with the other regimental battalions we landed at first light. To the west was Omaha beach with Juno and Sword to the east. The whole panorama was a sight you will never see again. We were part of the largest invasion force ever launched and although the beach had been secured by the time we arrived it was nonetheless a harrowing experience.

'I exited the landing craft alongside many boyhood friends including 'Emma' Riggs from Blandford, who was awarded the Military Medal for his heroic actions on that very morning. He was always known as 'Emma' - I never knew his given first name.

Edward 'Emma' Riggs MM in 2001

Many young men who accompanied me on that fateful day were never to return. One young man, Private Baggs, a Londoner, was literally dragged from beneath the waves by Sergeant Les Rideout of the 4th battalion and saved from an untimely death. That episode became quite a famous story told and re-told many times over the years. We were ordered to ignore those who fell and press ahead regardless but Sergeant Rideout's words were to become a by-word in Dorset regimental folk lore.

"I was the nearest thing that boy had to a father and fathers do not leave their sons behind, sergeants don't leave their men and come hell or high water there was no way I was going to leave a twenty year old boy to drown on a French beach."

Sergeant Leslie Rideout 18 Oct 1996

"Our advance was fast and furious and within five days we were outside Arromanches and although under heavy fire we were advancing at a pace. Our inevitable goal was The Rhine and victory."

'It was pretty scary at times but we were well trained, kept our heads down and ploughed on. The colonel had decided prior to embarkation, despite orders to the contrary, that the instruments of the regimental band were going with us. They had been loaded onto a lorry in England and ferried across the channel. None of us know to this day how he managed to get them aboard the landing craft but I recall him saying: "When we reach Berlin the Dorsets will march in a victory parade to our own music." However events were destined to change all that.

'Just outside Arromanches we came under heavy fire and a German shell hit the lorry blowing most of the instruments to smithereens. I was within yards of the explosion and saw everything but before making for safety I spotted the regimental bugle lying a few yards away in the mud. I made a grab for it then dived into the hole gorged out by one of the hundreds of enemy shells that rained down for what seemed like an age. Then suddenly all was quiet. I raised my head and it was utter carnage. Trucks and injured soldiers were everywhere and the musical instruments were a tangled mass of metal, apart from the bugle which I rammed into my back-pack.

'Medics were working furiously amongst the wounded while those of us who were unharmed were immediately ordered forward. The battalion wag was heard to shout out; "Once more unto the breach, dear friends." In the heat of battle the spirit of the British soldier shone through and those of us who knew of which he spoke recalled the great victory of Henry V at the battle of Agincourt, Friday 15 October 1415. We were in the same place all but a few miles, albeit fighting a different enemy and a much worse tyranny, but the spirit was the same, except instead of longbows we had the trusty old Lee Enfield, which in the right hands could knock the head of a gnat at 1500 yards.

'The bugle stayed with me right across France and into Holland and although badly damaged, when victory was declared on 8 May 1945 the regiment paraded and I played the Last Post followed by Reveille to declare Europe free on the only regimental musical instrument left intact. On demob in June 1946 I went to hand the bugle back to the colonel but he graciously allowed me to keep it. "You saved it sergeant, you care for it." were his words.

'It was pretty badly dented and needed a new mouth-piece and on my return to Blandford I had it restored. It cost £100, the price of a decent sized cottage in those days but well worth the investment.'

Percy with medals plays last post in 2001

For the next 55 years Percy played the bugle at the annual Dorset Regiment Memorial Service at the Cenotaph in London. The service was always held the Sunday following official Remembrance Sunday. He played for the final time in 2000 when he said it was becoming too difficult for him to make the journey. Percy was 88 on 22 February 2008 and still remembered clearly the comrades he left behind in France. Then he added these poignant words.

'I want this story and my last effort at playing the bugle to be dedicated to the service men and women in Iraq and Afghanistan who are doing a thankless and dangerous job. Many are still only in their teens and are forgotten. When we went to war it was with a fanfare and great farewell parades. Songs like 'White Cliffs of Dover', 'We'll Meet Again' and 'Keep the Home Fires Burning' rang throughout our service years. We were bolstered by the men, women and children from home who sang our praises and talked about our exploits from morning until night. The whole nation was behind us. Sadly the servicemen and women in Iraq and Afghanistan haven't that same support. Well, you let them know, through the pages of newspapers and magazines, that one old soldier from Blandford is thinking about them. I can't do much but you tell them that I haven't forgotten and if I had the energy I would go out there and play Reveille for them on a war ravaged bugle'

Sotheby's valued the bugle at £2,500 on 1991 and to this day it remains a fitting tribute to the men of the Dorset Regiment and indeed to all members of our armed forces who fought and died that we might be free.

Percy Matthews lived in Anne Close, Blandford right up to the time of his death. He had two daughters, two grandchildren and two great grandchildren who all visited him regularly. His wife Iris (Biddy) died in 1991.

The 4th battalion Dorset regiment lost 266 men during the campaign.

At Maiden Castle

Mark Duxbury

Lurcher George clears the electric fence effortlessly;
Charging on down into the mustard- yellow rape- field
Chasing his third hare of the day;

Members of soon to be Vespasian's Second Legion
Toiled these earthen- steep ramparts,
Under hails of flung sling stones,

A cacophony descended too;
A Confederation of defending Durotriges;
Britons' tribal raging.

The burning of the gates,
Quadrangular Ballista bolts and ferrous arrow- heads
Won Rome the day.

Finally, after a call to cease,
Savage slashing swords were lowered
Over smouldering home- hut ashes.

A 'war cemetery' was dug perhaps,
By Eastern Entrance Inner Bank
Where George began both his prior hot pursuits.

Hares are swift runners, so too are sighthounds.
I do my best; this time to level ground.
Amidst the crop, dog and leveret play Life and Death!

Combatants dart to and fro until the hare escapes;
Whilst helpless to intervene at such speeds as these,
I Look back over my shoulder.

The Maiden mound has lost its green;
Seeming sinister now in dark
Southern sunshine silhouette.

Exhausted George collapses at the roadside, I follow suit.
We are nose- to tail, head to foot, egg- yolk honey- dust
In an Iron Age War Zone!

Building repair & maintenance | Home refurbishments | Facilities management services

Serving all your interior & exterior maintenance needs

- Heating & Plumbing
- Boiler Installations
- Home Refurbishments
- Commercial Refurbishments
- Carpentry
- Kitchen Fitting
- Bathroom Fitting
- Wall/Floor Tiling
- Plastering
- Hard Landscaping
- Painting & Decorating
- Roof Repairs
- Electrical Installations
- Electrical Test & Inspections

01747 826656
info@franksgroup.co.uk
www.franksgroup.co.uk

The Charm

Hayne Russell

"You'm lookin as though thee baint too 'appy" said Granfer Watts when he was joined by Albert in the Bunch of Grapes. "I be alright, tis the missus" said Albert "What be wrong wi' 'er then?" asked Granfer "Er got tuthache and gi'en I a turrible time Zee tis long time vor Can'lemas when thick doctor bloke t' cum round. Zo I caint zee what I kin do vor 'er" said Albert. "Why don' 'ee go an' zee Zebedee Smith ee'll charm in ver 'ee" said Granfer "Ee be a wizard in 'er? Caint see 'ow 'ee kin 'elp" said Albert "Won't do nar 'arm" said Granfer.

Albert later made his way home wondering just whether he might be able to persuade his wife to visit Zebedee Smith who had a reputation for being able to charm away various problems and ailments although many were fearful of his legendary powers. As expected she was adamant that she would rather suffer the pain. "I ain't goin' near 'ee. Volk do zay 'ee can maeke spells on 'ee"

However, the pain did not diminish and this was at a time when isolated villages had no access to dentists and the only solution was often to await the arrival of the "quack doctor" for a painful extraction or rely on local folk remedies. So finally, when pain became unbearable Albert persuaded his wife to go to see Zebedee Smith. He listened without comment to what they had to say and then wrote something on a piece of paper which he folded into the form of a "true lovers knot" He then told Albert's wife to sew the piece paper into her stays and that when she woke up the following morning her toothache would be gone. She did as told but said to Albert "Cain't zee 'ow this kin do I any good" However, the next morning to her great relief the toothache was gone.

Some time later she bought new stays and before throwing away the old her curiosity got the better of her, so she removed the piece of paper unfolded it and saw that written on it were the first letters of a well know bible text. Considering that after such a long time she could safely get rid of the paper she threw it into the fire where it sparkled and spat with some ferocity and in that instant her toothache returned with a vengeance. The moral of this tale is that you should always remember that "curiosity killed the cat" but you keep your faith to the bitter end whatever the consequences!

Witches and Wizards

by Hayne Russell

Towards the end of the 19th century it appears that belief in witchcraft was still quite widespread in the villages and small towns of Dorset which the following two stories clearly illustrate.

In September 1884 public interest was aroused by a case which came before the Sherborne Magistrates Court which had all the elements of an allegation of witchcraft. A married woman named Tamar Humphries was the defendant having been accused of an assault on her next door neighbour Sarah Smith. Both lived at an area known as Coldharbour which at the time was described as being in the "poor north eastern area"

It appears that Tamar Humphries entered the back garden of Sarah Smith who was described as being aged "around eighty" whilst she was engaged in digging some potatoes. She shook the old lady by her shoulders and said "Oh Sal Smith what's thee done to my child. You'm a witch an' I'll draw blood o' thee" She was holding a stocking needle in her hand with which she stabbed repeatedly into Sarah Smith's arms and hands. When questioned by Sydney Walker the defending solicitor Sarah Smith said that they had been neighbours for 30 years and had never quarrelled before. In mitigation he could only plead that his client had been given a bad name by Sarah Smith and that the violence used only amounted to a push. He said that Tamar Humphries was upset because her daughter was crippled with rheumatism for which she blamed Sarah Smith.

The magistrates however, took quite a serious view of this case of blood letting in a back garden and considered it to be a disgraceful assault on an inoffensive old woman.

Tamar Humphries was fined £1 with 11s 6d costs which was quite a heavy fine for the time and more than a token penalty.

No doubt Sarah Smith had, whether true of otherwise, gained a reputation as a witch in the neighbourhood and the use of a needle for blood letting was of significance in witchcraft.

Root and Branch

The Slades have been in Dorset
Since almost time begun
The first time we a tax bill met
Was 1341.

Another Slade, John he's called;
Sooner him than me,
Was hung and drawn and quartered
In 1583.

The first I know of my own line
Was not in Dorset bred:
He, coming down from Closworth,
A Martinstown girl wed.

I don't know what his roots were:
In Somerset or here,
'Cos Slades had been in Martinstown
A hundred years before.

The fam'ly was quite lowly,
In service or in toil
And never very holy:
In workhouse, but not gaol.

In 1870, one of us
Achieved some lasting fame
For when he took his wedding vows
Could sign and write his name!

From then on we could prosper
As well as scrimp and save
And Granddad had a proper
Stone to mark his grave!

My Father, at the village school,
When they were on parade,
With 40 pupils it was full
And 10 of them were Slade!

Father was at first a groom;
A gunner in the War,
Surviving many a blast and boom,
Field Regiment 94.

He finished as a Sergeant
And then rejoined my Mam
And gardened for a local gent,
Then laboured on a farm.

His children: Brother, Sis and me
Are scattered far afield.
Brother's now in Yeovil he's
Near Closworth: ain't that weird?

My Mother, in her nineties,
Was living in a home.
Ev'ry year upon her birthdays
We'd all meet in Martinstown.

Father died some years ago
In 1994.
Now it's time for Mum to go.
They'll meet at Heaven's door.

Chris Slade 25/26 June 2010 (whilst getting outside of a bottle of 1998 elderberry). Updated on 18th April 2011 following Mum's demise.

The Blackmore Vale Trip

Marion Tait

One of the highlights of the William Barnes Society's Programme was the trip to the Blackmore Vale. A group of 25 Society members met at the Parish church of St Thomas A Beckett, Lydlinch, on a warm sunny afternoon in July. Lydlinch is a village about 3 miles west of Sturminster Newton in the Blackmore Vale in North Dorset. The parish includes the village of King's Stag to the south and the hamlet of Stock Gaylard to the west. It is bounded by the Lydden to the east and its tributary the Caundle Brook to the north.

We were met by the church warden Mr Barratt who kindly gave us an informative talk on the church. The earliest Rector was Henry Haddon who was instituted in 1303. The church has a 12th-century font which is carved from a solid block of stone. The present building, which is Perpendicular in style, was erected in 1479 and the addition of the South Porch dated from the first major restoration in 1753. In the 19th century the north aisle was rebuilt and the north vestry added, the building being twice restored. The Hooper family gave a new stained glass window which was fitted to the east window over the Alter; no relation to Keith Hooper who is a society member

There are three sundials in the church; one is over the Porch, and one each on the North and West corners of the Tower. The Tower was refurbished in 1959 when new clock faces were also fitted. The five bells were also re-hung the same year.

An interesting fact is that in the church porch there are scratch marks and graffiti known as 'apotropaic symbols'. They were used to protect the building from harm of evil spirits and witches curses. Most that have been found elsewhere in Britain date from the 16th to the 18th centuries.

Lydlinch Church

The beautiful church of St Thomas A Beckett is set in picturesque surroundings. It is a Grade 11 listed building and well worth a visit. William Barnes was born just outside the parish in nearby Barber and wrote 'Lydlinch Bells' in the Dorset dialect.

"Still Lydlinch bells wer good vor sound, An' liked by all the naighbours round".

After the much appreciated talk by Mr Barratt we were treated to the poem 'Lydlinch Bells' read beautifully by Charles Buckler, Brian Caddy, Keith Hooper, Brian Button and Rod Drew. This was then followed by Brian reading "The Church An' Happy Zunday". A perfect end to the first stop of our summer outing.

Onward to Sturminster Newton Mill, our second stop, where we were met by Peter Loosmore, the Mill Supervisor. Peter was very knowledgeable and started the tour by giving us an in-depth history of the mill. The mill was built on the river Stour over one thousand years ago. There were originally two mills, one a fulling mill, the other a grist mill with separate mill wheels sharing a common pit in the centre.

The present L-shaped building consists of the South and North wings. The South wing sits on the river bank and was rebuilt in 1650. The North wing which juts into the river was originally a completely separate fulling mill.

The fulling mill involved the cleansing of newly woven woollen cloth to eliminate oils, dirt and other impurities and in turn make the wool thicker. This cloth became known locally as Swanskin. This cloth was produced for over 200 years. In 1904 the two wheels were replaced by the single Armfield turbine which still operates to this day. There was evidence of Daisy Wheel Scratch Marks in the mill doorway which were used to trap evil spirits. These marks often applied to entry points in a building and dated back as far as the 16th century.

Sturminster Newton Mill

The demonstration of the complete working process covered three floors which was fascinating. We learned how the grain was fed down into the millstones from the upper story resulting in the flour being collected into the sacks, then weighed and packed into bags ready to sell in the shop. There was a new display centred on the fulling mill, the fulling process and the strong links with Newfoundland where much of the Swanskin was exported for use by the cod fishing industry.

Between the months of October and March is a busy time at the mill with maintenance being carried out and repair of the machinery. During this period all equipment on the ground floor is stored on the first floor just in case there is a flood. The deepest flood was in 1756 when the water rose to 5 foot above floor level. The latest flood was in 2013 when the water rose to four foot four inches above floor level.

Once more we were treated to a wonderful dialect reading by Charles Buckler and Brian Caddy-'John Bloom In Lon'don'.

John Bloom he wer a jolly soul, A grinder o' the best o'meal.

In the 1990's, due to the food hygiene, health and safety regulations the mill faced closure. It was then taken over by the Sturminster Newton Museum Society, and is now run as a visitor attraction.

The visit to the Mill had been very enjoyable and informative tour and many of us carried bags of flour back to the car with the promise of baking some rolls. Sturminster Mill is well worth a visit, a must for the diary.

From here we drove through the beautiful, peaceful hamlet of Bagber where William Barnes was born at Rushay, not far from Pentridge. We continued to the Manor House, a splendid looking Victorian house set in idyllic grounds with chickens and ducks in the driveways. The stone pillars, low stone walls and stable blocks survived from when the house was rebuilt along with the Shirley family coat of arms dated 1599 which also adorned the front of the house of which William Barnes was so fond.

We walked up the drive and under the lilac flower and rose arch to the front of the house. There were daisies growing on the terrace outside the front door while swallows were breeding in the porch.

Our hosts James and Tamsin Holroyd welcomed us to their home and we were led to the kitchen area for refreshments. The table was laden with delicious triangular sandwiches, cake, home-made scones, jam and cream not forgetting priceless cups of tea. It was so very kind of Tamsin and James to invite us into their home and provide such an excellent spread. Tamsin was presented with a bouquet of flowers and a subscription to the William Barnes Society for a year.

After tea we were entertained again to some of Barnes's dialect poetry including: 'A Ghost,' 'Shirley's House,' (John Shirley a magistrate once lived in the house) 'Easter Zunday,' 'The Carter,' 'The Girt Woak Tree That's in the Dell,' and 'Evenen in the Village,' read by Brian, Charles, Rod, Ann and Keith.

Brian and Charles read the Eclogue: 'A Ghost', which was so surreal, being in The Manor House which Barnes referred to as 'The Haunted House'. It was on the halter path that Barnes' grandfather told of the haunting of the Manor House and encountered a spectral Black Dog that inspired Barnes to write 'A Ghost'.

After listening to Barnes' poems a group of members decided to put their best foot forward, the need to experience the special Girt Woak Tree for themselves.

'Aye, up that lane for one short mile I went, at evening, time on time,' 'Shirley Hall,' is the inviting Halter path leading to Barnes' Oak. The path runs from The Manor House to Sturminster, and is an enchanting walk of trees and fields: the cattle were grazing and horses playing in the fields. 'The Girt Woak' was recited a second time and the magical feeling returned. To stand on the spot and touch the tree that Barnes so loved and see opposite the site of 'Golden Gate,' the house where Barnes and family had lived was incredible.

The history of Barnes' childhood suddenly came to life and how privileged I for one felt. It had been a wonderful visit to the Blackmore Vale, a day I think we will never forget.

40 Years of Dancing in Dorset

Chris Preece

A little over 40 years ago an after-school club was formed at what was then Thomas Hardy's School for boys. One of the activities was Morris dancing. Exactly how, is a dimmed memory, but from these roots young Dorset men got together and Frome Valley Morris was born.

Frome Valley Morris 1978 - 2018

A reputation was soon gained for robust and precise Cotswold Morris dancing, a reputation for enjoying life and for entertaining with enthusiasm. Every Thursday evening during the summer, for the last 40 years, green, blue and white ribbons have been seen as Frome Valley Morris danced in pubs throughout West Dorset, entertaining local people and enjoying the local beer. A remarkable achievement I think, and not only did the team perform locally but also in folk festivals such as Whitby and Sidmouth and other events around the country and in Europe.

Sidmouth 1982

FVM wear white shirt and trousers with a sash over the right shoulder and a rosette over the left hip, all in green. The ribbons are worn around a top hat which is also adorned with a Dorset button in the same colours. The Dorset button came about because in the very early years FVM danced out with a women's Morris team based in Swanage, called Dorset Buttons, the first male team to do so at a time when chauvinism still ruled many attitudes in the Morris world. To commemorate the occasion FVM were presented with a Dorset button in red and green. From that time on, buttons were made in FVM colours and became part of the kit.

During the 80's and 90's FVM was a large team of young men. In those early days it was generally accepted, erroneously, that Morris dancing was a male occupation. Women, though, have always been important musicians with FVM.

The dance styles have always been mostly from the Cotswolds, from villages that include Adderbury, Bampton, Fieldtown and Longborough. There was a style of their own, imaginatively called the Frome Valley style. There have also been flirtations with dances from the Border and Longsword traditions.

Most of the music used by FVM has been traditional Morris tunes, but they have been added to by some of the musicians. Tunes such as 'The Wise Man', after the pub in the village of West Stafford, 'Cross over Jordan' and 'Pulpit Rock' after local landmarks.

Outside the Wise Man 1980

Soon after the beginnings at Hardy's school the team moved to West Stafford where the village hall was adopted as the place of practise, on the banks of the mighty River Frome, hence the name Frome Valley Morris. The last few years have seen a move to the Old Town Hall in Weymouth.

Royal Manor Morris; a good day on Portland

In 1990 FVM was joined by some of women from Royal Manor Morris who danced on Portland until that year. With them came stave dances, dances that originated in the West Country from Friendly Societies, the forerunners of today's workers unions. The early stave dancers have been remembered in the poetry of William Barnes:

Zoo off they started, two an two
wi' painted poles an' knots o' blue,
An' girt silk flags,
While fifes did squeak an' drums did rumble,
An' deep beazzoons did grunt an' grumble.

Dancing with FVM has had a huge impact on the lives of many dancers, if not changing them. Glories and triumphs are remembered. Lifelong friendships have been formed, not only within the team but also within the wider Morris community of Dorset and West Somerset, a community of which FVM are proud to be part. There is also at least one Dorset Ceilidh band that traces its roots to Frome Valley.

FVM is not as big a team as it was and the days of energetic and strenuous Longborough dances have passed for some, but the enthusiasm and commitment is still there and there is the hope that in another 40 years a group of dancers and musicians from Dorset will be celebrating and remembering past glories.

Nearly together

The Hardy Tree – St. Pancras

Graham R Allard

A Tale of times gone by, but not forgotten

Should you ever find yourself at St Pancras Station (Eurostar) and Midlands, having a little time upon your hands nothing could be more of interest than visiting the St Pancras Gardens. The St Pancras Gardens were in fact the cemetery for what is reputed to be one of the oldest sites of Christian Worship in Europe that being 'The Old St Pancras Church' in Somers Town. The church was built upon the site where prayer and worship have been carried out since 314AD. In 1847 it sat derelict and so it was restored in 1871, it was then restored further again in 1888. Sadly it had to be restored yet again after World War 2 following bomb damage that it received during the Blitz. A new St Pancras church was built eventually and the old church building was designated a Grade II listed building status on 10 June 1954.

The Hardy Tree

As interesting as the old church is, what I found of more of interest was that of the old cemetery itself. Apart from it having many sinister stories relating to it about body snatching and also being mentioned in 'The Tale of Two Cities' by Charles Dickens who knew of its reputation was that this cemetery had held many thousands of bodies over the generations of its existence, it was known according to records that 26,676 were interned up to 1854 when it was closed. This cemetery had been used of course over the years for parishioners and other Roman Catholics from all around London. Buried within the cemetery were many, many, names of note, in fact far too many to list. St Pancras as we know it today is of course the main railway station from which one can board the Eurostar. Back in the mid 1860's the cemetery ground was required in order to expand

and build the railway network for the Midlands leading out of St Pancras, thus despite a lot of objections the church sold a very large part of the cemetery to the railways.

The Bishop of London, who was responsible for the St Pancras graveyard, commissioned a Mr Arthur Blomfield (1829-1899), a very well-known architect from Covent Garden, with the task of exhumation of the human remains and the dismantling of the tombs and gravestones, notwithstanding the re-internment of all the remains of the deceased. This was such a very delicate subject and at the time the general public, as well as the parishioners of St Pancras, were not at all happy about the idea of disturbing the bodies of the dead. Blomfield who had accepted the commission, but who was also very wary of public reaction decided to pass the project to his young protégé, Thomas Hardy (1840-1928) to carry it out. Thomas Hardy was a junior architect who was as we members of the 'The Society of Dorset Men' also know was destined to become a very well-known, in fact famous, author of tales about Wessex in his later life.

Spokes of a Wheel

In 1865 Thomas Hardy squeamishly commenced with the project by having all the tombs dismantled, headstones removed and then graves dug up. He then had the majority of the remains that were exhumed cremated with the utmost respect and dignity; these ashes were then buried in neighbouring cemeteries with suitable memorial plaques. His next problem though was the disposal of the headstones, a very expensive commodity to transport in those days due to their size and weight. However he came up with the idea of turning them into the spokes of a wheel and actually using them on site it would save any further transportation expense to the project. A large hole was dug and the remaining bones and ashes were reverently laid to rest. Filling in the now resting place of hundreds of people he made the gravestones into these spokes as seen on a cart by placing two rows of stones back to back.

In the centre he planted a young Ash Tree (Fraxinus Exelsior) which was about fifteen years old. This was of course some 151 years ago now, so inevitably the tree today is around 166 years old. It has grown immensely and its roots now ooze over and even through some of these old weathered headstones. The 'Hardy Tree', as it has now become known, has become one of London's most cherished landmarks. After all Thomas Hardy had shown the people of London despite how harrowing a task it was that the disinterment and re-internment of the dead could be tastefully done. The Hardy Tree therefore serves as a monument to the dead of St Pancras Graveyard and to Thomas Hardy himself, who was never to forget this daunting task that he had been delegated. One of his poems 'The Levelled Churchyard' was inspired by the hate that he had for the moving of graveyards and cemeteries.

Footnote: Also within St Pancras Gardens are two Grade 1 listed memorials, the first being the Burdett-Coutts Memorial Sundial which is most elaborate and the other being a memorial to Sir John Sloane. This memorial is said to have inspired the Red Telephone Box. Both of these memorials are certainly worthy of a visit along with 'The Hardy Tree' should you ever have 'The time to stop and stare'.

"The Levelled Churchyard"
"O passenger, pray list and catch
Our sighs and piteous groans,
Half stifled in this jumbled patch
Of wrenched memorial stones!

"We late-lamented, resting here,
Are mixed to human jam,
And each to each exclaims in fear,
'I know not which I am!'

"The wicked people have annexed
The verses on the good;
A roaring drunkard sports the text
Teetotal Tommy should!

"Where we are huddled none can trace,
And if our names remain,
They pave some path or p-ing place
Where we have never lain!

"There's not a modest maiden elf
But dreads the final Trumpet,
Lest half of her should rise herself,
And half some local strumpet!

"From restorations of Thy fane,
From smoothings of Thy sward,
From zealous Churchmen's pick and plane
Deliver us O Lord! Amen!"

T.H 1882.

The Royal Navy's Forgotten Graves

Kevin Patience

Some years ago while working in Zanzibar I was researching records of the Royal Navy's anti-slave trade patrols off the East African coast in the late 1800s, when I came across a reference to a small naval cemetery on Funzi Island, off the west coast of Pemba, the adjacent island to Zanzibar. Funzi, and the neighboring island of Misali, had been forward supply bases for the Royal Navy's sailing and latterly steam cutters involved in the day to day interception of dhows running from the mainland to the towns of Chake Chake and Wete on Pemba. The bases had most probably been largely tented camps with some wooden buildings storing ammunition, coal, food and water for the boats, with supplies being regularly replenished from stocks in Zanzibar. The headquarters of the navy in Zanzibar was for many years the former 2nd rate sail/steam ship H.M.S. London which became a harbour store ship in 1874.

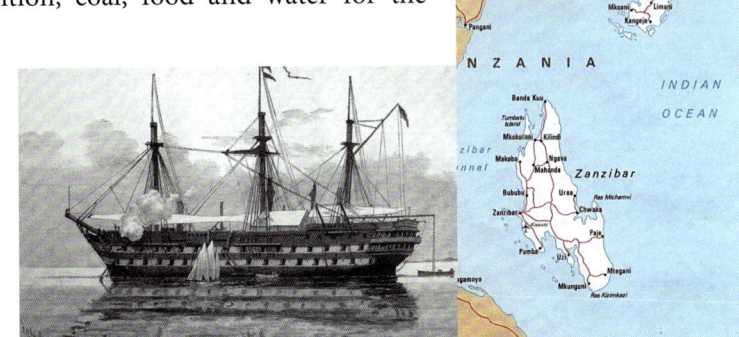

As with nearly all campaigns that British forces have been involved in, there were casualties, although in many cases not all resulted from conflict. Around one hundred naval personnel died at Zanzibar between 1860 and 1900 and are buried on Grave Island, a small island in the middle of Zanzibar harbour. The cemetery was opened in the 1840s for the burial of Christians serving with the missions and consulates, as well as for seamen from visiting ships. With the escalation of the anti-slavery patrols and increasing naval casualties, Sultan Bargash bin Said, the ruler of Zanzibar, bequeathed the cemetery to the Royal Navy in 1879. I was particularly interested in those that had been killed in action with slave dhows. The most prominent individual had been Captain James Brownrigg, Captain of the R.N.'s flagship H.M.S. London, killed with three seamen in a shoot out with a dhow in December 1881. His story was well documented and his grave marked by a large pillar. The burial records indicated that at least six other men had died while checking for illegal cargoes of 'Black Ivory' as slaves were commonly referred to, and one of those was buried at Funzi; others had drowned, died of disease, fallen from the mast or had been killed in explosions aboard ship.

Since Funzi Island is around a hundred and twenty miles north of Zanzibar town it would seem logical to have a cemetery there for casualties in that area. The cemetery records in the Zanzibar Archives contained a drawing of four graves, each with its individual teak cross. The first burial was that of Able Seaman William Hawke of H.M.S. Briton who

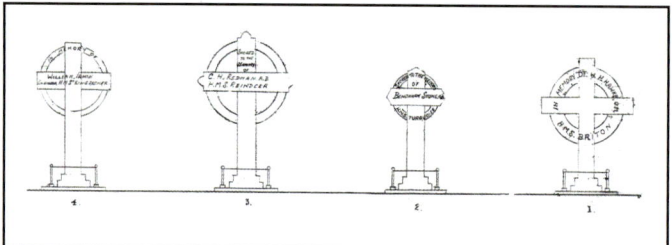

drowned on 25 August 1886. The next year there were two; Able Seaman Benjamin Stone of H.M.S. Turquoise, who died on 10 June 1887 from a gunshot wound that went gangrenous, and Able Seaman C.H. Redman of H.M.S. Reindeer who drowned on 1 July 1887. The last burial, on 30 December 1890, was that of Engineer William Irwin of H.M.S. Kingfisher. The naval camp on Funzi Island was abandoned in the early 1890s when the slave trade was beginning to be contained, and the coastal regions were opening up following the establishment of the two protectorates of British and German East Africa. The Zanzibar Archives indicate that the navy maintained these graves for many years afterwards and that they were last tended in 1929.

Seventy five years later I organised a trip to Funzi to locate the graves, catching the fast ferry to the port of Mkoani in Pemba, and travelling the

remaining twenty five miles in a small powered dhow.

On arrival I spoke Swahili to the local fishermen who vaguely recollected hearing a tale of English graves deep in the tropical undergrowth. Everyone turned out to help. Slashing and cutting the creepers and bush proved to be backbreaking work and before long everyone was soaked. The temperature

and humidity were high and the insects had a field day. Within an hour we located the grave site, deep in the forest. Only a small section of concrete was visible and how anyone had spotted it in the gloom was incredible. It was totally overgrown and daylight barely permeated through a thick canopy of palm trees, creeper and nasty spiny plants. The thicket was cut back revealing a large concrete slab twenty feet by seven, with four individual humps, but no crosses. These had fallen over and were replaced in the correct order from the drawing, the names being barely legible. Apart from the heavy undergrowth covering the slab it had been cracked and lifted by the roots of surrounding trees, which in turn had knocked over the crosses. Once the site had been cleared, photographs were taken and we returned to the beach where the most unexpected aroma was in the air. The local villagers had found a large pile of coal in the forest left by the Royal Navy over a hundred years ago and were using it in lieu of wood.

Back in the Zanzibar Archives I found the relevant R.N. file about Funzi. It now became obvious what had taken place all those years ago, the maintenance of these graves by the Royal Navy had become an issue not from cost, but from the time and effort required to reach the site. A warship would anchor off the island and launch a boat with the maintenance crew to cut the vegetation back, tidy the graves and repaint the wooden crosses Eventually a decision was taken by the navy to concrete the four separate graves into one, and replace the original wooden crosses with concrete in the hope that the graves would survive for the foreseeable future with minimal maintenance and a stipend was paid to the Zanzibar government to carry out the maintenance. That may well have continued until 1963 when the Sultan was overthrown and the revolution changed the island forever.

Once back in the U.K. I checked the casualty names in the Admiralty files and ship's logbooks in the Public Records Office in London, and also passed the names to the Naval Casualties Department in Portsmouth. The Admiralty files were extremely detailed with respect to the dhow incident in which Stone died. Both sources came up with details of the four men's naval service.

William Hawke was born in St Ives, Cornwall, on 9 April 1855, and was a labourer before he enlisted, in February 1871, as a Boy 2nd Class in H.M.S. Agincourt. He rose through the ranks to Petty Officer 1st Class and, as Captain of the Quarterdeck, joined H.M.S. Briton on 5 April 1884. The ship's logbook shows he died aboard the launch Olga while on patrol off Pemba with no cause of death shown.

George Redman was born in Ryde, Isle of Wight, on 31 January 1867, the son of James and Anne Redman of Dover Street, and had been baptised with his two brothers Charles and Frank at All Saints Church, Ryde, on 26 October 1873. Before he enlisted in the Royal Navy, as a Boy 2nd Class on 12 October 1883, he was a gardener. He joined the composite sail/steam gunboat H.M.S. Reindeer on the East Africa station as a Boy 1st Class on 14 January 1885 and was promoted to Able Seaman in October 1886. During an anti-slavery patrol he fell overboard from the launch Helena and drowned at Dry Gap, a narrow channel between two of the outlying islands, off the west coast of Pemba.

William Irwin was born on 5 May 1846, and joined the Royal Navy as an Assistant Engineer 2nd Class on 25 February 1867. He was promoted to Assistant Engineer 1st Class on 25 February 1870, and to Engineer on 20 December 1877. He joined H.M.S. Kingfisher on 30 January 1890 in lieu of a Chief Engineer, and was discharged dead from the ship in 1890, with no cause of death shown.

But it was Benjamin Stone, killed by a slaver's bullet, that intrigued me, and I was keen to find out more about him. With the help of the Naval Casualty Department in Portsmouth, the National Archives at Kew, and the Dorset County Records

Office in Dorchester, the following story came to light.

Benjamin Edward Stone was born on 1 February 1867, one of six children of Benjamin and Sarah Stone of Wakeham, Portland, Dorset. He enlisted in the Royal Navy on 24 July 1883 as a Boy 2nd Class and, after training, joined his first ship the iron screw corvette H.M.S. Euryalus in November 1884. On 10 April 1885 he joined H.M.S. Turquoise, on the East Africa station, and was promoted to Ordinary Seaman in February 1886.

On 30 May 1887, Stone was a crewmember of a sailing pinnace, under the command of Lieutenant Frederick Fegen, on station near the island of Fundo, off the west coast of Pemba. The pinnace was anchored in a channel leading to Wete when a dhow was sighted, heading towards them. The dhow ignored an order to heave to, and just before the vessels collided, the Arabs opened fire with Snider rifles, wounding Stone in the leg. A fierce hand to hand engagement ensued during which Fegen, and three other crew members, were severely wounded. The dhow veered off, ran aground, and capsized, and fifty-three slaves were rescued from drowning by the pinnace and taken to Funzi. For some unknown reason Stone was not transferred to Zanzibar, but taken ashore at Funzi, and some nine days later operated on by Surgeon William Norman from H.M.S. Reindeer but gangrene had set in and despite the amputation of his leg he died the following day. He was buried later that day by a funeral party from the ship with a cross made from ship's timber. Lieutenant Fegen, and the three wounded crew, were hospitalized at Zanzibar. For their gallantry all were recommended for promotion, with Fegen being promoted to Commander in October that year. He retired as a Vice Admiral, and died on 20 March 1911. His son, Captain Edward Fogarty Fegen, was awarded a posthumous Victoria Cross, while in command of the armed merchant cruiser H.M.S. Jervis Bay, for his gallant defence of a convoy against the German pocket battleship Admiral Scheer in November 1940.

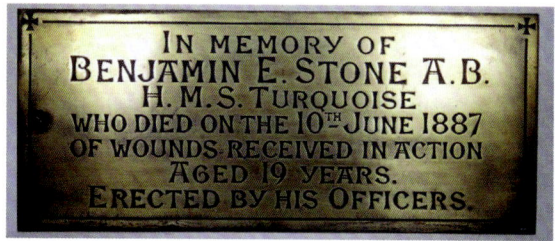

My research of births, marriages and deaths in the archives in Dorchester led to a meeting with a nephew descended from one of Benjamin Stone's sisters. He in turn showed me a brass plaque in St. George's Church, Reforne, Portland. Erected by his shipmates, it commemorates Stone, but fails to mention where he died.

Recently, while visiting a new gallery in the House of Wonders Museum on the Zanzibar seafront, I was amazed to find the wooden cross from Redman's grave hanging on the wall, together with a small notice alongside. Enquiring as to the origin of the cross, I was told that it had come from a store in the old Peace Museum in town. A trip to the store revealed two other crosses, those of Irwin and Stone, but as they had some parts missing they had been considered unfit for display. Stone's cross had the Following inscribed on it, 'O comrades stay as you pass by, as you are now so once was I. As I am now you must be prepared for death to follow me.' The House of Wonders was originally a palace, built in 1883, for Sultan Bargash and, because it was the largest building in East Africa at the time, it became known as the 'Beit al Ajaib' or House of Wonders by the Arabs. The crosses had apparently been brought back to Zanzibar from Funzi Island by the Royal Navy and presented to the museum in 1929. That they had survived for nearly seventy-five years was surprising, considering Zanzibar's recent turbulent past. It was an interesting finale to a story that had started in the 1990s with the finding of the drawing of the Funzi graves.

While researching logbooks of the ships that had operated in the area I noticed that Misali often appeared as an anchorage. Almost a year after the Funzi grave incident, I was diving with a friend off Misali and found an Admiralty pattern anchor laying in deep water, its chain ran up the reef into shallow water. Judging by its size, it probably came from one of the many composite sail steam sloops like H.M.S. Reindeer that had anchored in the lee of the island over a century ago. It may have become entangled in a coral head and, despite the best of attempts to free it, the whole lot had been jettisoned. Misali is now a marine park but there is nothing to tell the visitor of the interesting and turbulent past the island has seen. The main story on the island is that of 18th Century buried treasure which, for many, is far more interesting.

Acknowledgements: National Archives, London - Admiralty Personnel Files, East Indies Correspondence and Ship's Logbooks, Dorset County Record Office, Dorchester – Births, Marriages and Deaths Records. Ministry of Defence – Naval Personnel Records, Zanzibar Archives – Cemetery Files, Grave Island Cemetery Committee.

Book Review

'Yells, Bells and Smells'

Christopher Jary

The Story of the Devons, Hampshires & Dorsets in the Siege of Malta 1940-43

Size, they say, matters. As a piece of real estate, Malta has but 12.5% of the area of our own county of Dorset. During WW2, however, it was pivotal in the battles in North Africa and the Mediterranean which, when won, enabled the Allies to proceed to eventual victory. For it was not the size of Malta's land mass that mattered but the size of its heart. It is not too fanciful to suggest that the loss of Malta could have led to the loss of the war. This excellent little book tells us why.

Geography has placed Malta at the crossroads of the Mediterranean, between Italy and North Africa and between Gibraltar and Suez. Fate – and army postings – decreed that its defence should be entrusted, among others, to the regiments of Devon, Hampshire and Dorset. That this defence succeeded is a source of justifiable pride to those regiments and a cause of relief to the rest of the world.

This geographical situation has given Malta a chequered and lively history and here we can read of but three years of the thousands it has endured. The narrative is by Christopher Jary in his own inimitable style but he is quick to point out his indebtedness to an excellent team of researchers from the Keep Museum in Dorchester – Nick Speakman, James Porter, Andrew Edwards and Laurence Thornton-Grimes – and a dedicated band of willing helpers anxious to help ensure this thrilling tale is brought to the public arena.

'Yells, Bells and Smells' may appear, at first glance to be an unusual title for a book on military endeavour but it was an epithet used to describe the island by British soldiers themselves in the late nineteenth and early twentieth centuries and, to those of us who know Malta, it neatly encapsulates the flavour of life there.

During the siege, Malta became the most heavily bombed place on earth. It was succoured at great cost in life and materiel, by the Royal Navy and Merchant Marine, including the famous Operation Pedestal when the tanker Ohio was virtually carried into Valetta by warships. Its population and their defenders lived a good deal of their lives underground and on starvation rations – but they never succumbed.

The three regiments involved were brigaded together and later known as 231 Malta Brigade. They took as their badge the red and white cross of Malta, which their soldiers carried on their sleeves when they landed on the beaches of Sicily, Italy and Normandy, and in their bloody advance – through France, Belgium and the Netherlands – to Germany.

This book is a must-read for any serious lover of Dorset and of its proud Regiment. Priced at £15, copies can be obtained for £12 from the Keep Military Museum in Dorchester.

Yells, Bells & Smells

The Story of the Devons, Hampshires & Dorsets in the Siege of Malta 1940-43

Christopher Jary

with Nick Speakman, James Porter, Andrew Edwards
& Laurence Thornton-Grimes

Dorset Christmas 1950's

Bev Lenthall

"C'mon you kids!"
Dad's voice yelling up the stairs, 7 o'clock, a week before Christmas.
My sister Susie and I clattered down the back stairs to the kitchen. Dressed, vaguely washed, as Mum called it, a lick and a promise.

A cup of beige tea was waiting and a hastily boiled egg, ugh, the white hardly set. I always left mine, but, that was all Dad could cook, so, like it or lump it. Coats, gumboots, gloves, we bundled into the farm truck with Nellie the collie struggling for space.

Every year we went over to Dad's friends the Fooks family at North Poorton to get the turkey, the tree, a sack bag of swedes for Christmas, down through the muddy, icy lanes, Dad calling it the back of beyond. 20 minutes later we were there, scrambling out of the truck in a tumble of old sack bags, baler twine, bits of straw and a dog desperately trying to get out first, straight into the warmth of the kitchen. Always a few cats in front of the Rayburn, a couple of small children having breakfast, Mrs Fooks, a tiny woman, smiling, with sparkling brown eyes, at the sink or the oven and a greeting from Wilfy always in britches, gaiters and hobnail boots.

"COR, Bunny, how be you then, and look at these dear little souls, well I'm buggered, how they do grow, come on in and sit down, you'll stop a while, won ee?" brushing a cat off a chair. "You'll have a drink, won ee? COURSE you will, get Bunny a glass, m' dear." Dad always protested feebly that it was too early for that. "You want SOMETHIN hot in weather like this, 'sides it'll be Christmas in a wick." Suddenly a steaming half pint tumbler of whisky, hot water and sugar would be handed over, Wilfy having one too. "Cheers, here's to ee all, a Happy Christmas and Prosperous New Year."

Oh God, we groaned, munching away on Mrs Fook's biscuits, it'll be hours, and boring hours. Dad and Wilfy both had prize winning flocks of Dorset horns, and competed against each other at various shows, always in friendly competition. But, Melplash show was the one where the competition was the fiercest. We sat, and sat.

Melplash Show with Eli Lenthall in the straw hat, Bob Gale and Bunny Lenthall behind the hurdle.

"Now, Wilfy, that T 20 was the best ram you EVER bred, don't let that'n ever leave the farm." "Well, Bunny, tis like this, I think you may be right, but that bloody gert stoop of a judge, what cann'er ave bin thinkin' of to put n down third?" After an hour of this Dad rose from his chair, our hopes rose with him, but no, it was not to be.

"You're not goin' yet, surely. Here Betty, get Bunny another drink?" Oh God. Susie and I, stuffed with biscuits, while these two went on and on, the yarns getting funnier, the rams more fabulous, the competitors even more sinister.

Wilfy Fooks with his England's Best Ram, Poorton T 20

Eventually, Dad lurches to his feet with the magic words, "well, where's thick old turkey Wilf? Hope they bloody cats ant had a go at un!!!! You got some swedes for us too? I better get these kids home before I get as drunk as a handcart."
We pick up the naked turkey from the outhouse, by some magic, none of the cats have had a go at it, although one Christmas they ate half a goose which had been plucked ready for Wilfy's Christmas lunch.

The tree, a lovely fir, about 6ft was propped up against the barn. We lug it, and the net bag of swedes towards the truck and Dad's attention has been grabbed by the sight of half a dozen sheep in the paddock. He's clutching the naked turkey to his chest, the dog is jumping up and barking. Dad's yelling at it to LIE DOWN while he and Wilfy have another discussion on the finer points of the stud rams.

Eventually, we pile into the truck. Everyone comes to wave us off, with lots of Happy Christmases echoing down the track. Dad is giggling over something and says, "keep an eye on that tree, we don't want it falling off, what would your Mother say, hah, har har?"

We are so happy to be going home, we forget to watch the tree through the back window. Suddenly Susie pipes up. "Daaaad, I can't see the tree anymore."
"Well, did you see it fall?" "NO," says Susie "Well that's alright then."
5 minutes later, the truck lurches to a halt. "Spose I better have a look at un." Seconds later a very rude word, then "We better bloody go back and find un, why didn't you kids keep an eye out."

Turning the truck around in a narrow muddy lane, with much cussing, after half a pint of whisky, we go back up the road. There's the tree, half in the ditch. We lurch to a stop .Dad slithers down into the muddy ditch, "I'll push, you two pull. It gets snagged in the brambles, Dad gets the giggles at this, so do we. We pull it out, haul Dad out of the ditch. The dog Nellie and now the tree are safely in the back. "Don't you damn well take your eyes off that tree, you kids."

Home, still giggling, we pull up in front of the house, Mum comes out, and at the same time all the swedes escape from the bag and roll off down the drive. Dad hugs her. "Beautiful tree," she says.

The Vikings on Portland

Paul Snow

In AD 793 the Vikings famously landed on the Holy Island of Lindisfarne, putting the monastery to the torch and killing the monks and any others that they found. The incident caused shock waves to reverberate around Britain's Anglo Saxon world and was reported in the Anglo Saxon Chronicle. 'The heathen miserably destroyed God's church in Lindisfarne by rapine and slaughter.' (Laud Chronicle. The Anglo-Saxon Chronicle. J M Dent, 1975) This was not Saxon Britain's first encounter with the Norsemen, for that we have to go back to AD 787-789 (there is some confusion over the exact date) and to the Isle of Portland in Dorset.

The Reeve's Tale

In that year three Viking longships landed on Portland, possibly in Church Ope Cove. They may have been heading elsewhere but forced to make landfall due to heavy weather. News of their landing spread fast and Beaduheard, the King's Reeve in Dorchester, with a group of attendants, was despatched to meet them. Nothing is known of the reception that the Norwegians received from the people of Portland, and nothing of Beaduheard's intentions. There is speculation that they were mistaken for merchants and the King's representative had been sent to collect taxes from them, or to escort them to Dorchester where the purpose of their visit could be ascertained.

Whatever their treatment at the hands of the locals and whatever the Reeve's intentions, the meeting did not go well. Beaduheard and his attendants were killed by the Norsemen who set sail soon afterwards, perhaps fearing reprisals from a larger force. The incident is recorded in the Laud Chronicle in the year 787 (789) (The Anglo-Saxon Chronicle. J M Dent, 1975):-

'…. came three ships of Norwegians from Horthaland (around Hardanger Fjord): and then the reeve rode thither and tried to compel them to go to the Royal Manor, for he did not know what they were: and then they slew him. These were the first ships of the Danes to come to England.' Thus, Bearduheard and his men became the first know Saxon casualties of the Norsemen on British soil.

Aftermath

This first Viking landfall in Britain was the start of 250 years of conflict and saw the conquest of much of Britain by the Norsemen. In AD 1016 Canute, son of Sweyn Forkbeard King of Denmark, became King of England and later united 3 kingdoms by becoming King of Denmark and Norway. His death at Shaftsbury in AD 1035 saw the beginning of the end of Danelaw and Viking power in England. William the Conqueror's success at Hastings, and Harald Sigurdsson's crushing defeat at Stamford Bridge a few days earlier, were the final nails in the coffin.

On a local level the people of Dorchester and Portland later avenged the death of Beaduheard and his men. In 2009, during excavations for the Weymouth Relief Road, 54 skeletons were uncovered on the Ridgeway. All were men, generally fit and mostly young aged from their late teens to about 25. All had been decapitated, their hands were bound and they were probably naked, as no evidence of clothing was found in their mass grave. 51 skulls were found, set apart from the bodies, the other 3 (of their leaders?) were missing, perhaps taken as trophies. Carbon dating showed the dates of death to be between 890 and 1030 the height of the Saxon-Viking conflict, and the origin of the men proved to be Scandinavia. This summary execution of what appears to be a Viking raiding party in sight of Beaduheard's ride from Dorchester to Portland, provided rough justice for the slaughtered Reeve and his men.

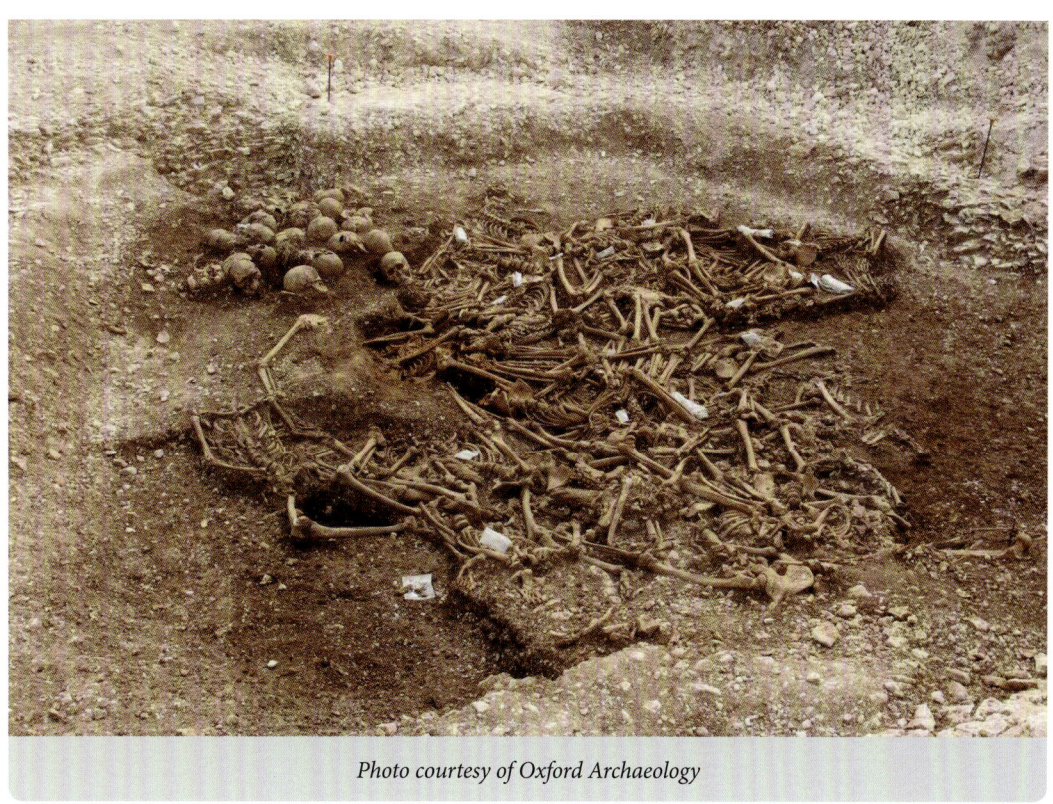

Photo courtesy of Oxford Archaeology

FIRST BLOOD

Paul Snow

We come from the North Lands,
The lands of the white bear.
We come in three ships
to this unknown shore
and the cold iron tongues of our weapons
thirst for southern blood.

We come the way of the whale
through storms
through many days and nights,
our axes and swords,
the bundled ash shafts of our spears
wrapped in the skins of wolf and deer,
covered with war shields
fill the flat belly of each boat.

Our dragon necked prow grounds,
grinding over big stones
up this strange beach,
and we stand,
new land under our boots,
scan the empty rim of the sea cliff.

At length
we rest, eat and drink on the high ground,
the sound of gulls above
and the water churning below.

A hand of horsemen
come from the north,
soft in body and lightly armed.
One, comes among us
without army, without armour
and with open hands.
Nothing we want, but first blood . . .

And first blood we have of him
and his companions,
our first
washing of the spears
in this place.
We feel the sun on our faces
and this land feels like home.

Your gods will not stop us,
your shields will not stop us,
your warriors will be
but meat and drink for our weapons.
We come from the North Lands
and our brothers will follow.

King Solomon's Pillars and Other Masonic Symbols on Coins, a Common Source?

Selwyn Williams

While being initiated into masonry through the three degrees to Master Mason I was constantly wondering whether there was a connection between the Pillars of Hercules and the pillars of King Solomon's Temple, as used in Masonry.

I had come across the Pillars of Hercules depicted on Spanish American pieces of eight. They are silver coins minted by the Spanish at Potosi in South America in the mid 17th century that I had found while diving on a local shipwreck off Chesil Beach, Dorset in the 1980s.

These are crude hand struck cobs known as pieces of eight.

Reading across the top of the obverse **P 8 E** with the **Pillars of Hercules** between them: -

P for Potosi is the silver mint in South America, **8** for eight reales the coin denomination, hence Piece of Eight, **E** is the Assayer – Antonio de Ergueta, the Spanish Official overseeing the production of coins.

PLV SVL TRA – Plus Ultra – further and beyond

Bottom Row **E 78 P**

E – Ergueta, **78** partial date referring to 1678, **P** – Potosi

The waves represent distance

A full edge date of **167**(8) is on the southwest edge while the right edge shows part of (POT)**OSI**

The columns represent the Pillars of Hercules, and the later milled edge pieces of eight or dollars became known as pillar dollars because of the design. America, on their independence, adopted the Spanish dollar with its variants of pieces of 8, 4, 2, 1 and 1/2 as their currency hence why there are still 8 bits to a dollar and why quarters (piece of 2) are still mentioned.

The reverse of the coin shows the arms of Spain amidst the **Cross of Jerusalem.**

Castles – in the top left and bottom right quadrants represent Castile, **Lions** – in the top right and bottom left quadrants represent Leon and the **pomegranate** on top of the cross represents Granada.

78 the partial (16)78 date on the bottom of the cross, **CAROL** (VS II) for Charles II King of Spain.

IARV is (HISPAN)IARV(M) – of Spain

My research has found that the Phoenician King Hiram of Tyre (970-936BC) had built a temple to Melqart, their God of the city of Tyre. Melqart was later renamed Heracles and Hercules is the Roman and western name for Heracles, the Greek God of the Sun and of course the Sun features heavily in Masonic symbolism both in the design of the Masonic temple and the location of the principal officers of the Lodge within the temple.

The Master is placed in the east *"As the sun rises in the East to open and enliven the day, so the Worshipful Master is placed in the East to open the Lodge, and employ and instruct the Brethren in Freemasonry"*.

The Senior Warden is placed in the west *"To mark the setting sun, to close the Lodge by command of the Worshipful Master, after having seen that every Brother has had his due."*

The Junior Warden is situated in the south *"To mark the sun at its meridian, to call the Brethren from labour to refreshment and from refreshment to labour, that profit and pleasure may be the result"*.

Herodotus writes in 450BC

"…I took a ship to Tyre in Phoenice, where I heard that there was a very holy temple of Heracles. There I saw it, richly equipped with many other offerings, besides that there were two pillars, one of refined gold, one of emerald,…"

King Hiram, the most powerful and richest monarch in the region at the time, recognised David as King of Israel and became allied to Israel through him and then his son, Solomon. In exchange for Israelite silver and yearly supplies of food, Hiram built a palace for David and two palaces and a temple for Solomon supplying building know how, including metal work in bronze, and also supplying building products such as cedar, spruce and pine from Lebanon. King Hiram sent his architect Hiram Abif, who had built the Temple to Melqart, to oversee the building of King Solomon's Temple, as the Israelites had no tradition of building, being a largely nomadic people until the building of Solomon's Temple.

The Phoenicians were also great maritime traders and each Tyrian colony already had a temple dedicated to Melqart, such as at Kition, Gades and Carthage. Gades (Cadiz) was the most important Tyrian colony in the western part of the Mediterranean and the pillars were said to be inscribed "Ne Plus Ultra" – "nothing more beyond", a warning about sailing through the pillars, the end of the world, an exit into the unknown. However when the Spanish subsequently discovered South America the Spanish coins featured the pillars and the words "plus ultra" meaning "further and beyond."

The Pillars of Hercules are said to be Mount Calpe (the Rock of Gibraltar, Gibraltar is a corruption of Jebel Tariq), and Abila (Jebel Mousa/Mount of Moses) in Ceuta on the opposite Moroccan coast.

The Pillars of Hercules first appeared on Spanish coins in the early 16th century and a pomegranate was part of the Spanish Arms on the reverse of the coin representing the Kingdom of Granada. Granada's name is derived from pomegranate, as they were abundant in that lush agriculture-based Kingdom, having been brought there circa 800 AD by the Moors.

Together with some Masonic colleagues I visited the United Grand Lodge of England temple in London and afterwards we made our way across the road to a local hostelry..

The 'Hercules Pillars' featuring a bust of Hercules.

This confirmed what I thought, that there was indeed a strong connection between the Pillars of Hercules and Masonry.

In 1584 the Mariners Mirror, by Lucas Janszoon Waghenaer from Enchuisen, Netherlands, was published containing sea charts aiding navigation to the New World. The original Dutch version shows a columned portico surmounted by two pillars, one with a celestial globe and one with a terrestrial globe, both feature as Masonic symbols. An hour-glass (itself a Masonic symbol especially in American Freemasonry) is on either side on the

roof but in the middle is a round mirror; could this represent the sun or the All Seeing Eye, again both are Masonic symbols? To each side of the portico, is a square of 90 degrees, above an astrolabe for use with the stars in astronomy and in navigation. All are connected by a lead sounding line similar to plumb bobs. Behind each is a cross-staff used to measure the angle of the horizon with the star Polaris to determine a ship's latitude but it can also be used to determine the distance from a building of known height. (As the Phoenicians were great sailors Hiram Abif could have used a cross-staff in laying out the design of the Temples). Either side of the portico's columns is a sailor, again each with a lead sounding line in their hands. At the bottom in each corner is a compass for navigation. Square and compasses, as well as plumb lines, are very strong Masonic symbols.

The Greeks in the Labours of Heracles say that Heracles in his tenth trial set out for the far west and when he reached the extremity he erected the Pillars of Heracles where Europe was opposite to Africa and the Pillars were Gibraltar and Jebel Musa.

Roman sources such as Seneca & Pliny, state that Hercules while on his way to the garden of the Hesperides in his 12th trial had to cross the Atlas Mountain but instead Hercules smashed through it and at the same time made a connection between the Atlantic Ocean to the Mediterranean Sea, forming the Strait of Gibraltar. One part of the split mountain is Gibraltar and the other is Jebel Musa. These two mountains have since been known as the Pillars of Hercules, though others think that the pillars in the temple to Melquat/Heracles at Gades (Cadiz) are the true Pillars of Hercules and they featured on Spanish coins such as pieces of eight because the Spanish had gone further and discovered the New World. Indeed the Pope on hearing this gave them the World.

Weymouth privateer and 5 times Mayor of Weymouth John Bond had sailed with Basil Ringrose to St Domingo where he found the Spanish had a stone globe surmounted by the Latin inscription "Non Sufficit Orbis" and he thought that would make a good motto for his estate in Lutton near Swanage. The translation is "The World Is Not Enough" and when Ian Fleming went to school near Swanage he came across it and it became a title of one of his books and subsequently of a Bond film.

There seems to be a common pattern with both the Pillars of Hercules and the Masonic Pillars of King Solomon's Temples that by passing through them one gains greater knowledge. In one it was a barrier marking the edge of the known world, which the Spanish sailed through to find the New World and not fall off the edge of the World and in Masonry it led into the Temple to the Ladder, and the stairway to Heaven.

The Pillars of Hercules appear prominently on the engraved title page of Sir Francis Bacon's Instauratio Magna ('Great Renewal'), 1620, the foreword to his Novum Organum. The motto along the base says 'Multi pertransibunt et augebitur scientia' ("Many will pass through and knowledge will be the greater").

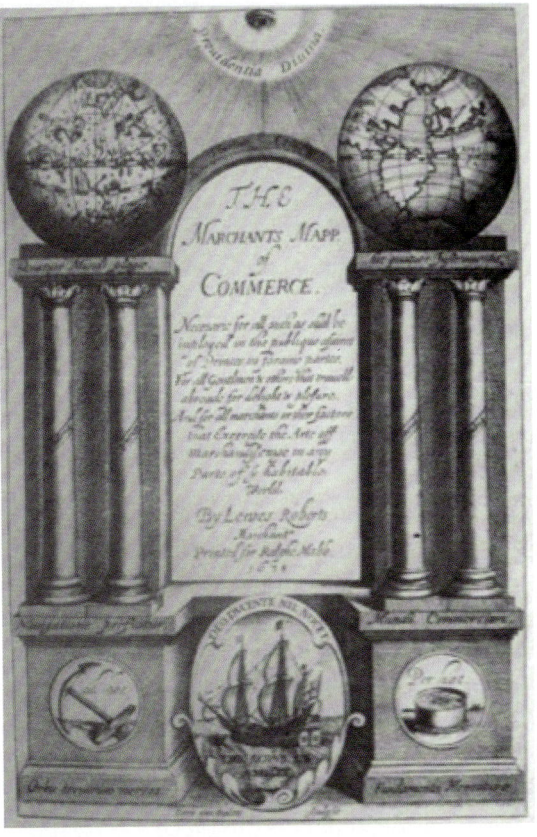

The slightly later Merchants Mapp of Commerce by Lewes Roberts is a book published in 1638 on maritime trade and its title page engraving shows four columns, the first pair surmounted by a celestial globe and the second pair surmounted by a terrestrial globe. Above the pairs of columns is providential divina, - by Divine Providence, better known as the All Seeing Eye, later adopted as a Masonic symbol.

The evidence suggests that Masonry shares many symbols, beside the Pillars of Hercules, with the coins and with seafaring; the Phoenicians being a great maritime power under King Hiram's reign. The Spanish used the symbolism of both the Gibraltar and Cadiz Pillars of Hercules as exploration statements on their pieces of eight.

In 2016, I and my partner Fliss travelled to Andalusia in Spain to undertake some maritime research and to visit Seville, the main port for the Spanish South American trade. The pillars feature in the Spanish flag and sure enough we came across pillars in one of Seville's parks.

We then made a day trip by train to Cadiz to see if we could find the original famed Pillars of Hercules there. We went around their museum, which featured their maritime history and we came across a tile featuring the early arms of Cadiz, namely Hercules and the pillars. "Cadium Dominator que Hercules Fundator" with NON PLUS ULTRA (no further) around the pillars suggesting it dated from before Spain's discovery of the New World.

This later exhibit shows PLUS ULTRA. We asked the curator of the museum where the Pillars of Hercules were in Cadiz and he said there were none so after touring the magnificent city we made our way back to the railway station next to where the cruise liners tie up and there we found…..

So although the original ones do not survive they do indeed have new ones. The left hand pillar is surmounted by the Pillars of Hercules together with the arms of Spain as depicted on the piece of eight.

We have connections with both Hercules and his pillars in Dorset. Hercules has been suggested as the Cerne Giant with his club and feint signs of his cloak and when you drive to Portland you will see a pair of pillars on the green where the old railway station used to be off Victoria Square. They were erected by the six local Masonic Lodges of Portland, located in Victoria Square, and were originally going to be placed on either side of the road after crossing the Ferrybridge from Weymouth and were to have Masonic Terrestrial and Celestial globes on top but that was turned down by the authorities and they were changed to have beacons on top to mirror the warning beacons that were historically lit around the coast and also to commemorate 50 years of Queen Elizabeth II.

We have come full circle back to Chesil Beach where the pieces of eight came from. So when you drive onto Portland will you fall off the end of the World or pass through them to gain greater knowledge? NE PLUS ULTRA or PLUS ULTRA. It is a mystical place in either case.

References:
English Merchant Shipping and Anglo Dutch Rivalry in the 17th Century – National Maritime Museum
Greek and Roman Mythology – Michael Stapleton
Cover illustration of the Mariner's Mirror - the Journal of the Society of Nautical Research
Pieces of Eight – Selwyn Williams
Las Monedas Hispano Musulmanas y Cristianas - Caston & Cayon
The Practical Book of Cobs – Daniel Sedwick and Frank Sedwick

A-Maze-Ing

Adrian Fisher

Adrian Fisher Design is the world's number one maze company, operating from studios at Portman Lodge, Durweston since 2002.

They are one of Dorset's most idiosyncratic export companies, having created over 700 mazes worldwide across 40 countries and setting nine Guinness World Records.

Within the gardens Adrian has created a yew hedge maze, with a central folly tower using the distinctive Dorset style of "brick and flint".

Within the tower, there is a mirrored chamber lit with ever-changing coloured lights; a blue spiral staircase leads to a walkway around the battlements above.

This unique garden feature makes an unforgettable impression on friends, guests and overseas clients alike.

Alan's adventures in Newfoundland

The Society of Dorset Men's Alan Perry is the only European ever to have received the Order of Newfoundland and Labrador. Roger Guttridge tells his story.

When film-maker Otto Tucker walked into a wine warehouse on Poole Quay thirty years ago looking for a distant relative of his wife, his interest turned out to be based on a false assumption. Yet it proved to be a key moment in re-establishing the historic links between Dorset and his home province of Newfoundland, Canada – and a life-changing moment for a number of individuals, not least Society of Dorset Men life member Alan Perry.

The year was 1983 and Otto was in Dorset with a film crew to make a film on the connections. The warehouse belonged to wine shippers Perry & Perry and the Newfoundlander asked to speak to 'Mr. Perry'.

'He said he thought I must be related to his wife Ruby because her family were named Perry and lived in Poole 150 years ago before settling in Newfoundland,' says Alan. 'I said, "I'm afraid not, because I was born in London and lived there until we were bombed out during the war".'

In fact Alan's first involvement with Dorset was in 1957, soon after he married his wife Jill. Having tasted rural life as a wartime evacuee in Scotland and Buckinghamshire, he suggested setting up home in the country and they bought Southview Nurseries at Corfe Mullen. Alan already knew he had green fingers, having been put in the 'gardening class' at school because of academic limitations that we would now call dyslexia. This too was a life-changing moment. Alan took readily to gardening, left school at 14 and began a four-year apprenticeship in a nursery. He was soon to discover that as well as green fingers, he also had the Midas touch as a businessman.

'I worked extremely hard and after 12 years I bought the other two nurseries at Corfe Mullen,' he says. 'Then I was extremely lucky and got planning permission for 23 houses at the Haven Nurseries in Hillside Road. That was a wonderful thing moneywise. I was going to sell it but my solicitor said the amount of tax on land with planning permission was very high and the only way to get over it was to build the houses myself. My father said he would help me, we built those houses and business was so good for us that we finished up building 66 houses and bungalows in Corfe Mullen in the late 1970s.'

The nurseryman-turned-developer sold the property business, took a holiday in France and, after discovering he could buy a decent bottle of wine there for £1, enrolled to study wine at evening classes. Ever the entrepreneur, he then launched Perry & Perry on Poole Quay. Soon he was employing two salesmen across Dorset and needed a bigger warehouse at Parkstone. He then accepted an offer to sell that business to Majestic Wines in London.

In the meantime time Otto Tucker's visit to Dorset had inspired the formation of the Wessex Newfoundland Society in Poole (with Alan as vice-chairman) and its sister organisation in Canada, the Wessex Society of Newfoundland. Financially secure and with time on his hands following his various business deals, Alan recalled Otto's visit and suggested to Jill that they visit Newfoundland. Their first visit in 1987 was to be the first of sixty-three visits over the next thirty years. 'We got to know Otto and his great friend Cyril Poole and they and their friends looked after us tremendously,' says Alan. 'We really loved it there.'

Among the places they visited was a picturesque harbour village called Trinity and it was there that they saw the remains of a brick house. 'The only things that remained were the two brick walls where the chimneys were,' Alan recalls. 'It took me by surprise because it was the only

Trinity from the air. Photo by Roger Guttridge

L-r Alan Perry, Lady Digby, Lord Digby and Chris O'Dea outside the Lester-Garland ruin in 1993

brick thing I had seen. Everything else in Trinity was constructed from timber. Making inquiries, I met a gentleman called Rupert Morris, who was the curator of the little Trinity Museum. I said wouldn't it be lovely to rebuild the house. He said there was no chance because they could never afford the one million Canadian dollars it would cost. That was worth about £500,000 then.'

Alan learned that the house was the first brick house to be built in Canada. It was built in the 1760s by Benjamin Lester of Poole, whose family's ships were among 300 that left Poole every spring to fish for cod off the coast of Newfoundland. The cod would be put in barrels of salt for preservation and taken to Britain, the Mediterranean or the West Indies in the late summer. 'They didn't have fridges of course so anything that you could keep for 12 months was sought after. The Navy used to buy large quantities of it,' says Alan. 'There were six very rich families in Poole at that time. The Lester-Garlands had thirty ships, which was the biggest fleet. All the big houses that were built in and around Poole from about 1750 to 1820 were built from the profits of the cod trade, including the Mansion House, Upton House, Joliffe House and Post Green, Lytchett Minster.'

The remains of the Lester-Garland House in 1993

Alan quickly learned that although forty other West Country ports were involved in the Newfoundland trade, Poole came increasingly to dominate it in the eighteenth and early nineteenth centuries. This in turn boosted other trades, such as rope-making at Bridport and the manufacture of a coarse woollen cloth called swanskin at Sturminster Newton, Shaftesbury and the Blackmore Vale villages. It also led to direct and indirect recruitment from Dorset's villages and market towns. Those who migrated to Newfoundland naturally took their customs with them. Two to three centuries later, Dorset surnames remain commonplace, the Dorset dialect is still spoken by many while in some places you can still find traditional Dorset furniture and fishing boats based on Poole harbour designs. Even the endangered Newfoundland pony is descended from the New Forest, Dartmoor and Connemara ponies that were shipped across as working animals.

It was these remarkable connections that really captured Alan's imagination. 'I was already very interested in the history of Poole and as I made inquiries in Newfoundland, so much of it led back to Dorset,' he says. 'The very strong links intrigued me. A university professor, Gordon Handcock [a descendant of the Hancocks (sic) of Sturminster Newton] had worked out that even today 45 per cent of the population are descended from people who originated in Dorset. Most of the other ancestors were from other parts of the West Country or Ireland, where the ships stopped at Waterford or Wexford for supplies and crew before crossing the Atlantic. It's also interesting because Newfoundland has a population of only about half-a-million – less than that of Dorset – on an island the size of England and Wales combined.'

By the time of his third visit to Trinity, Alan was ready to announce an ambitious plan to raise the £500,000 needed to rebuild the Lester-Garland house. Rupert Morris promised that the Trinity Historical Society would help with anything he organised. The first thing Alan asked him to do was stop selling off the dwindling remains of the house at $1 per 100 bricks to local people for their own use. Alan then launched two charities – the Trinity Trust in Dorset and an equivalent organisation in Newfoundland. He also persuaded Lord Digby to become Patron of the Dorset charity with the then Governor of Newfoundland, Fred Russell, fulfilling the equivalent role on the other side of the Atlantic. Mr. Russell, a former Canadian fighter pilot, had been stationed in the New Forest during the Second World War so had a particular affinity with this part of England.

'Seeing the remains of the first brick house in Canada, I thought what a wonderful thing it would be to rebuild it and unite Dorset and Newfoundland again,' says Alan. 'My idea was to open it as a museum and learning centre about the history of the link between our two countries. Nobody was against the idea at all. The only problem was raising the money.'

By 1993 Alan was in a position to launch his project with a formal event in St John's, the Newfoundland capital, followed by a more informal one in Trinity itself. Both were attended by dignitaries including Lord and Lady Digby, Mr. Russell and the Newfoundland Minister of Tourism, Jim Welsh. Fund-raising events were held on both sides of the Atlantic and there were several notable donations including $10,000 from Paul Johnson, a Newfoundland businessman, who had been involved in other historical projects in the province, and £5,000 from Dorset County Council. Trinity Trust Newfoundland chairman Chris O'Dea organised an auction at St. John's featuring historical lots from both sides of the Atlantic. The Dorset folk group The Yetties played fund-raising concerts at both Wimborne's Tivoli Theatre and in Newfoundland, where they proved very popular. They included both Dorset and Newfoundland songs in their shows.

Alan also commissioned Roger Desoutter, one of Britain's leading marine artists, to paint a picture of the Lord Nelson, one of Poole's Newfoundland trading ships about 200 years ago. 'I commissioned him to paint it which he did it wonderfully,' he says. 'When I went up to collect it, I told him I was going to get 250 numbered limited edition prints made and he said, "You can't do that because you haven't bought the copyright." It doubled the price of the picture. I got Lord Digby to personally sign all 250 prints, then I took them all to Newfoundland, which was quite a job. When Frederick Russell had also signed them, I left 125 for sale there and brought the other 125 home for sale in England. That raised a nice bit of money.'

Alan presented the number one print to the Queen when she visited Lord and Lady Digby's home at Minterne Magna. The occasion was professionally photographed for posterity and the Queen called over a granddaughter of Lord and Lady Digby to be in the picture. 'Lord and Lady Digby were extremely supportive and helpful in raising money over many years,' Alan adds.

Alan presents the number one print of the Lord Nelson painting to the Queen at Minterne Magna as the Duke of Edinburgh and Lord and Lady Digby's granddaughter look on.

The highest profile fund-raiser was when Alan rode a penny-farthing from Trinity to St. John's – a 164-mile journey. He was accompanied by Ringwood cycle shop owner David

Benn, a penny-farthing expert, who normally used his skills by doing stunt work in films. The journey took six days and every evening the cyclists and their back-up crew marked the point they had reached with a piece of wood. The sight of two eccentric Englishmen on penny-farthing cycles guaranteed huge publicity across Newfoundland and the ride raised £60,000 for the Trinity Trust project.

Alan Perry gives a young Trinity resident his first penny-farthing lesson in front of the Trinity ruin.

Alan Perry (left) and David Benn arrive in St. John's on their penny-farthings.

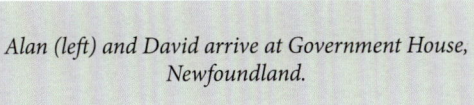

Alan (left) and David arrive at Government House, Newfoundland.

'We got excellent media coverage. Very few people in Newfoundland had ever seen a penny-farthing,' says Alan. 'People came out in the villages to put money in our boxes and the truckers on the Trans-Canada Highway tooted as they passed. All that added to the fun of it. I fell off once and broke my elbow. Getting off is the hardest bit. Fortunately there were no traffic lights between Trinity and St. John's. But there were in St. John's itself, which was a problem because you can't stop without the bike falling over. Luckily I knew the Mayor and he was kind enough to provide a police escort through the city. Our destination was Government House, where I rode into a garden party.'

Another challenge Alan had to solve was acquiring the 25,000 British bricks required for the rebuild and shipping them across the Atlantic. When Lord Digby hosted a dinner at the House of Lords and asked Alan to invite two or three special guests, one of the invitees was the managing director of Hanson Bricks. By the end of the dinner he had agreed to donate the 25,000 bricks. Next the irresistibly persuasive Mr. Perry approached Maersk, the world's biggest container shipping company – and they agreed to ship the bricks to Newfoundland free of charge.

The almost total absence of brick buildings in most of Newfoundland also means an acute shortage of appropriate labour – and Alan's builders had to import bricklayers from St. John's 164 miles away to do the work. Alan himself made five visits to Newfoundland to supervise the project. His aim was to have the house built by June 1997, when Newfoundland would be celebrating the 500th anniversary of its discovery by John Cabot, a Venetian sailor formerly known as Giovanni Caboto. In 1497, five years after Columbus's discovery of Central America, Cabot sailed from Bristol and effectively discovered North

The Queen with the captain of the Matthew in 1997. Photo by Roger Guttridge.

America (or more accurately 'rediscovered' it, as the Vikings and possibly others had already trodden this path). Cabot also discovered Newfoundland's cod-rich waters – so rich in fact that it was apparently possible to throw a basket into the sea and haul it back up overflowing with cod. Although Cabot was lost during his second trans-Atlantic voyage, Newfoundland's secret was out and soon growing numbers of ships were sailing from the West Country to exploit this great natural resource.

The 500th anniversary celebrations were centred on Bonavista, which is believed to be the point of Cabot's first landing in 1497. On June 24, 30,000 people converged on the single road into this small coastal community (population 3,500), including the Queen, the Duke of Edinburgh and the Lord Mayor of Bristol, who had chartered an airliner to take himself and his guests on a ten-day visit to Newfoundland. The highlight of the festivities was the arrival of the Matthew, a reconstruction of the ship in which Cabot crossed the Atlantic five centuries earlier to the day. Newfoundland is famous for its fog as a result of the warmer waters on the edge of the Gulf Stream meeting the colder Atlantic current. The magical sight of a medieval sailing vessel emerging out of the coastal fog off Bonavista in 1997 was something that no-one present will ever forget.

The Matthew following her arrival at Bonavista in 1997. Photo by Roger Guttridge.

The newly rebuilt Lester-Garland House in 1997 with the timber Ryan's Store to the right.

Outside the rebuilt Lester-Garland House in 1997 (l-r) Alan Perry, Lord Digby, Fred Russell, Mayor of Trinity David White, John Lester-Garland and Britain's Canadian High Commissioner Anthony Goodenough.

Next day a few of the 30,000 headed for Trinity, where Alan had assembled his own group of dignitaries for the grand unveiling of the rebuilt Lester-Garland House. They included members of the Newfoundland Government, forty members of the Wessex Newfoundland Society from Dorset and members of the Ryan family, who were the last occupants before the building fell into disrepair and was partially demolished for safety reasons in 1964. Also present was John Lester-Garland, from Bath, the last direct descendant of the family who built not only the house at Trinity but Post Green at Lytchett Minster and the Mansion House in Poole. The Trinity house was built two or three years after Post Green and was originally identical although it was later modified as its double gable or sloping roofs trapped snow which turned to ice and repeatedly caused damage. After the Trinity event, Alan, Jill and some of their guests attended a dinner at St. John's, where the Queen was again present.

Trinity Trust Patrons Fred Russell (left) and Lord Digby ring the Trinity Bell to mark the rebuild in 1997. Photo by Roger Guttridge.

The following year the Queen presented Alan with the OBE in recognition of his services to Canada. Jill, their son Simon and their granddaughter Emma joined him at Buckingham Palace. The invariably well-informed monarch asked Alan: 'How is your house in Trinity?' He replied: 'It's going exceptionally well, Your Majesty.'

Two decades on, it's still going exceptionally well. The rebuilt Lester-Garland House is flourishing as a museum and learning centre for young people and a celebration of Trinity's historic links with South West England and Poole in particular. The house even has paintings and period furniture that Alan has shipped over from England, much of it acquired from John Lester-Garland during his lifetime or from his estate following his death. The fixtures and fittings also include a large bell (known as the Trinity Bell) and two stained glass windows that Alan bought from Sopley House near Ringwood before it was demolished.

The cement holding the Lester-Garland House's bricks together had barely dried when Alan was approached in connection with a new project. Residents at Cupids (population 790) were planning their own celebration in 2010, a date which marked the 400th anniversary of the first English settlement in Canada. It was founded by James Guy, a Bristol merchant who lobbied King James I to establish a colony following a scouting mission in 1608. Two years later he returned to what was then called Cuper's Cove with a party of 39 men and a cargo of grain and livestock and the aim of 'securing the trade of fishing'. He immediately became the first Governor of Newfoundland and returned in 1611 with some more livestock and the female settlers that were required to create a proper colony. By 1612 he had established a link with the native inhabitants, known as Beothuck Indians, sharing a meal with them, exchanging gifts and establishing a fur trade. Guy's biggest problem appears to have been the pirate Peter Easton, whose predatory plundering forced Guy to fortify the settlement and hand over livestock as a protection payment.

Organisers of the 2010 Cupids event invited Alan to become their UK representative for the celebrations. There was no fund-raising involved this time but he helped them in various ways. The celebrations were launched in November 2009 at a ceremony attended by Prince Charles and Camilla, Duchess of Cornwall. Alan was carrying a copy of the Encyclopaedia of Newfoundland and asked one of Prince Charles's aides if he would be able to sign it.

'No way,' said the aide, gently pushing him aside. 'He's 15 minutes behind schedule already.' However, when Charles emerged from the event, he saw Alan standing there with his large book and a pen and said: 'Do you want that signed?' 'Yes, please,' replied Alan, handing the heir to the throne a biro. 'I have a better pen than that,' said Charles. After signing it himself, he called his wife who also signed. This in turn aroused the curiosity of the Prime Minister of Canada, Stephen Harper, and the Premier of Newfoundland, Danny Williams, who added their signatures.

'What a scoop!' says Alan.

Alan's duties included helping to raise the Cupids Union Flag. 'It's the biggest Union Jack in the world and I was one of four people raising it,' he says.

The book signed by Prince Charles, the Duchess of Cornwall and other dignitaries.

The celebrations in August 2010 included a three-hour re-enactment of the events 400 years earlier.

Up She Comes   **Cupids, Newfoundland Labrador**   **Photography by Dennis Flynn**

Alan Perry (third from right) helps to raise the world's biggest Union flag at Cupids.

Soon after the Cupids event, Alan was invited to Government House in St. John's for another unique occasion – his appointment to the Order of Newfoundland and Labrador for services to the province. 'It is the highest honour the province can bestow – equivalent to a knighthood in this country,' he says. 'They said there were 500 million people in Britain and Europe and I am the only one ever to have received it. It's quite an honour.'

He has also been awarded honorary doctorates by both the Memorial University of Newfoundland and Bournemouth University. As a result of his influence, the two universities set up an exchange scheme for students and staff. That is just one aspect of the vast Dorset-Newfoundland legacy resulting from Alan's boundless enthusiasm for all things Newfoundland.

'Newfoundland has been the most exciting thing in my life,' he reflects. 'We made and still have wonderful friends over there.'

If Alan and Jill go to Newfoundland again, it will be his sixty-fourth visit – though not quite so many for Jill. But whether they will is uncertain.
'Some of our friends have sadly died, including Otto Tucker and Cyril Poole,' says Alan. 'Jill and I are both now in our eighty-second year. It's a lot harder than it was when we were in our fifties and sixties.'

Something Fishy Going On

Chris Slade

First as a child, then with my kids
I'd take a jam jar on a string
To any stream among the meads
And cast the empty jam jar in.

Within two minutes, three at most,
The first few minnows would appear
And then a dozen, then a host,
And in the jam jar they would peer.

You waited 'til they'd gone inside
Then jerk the string to raise the jar
And bring it brimming to the side,
Then at the tiny fish you'd stare.

Retired now, with time to waste,
I thought I'd play that game again
And Walton's Minnow Tansy taste
But find my quest is all in vain!

I stalk the haunts of coot and herne.
I dabble, paddle, even swim!
But now I find, to my concern,
There is no stream with minnows in!

No kingfisher beneath the bridge;
They're just a mem'ry now, a dream;
Not much by way of fly or midge.
Pollution's poisoned ev'ry stream!

GRASSBY FUNERAL SERVICE

*Still a family run business,
serving the local community since 1861*

**8 PRINCES ST,
DORCHESTER** DT1 1TW
Tel. **01305 262338** (24 Hours)

www.grassby-funeral.co.uk

Weymouth Men and Q-Ships

by Greg Schofield

During the First World War, the threat posed by German submarines was a real problem for the Admiralty. Once submerged, there was no effective way of detecting a submarine; hydrophones were of limited use and the best that could be done was to post lookouts, who searched for periscope trails. If a submarine was detected, there was little that could be done unless it surfaced. However, 1918 was a turning point; the invention of SONAR and depth charges meant that submerged submarines could now be detected and destroyed.

The submarine was also faced with problems. Most could only carry about 12 torpedoes, and the temptation was to save these for use on warships and other tempting targets; there was no point in wasting them on an unarmed tramp steamer. Therefore, there was a tendency, when dealing with an unarmed merchantman, to surface and sink it with gunfire from the deck-gun.

The Admiralty saw this as an opportunity and requisitioned a number of insignificant merchant ships to act as 'wolves in sheep's clothing', and were known as 'Q-Ships'. They were manned with naval crews in civilian clothes, and to all intents and purposes looked totally innocent. However, concealed in collapsible deck housings was a gun which could rapidly be brought into action. The idea was to lure the submarine to the surface and then sink it; this frequently resulted in a prolonged exchange of gunfire, which, during the course of the war, resulted in the death of three Weymouth men. Two of them were involved in two of the most famous incidents involving 'Q-Ships'.

Assistant Cook Alfred John Newberry, age 32, died on 5th December, 1915. He lived at 151, Chickerell Road, and a brother was also killed in 1917.

The British steamer Nicosian, came under fire from U-27, but was in turn surprised by Q4 Baralong. After 34 hits, the U-27's crew abandoned ship as the U-boat sank, but instead of surrendering, made for Nicosian in order to board her. Baralong's men fired on them, killing most as they swam or climbed to Nicosian's deck. Baralong landed a boarding

party, who sought out and killed the survivors. The German government alleged the Baralong's crew had committed an atrocity. The dispute became known as The Baralong Incident.

Leading Cook's Mate William Sims, age 27, died on 3rd April, 1917. He lived at 3, James Court, West Parade.

Q2 Prize, a three masted topsail schooner was surprised by U-93, which came to the surface and opened fire with her 10.5cm gun at medium range. Prize was hit; the panic party went over the side and with the schooner apparently sinking, closed right in. At less than 100 yards, Prize opened up with her 3-12pdr guns, U-93 appeared to sink and her commanding officer Lt Cdr von Spiegel and two of his crew were picked up. The damaged Q-ship reached Kinsale, S Ireland on the 2nd May, but only with the German U-boat Captain helping to repair the engines. The badly damaged submarine also reached port.

Paymaster George William Turner, age 35, died on 13th August, 1917 when he was reported missing then confirmed dead. He was later mentioned in dispatches. He lived at 27, Avenue Road.

Q43 Bergamot was a sloop of war sunk by U-84. There were 14 casualties.

The Story of John Damer 1744-1776

Kay Ennals. MBE

Lord and Lady Milton of Milton Abbas might never have bought Milton Abbey if it had not been for Lord Milton's great-uncle, a very rich Uncle Joseph Damer. Joseph Damer born in 1630 was a trusted associate of Oliver Cromwell. When Charles II was restored to the throne Joseph bought up acres of land cheaply in Ireland. He amassed a fortune, being successful in selling land, in being a merchant, and in money lending, and other enterprises. In his will he named his two nephews one of whom was John Damer's grandfather. The inheritance was passed down to John Darner's father also a Joseph - Joseph Milton. He was well positioned in life already, and with the inheritance was very wealthy. Joseph - Lord Milton kept the name of Damer in the family. He married the daughter of the first Duke of Dorset Caroline Sackville.

Money was no object to Joseph, Lord Milton, and when he bought Milton Abbey he did not like the view of old village houses. He had the old buildings demolished and built new houses for the villagers. These are set in the main street of Milton Abbas and are greatly admired even today.

There were four children born to the Miltons; John, George, Lionel, and Caroline. John, the eldest, was heir to a £30,000 inheritance, and was given £5,000 a year by his father. He married well. His bride was Anne Seymour Conway, daughter of the Right Honourable Seymour Conway, who was a military man, reaching the rank of Field Marshal, and later becoming a Member of Parliament.

Anne married John Damer when she was eighteen and at first the couple lived a most extravagant life-style. They entertained their friends who were well known in literature and fashion, and the leading politicians of the time. But very soon there were signs that the marriage had problems. John noticed his wife was constantly away from home. This led him to following his own favourite interests. These were racing and gambling, and, it seems, women! He ordered suits of silk, lace and embroidery to meet his society. He also wanted to annoy his wife by showing her that men's clothes could be as fashionable as those of women.

But his wife returned from Paris declaring she was to separate from her husband. John was shocked and so were the whole family. John's gambling became worse, so much so that he was borrowing: from friends, and relatives. The borrowing agreements were always written down for the year with 10% added interest. Eventually his debtors pressed upon him for their money back, but it had no effect on John. He appealed to his father but his father had already paid some of his debts, and this time his father refused to help. He gambled ever more.

John enjoyed being in London and usually stayed at the Bedford Arms in Covent Garden. He sent a note to the landlord booking the 14th August at 10 o'clock for supper. He ordered Mr. Robinson the landlord - to provide, as well as supper, a fiddler, and some ladies. The supper was taken at about 11 o'clock and a fiddler called Mr. Burnet, who was a blind man, played on his violin.

About 3 o'clock in the morning, John Damer told Mr. Burnet to go downstairs and he would send for him in about 20 minutes. When Mr. Burnet went up again he found that the room smelt of gun powder. He called the landlord Mr. Robinson. When Mr. Robinson looked in the scene he shouted "The man has killed himself." Then Mr. Robinson saw a pistol on the floor and saw bleeding from Damer's head, his clothes bloodied. The women had gone.

There was an inquest into John Damer's death. At the inquest Mr. Burnet said he had heard no noise of a gun being fired. This was corroborated by others and Mr. Robinson. The jury was told that the ball of the shot had gone through John Damer's head. They arrived at a verdict that he was not of sound mind and was lunatic and distracted and committed suicide. That meant that all his chattels goods and lands had to be forfeited and the body buried in unhallowed ground. All debts were cancelled.

But a few days later a letter written by a Mr. Horace Walpole said "The ball had not gone through the head". He had found a scrap of paper on table near by with the words, "The people of this house are not to blame for what has happened, which was my own act." Walpole added that it was a tragedy for a man of 32, heir to many thousands of pounds, to have such a fate.

The Western Flying Post noted that John had applied to his father to help him a little with his latest debt. His father eventually decided to help and would pay in part. John Damer did not know of this, he had the notion that there was only one way to cancel all his debts, by committing suicide. Afterwards his creditors realised nothing could be expected back from what was owing to them.

The local villagers were very suspicious, because some said they had seen John Daniel in the flesh in his father's home on many occasions. Many did not believe John Damer was really dead. Could it all have been conspiracy? The villagers kept quiet, but they had their own thoughts and conversations, and conclusions. Were there more answers to more questions? It had become a mystery! As the years went by it became a legend!

Milton Abbey: Courtesy of Julia & Keld

Statues: Contrast and Compare

Chris Slade 29th June 2011

Hardy sits in effigy upon his plinth
The plinth sits on the ancient wall
of Durnovaria
Thomas minimus came from worthy stock
at Stinsford
He should have stayed there!

Instead, he used his formula:
Create a worthy character,
insert a knife
and twist.

This made him rich and famous
and a mean-hearted snob
little did he know that one day
His own cousin would be Mayor of Casterbridge!

I see a bird has shat
Upon his brazen head
I'm glad!

Two hundred yards away a better poet,
William Barnes, a scholar and a gentleman:
a gentle man and true
stands, also on a plinth,
outside St Peter's Church
in pious pose.

Riches, he neither sought nor gained
but taught and tended
his family and his flock.
He loved and was loved.

Another half a mile
set on Gallows Hill,
again upon the Roman wall
stands a group of three;
their figures not sharp hewn
like those before.

How could they be?
Their necks were stretched;
their entrails from their living
bodies ripped;
their corpses quartered and
displayed.

Alexander Briant
Thomas Hemeford
John Munden
John Adams
Thomas Pilcher
John Hambley
Williams Pike
Eustace White
Williams Pattenson
John Cornelius
Thomas Bosgrave
John Carey
Patrick Salmon
Hugh Green
and
John Slade

Newglaze
WINDOWS, DOORS & CONSERVATORIES

For the BEST in PVC-U, Timber and Aluminium Windows, Doors and Conservatories...

"Why Double Glaze when you can Triple Glaze?"

FREE PHONE 0800 41 31 29
www.newglaze.co.uk

The Horse With The Red Umbrella

Est. 1970

Proprietor: John Fiori

Tea Rooms and Coffee House
Home-cooked Lunches
Home-made Sponges & Cakes

Tel: 01305 262019
10 High West Street, Dorchester, Dorset DT1 1UJ
opp. Dorset County Museum

Lady of the Black Horse
- Mabel Annie St Clair Stobart

Graham Allard

In the quiet graveyard of St Nicholas Parish Church in Studland, Dorset I came across a simple gravestone belonging to Mabel Annie St Clair Stobart. Having not heard of this woman with such an impressive looking name I decided to find out who she was. I was just amazed at what a life this lady had and what she had achieved.

Mabel was born in Woolwich, London on the 3rd February 1862 to Sir Samuel Bagster Boulton and his wife Sophia. Sir Samuel was a wealthy merchant and so Mabel grew up amongst the well to do society, rubbing shoulders quite often with high society. She was a feminist and a firm believer in the suffragette movement. In 1884 at the age of 22 she married St Clair Kelburn Mulholland Stobart and they were blessed in their marriage with two sons, St Clair Eric Mulholland Stobart born in Falmouth in 1885 and Lionel Forester Stobart also born in Falmouth in 1887. Soon after the family moved to South Africa in 1903 where they had decided to give farming a go in the remote Transvaal, this just did not suit Mabel so she gave up the venture and returned to England in 1907 and settled with her sons in a cottage at Studland Bay, Dorset.

On the 9th April 1908, a year after Mabel and her sons had returned, her husband aged 46 died on his voyage back home to settle down with his family in Studland. Mabel had always had feminist values and views and now that she was widowed she became a far more vigorous feminist and had passionate views of women having great value in warfare alongside the men, so she joined the First Aid Nursing Yeomanry (FANY). Its female membership was trained to assist civil and military authorities in times of an emergency, however Mabel became dissatisfied with FANY and in the way in which it was run so she and many other supporters, who she encouraged, broke away from FANY in 1910 and formed the 'Women's Sick and Wounded Convoy Corps'.

By September 1910 Mabel and her team of around fifty ladies were holding their first exercise at Studland. They lived under canvas for a week and got up each morning to the sound of the bugle at 6am. Then after washing, dressing and having breakfast it was lessons in bandaging and stretcher drill, followed by foot drill as she insisted that they marched everywhere as did soldiers. This was then followed by a good swim in Studland Bay prior to lunch. After lunch there would be lectures on anatomy and physiology as well as subjects such as hygiene, ambulance loading and unloading and even more foot drill.

The majority of her fifty strong team were from well to do families and were fairly strong and practical females. Apart from marching everywhere which was unusual for women, they also wore a uniform which Mabel and her committee had designed. The uniform was a blue and grey divided skirt, Norfolk jacket, helmet and haversack. The primary aim of the Convoy Corps was First Aid and the evacuation of wounded soldiers from the front line back to a hospital as soon as possible. It was always Mabel's underlying hope that if women could be seen as useful in warfare as men, that it would help the cause for getting the vote.

In March 1911 aged 49 Mabel married John Herbert Greenhaugh who was a Barrister at Law born in Mansfield, Nottinghamshire. They married in St Johns Church, Westminster and lived mostly at John's cottage called Knapwynd in Studland.

Another large exercise for the Women's Convoy Corps took place at Studland in 1912 and after this exercise, with the help of Queen Eleonora of Bulgaria, Mabel took her Women's Convoy Corps to Kirk-Kilisse in Thance as the first Balkan War had broken out that October. Previously Mabel had gone to see the Chairman of the British Red Cross to suggest that her Corps and its training could be of assistance to the wounded in Bulgaria. Sir Frederick Treves the chairman was not impressed with her suggestion as he felt the treatment of casualties on the battlefield was men's work and women did not belong near a battlefield.

Ignoring his opinion she obtained funds for equipment and travel from her high society friends and took her Convoy Corps to Serbia where she set up a hospital not far from the battle front. Apart from the language barrier they certainly had to put their training to the test fighting injuries and disease. They did however treat the wounded and give great assistance until the end of the war in the spring of 1913.

In August of 1914 The Great War started and Mabel had the idea of forming a new women's formation that may be able to assist the wounded in battle, so she formed The Women's Imperial Service League. She went to Sir Frederick again for support in her cause, but he had not changed his opinion about women at all near the battlefield. So once again she ignored his opinion setting up two Field Hospitals, one in France and another in Belgium. Still having an allegiance to Serbia, in April 1915 Mabel and her husband and a team of 45 women, female doctors, nurses, cooks, and orderlies, plus 60 specially designed tents, an x-ray machine, and Ford ambulances travelled to the Balkans where they set up a hospital south of Belgrade. The main problem she and her team encountered, apart from battle casualties, was Typhus. This contagious disease meant that the team had to treat civilians as well as soldiers in order to contain its spread. The conflict turned for the worse and in November 1915 the Serbian Forces started a mass retreat to Albania, some thousand miles away over the perilous mountains of Montenegro and North Albania. Mabel was promoted to the rank of Major and given her own column to command as well

Painting courtesy of its owners, Studland Village Hall

as her team of staff, ambulances, ox-wagons, and an Austrian field kitchen, horses and carts. During this awful ten week retreat, Mabel commanded her column whilst riding upon a large black horse that was given to her by the Serbians, along with her promotion. Mabel riding on a black horse leading a medical column was actually depicted on the front page of The Tatler with a painting by George Rankin in 1916; it was called 'Lady of the Black Horse'. Her column eventually got to Scutari (of Florence Nightingale fame) for Christmas 1915. Thousands of Serbians had perished on that arduous retreat from wounds, injuries, starvation and hypothermia due to the freezing temperatures up in the mountains. Mabel returned to England and once more did several tours promoting the needs of women doctors and nurses in front line hospitals to care for the wounded.

She received in her lifetime no less than eleven decorations and medals for her heroism during these conflicts, including The Order of the White Eagle bestowed upon her by the Serbians who, even today, regard her very much as a true heroine. Sadly tragedy was to hit Mabel as both her sons were killed with the Spanish Flu epidemic in 1918, then in March 1928 her husband died aged 74. He is also buried in the graveyard of St Nicholas Church. The loss of her sons made her interested in Spiritualism and she became quite an authority on it holding many meetings and séances. It is also a fact that she often held these with Sir Arthur Conan Doyle at her cottage in Studland, as he was also very much into spiritualism since losing his son. Mabel remained at Knapwynd cottage and still swam in Studland Bay well into her eighties, then due to ill health she moved into the Cavendish Nursing home in Bournemouth where she died on the 7th December 1954 aged 93. She was laid to rest with her husband John in the cemetery at St Nicholas Church, Studland.

St Nicholas Church, Studland.

The Sweet Smell of Mill Street

David Forrester

The information in this story was given to me by a lady who attended our Mill Street Memories meetings, without which I could not have completed this story. I thank her and apologise for having lost her name, I know however she was very keen that this story be told, and hope that I can do it justice.

Anyone who has read my book on the history of Mill Street will definitely be surprised at this title. However despite the run down, poor, untidy area where the river was often used as a rubbish tip and where rats were quite often to be seen, there was on occasions a sweet perfume drifting over the area.

Over the corrugated iron fence in Hardy's Avenue stood the Dorset Farmhouse Sweets Factory. On days when they were working, this wonderful sweet smell of boiling sugar, and its various additives drifted over the streets and houses, where many could barely afford the price of a loaf of bread. Wonderful as this drifting aroma was, it must have been cruel to those who were poor, and very often hungry.

In 1933 Dorset Sweets, was the brain child of Oliver and Norah Boon. The factory opened in 1934 at No 12 Kings Road overlooking the water meadows. This property, now National Tyres, backed onto Hardy's Avenue.

The building, large and made of corrugated iron stood with the sign DORSET FARM HOUSE SWEETS displayed proudly high up on the top, until the business closed in 1964.

Oliver Boon was a member of the Boon family who owned the grocery shop in Cornhill. However going into the confectionary business was a huge change for both Oliver and Norah. Living in a tied cottage, well actually a bungalow in Kingston Russell, Oliver was the poultry man for Foster and Peggy Symes. He was helped in this by Norah, who really didn't like the country side, or the lifestyle and wanted to return to town.

No one really knows what started them boiling up sugar mixtures in a pan on an old primus, but it is clear they must have had some success and that this is what eventually encouraged them to make what was a huge change.

With the help of Commander Toms of Fordington House they rented the corrugated iron building from Bill Sansom (a local sign writer). Commander Toms became a fellow director, followed by a Mr Hardwick, a resident of Broadmayne and a Mr Lovell from Bournemouth. Exactly how these gentlemen became involved appears to have been lost in the sands of time.

The building was split into various areas, a boiling room with long steel tables with a slightly rough area in the centre. At one end stood a large gas fired square for the huge copper pans in which the butter, glucose, sugar and water were boiled to a very high temperature. Next to this was a separate wrapping room where the girls, at first, hand wrapped each sweet in small squares of grease proof or cellophane paper. Later these girls were replaced by a mechanical wrapping machine, wonderful when working, but quite often frustrating when it played up. Remember these were the early days of mechanisation!

There were two other rooms, one to store the tea chests, straw and Sweet Jars. The other room was where the girls left their coats and cycles, some of them having ridden some way, into work from the countryside. This room was also used for their tea break, where they would perch on the odd tea chest also stored here, no such thing as home comforts! They were of course not allowed to stay on the premises for their lunch hour. The other room was the office; the secretary must often have been cold as the only heating in this concrete floored room was a two bar electric fire.

Schools occasionally visited to watch the process of hard boiling, this consisted of pouring the hot mixture onto the greased table, adding flavourings, mixing by hand, turning it over and over until at a precise moment it was shaped into an oblong shape and fed through oblong rollers of assorted shapes and sizes. When cooled it was broken up into individual sweets ready for wrapping.

Originally these sweets were packed into 7lb tins then put into tea chests. These chests were collected by horse and cart and taken to the two Dorchester stations for distribution all over the South of England. These packages were charged for, and credited when returned.

Wrapped and unwrapped sweets were distributed locally in jars containing four pounds of sweets. After the war these glass topped jars were replaced by jars with Bakelite tops, which were packed into wooden crates surrounded by corrugated paper.

By the 1950s quarter pound tins were introduced for the tourist trade. These were often packed by evening workers, but by the 1960s Oliver's health had deteriorated and he was forced to sell the business.

In Harmony With Dorset

Kay Ennals MBE

There came a deep felt longing
    To return to open space,
        To find that boundless freedom
I once knew at a certain place —--1 really must retrace.
(It all popped up in memory -——• or was it nature calling me?)

I want to be back on those soft green hills
    That led down to sunny bays --—
        To where the constant frothy waves
Crept up on sandy shores --— in sunshine's radiant rays.

Just to wander without a care
    Along the Jurassic Way -—-
        Where historic wonders have been found
Revealing mysteries in its ground —— wonderful and rare!

I'd like to follow quaint village lanes
    To hear birds give their sweet refrains,
        To gaze at the spreading, amazing terrain —— views deserving a golden frame!
And 'I want to stand on Portland heights to enjoy its panoramic fame!

It would be great to wake at dawn
    When a promising day is born,
        To watch the mist fade and be restored
By an overflowing sky of blue -—- to make the world feel fresh and new.

I'll soon be busy —— getting it planned -—
    To follow the road to this charming land;
        Here is the freedom I think I can find,
Fulfilling my longing, and peace of mind —— in harmony with Dorset.

Major-General Mark Bond

An appreciation

When, following the end of the war in 1945, large numbers of prisoners were repatriated, there would be many who would discover that the homes and communities they left behind were much changed and, in many cases, no longer existing, due to enemy action. It was not expected that such altered circumstances would have been caused by what might loosely be termed 'friendly fire' but such was the experience of Mark Bond. Arriving at Wareham station in the wee small hours he slept on the waiting room table, a comfortable billet compared to some he had endured during the war, until, with the dawn, came his father to collect him.

Heading west from the station, rather than east, Mark was compelled to enquire as to their destination. He now learnt for the first time that the house, village and lands in Tyneham that had been the family home for some 300 years were now occupied by the military and had been since 1943.

Henry Mark Garneys Bond was born at Chideock on 1st June, 1922 and subsequently educated at Eton. It was somewhat ironic, therefore, that when he enlisted in the King's Royal Rifle Corps in 1940 he was sent to Harrow where the battalion was billeted. His war experiences could well be said to have put the 'active' into 'active service'. After eight months in the ranks he was commissioned and sent to the Middle East where he received a head wound at the Battle of El Alamein, but discharged himself and rejoined his platoon by hitch-hiking a lift to Tobruk.

In 1943, Mark was fighting in Italy and was captured at Naples, but managed to escape from the prison train when it was attacked by American planes. Quickly recaptured he escaped again when the planes renewed their attack. He headed east but later, in the Abruzzo mountains, he was recaptured again and this time there was no escape. He spent the rest of the war in PoW camps in Czechoslovakia and Germany. With peace came his return to England and his rude awakening at Wareham station.

Mark Bond rejoined his regiment and enjoyed a stellar career in the Army until retiring in June, 1972, when he was Assistant Chief of the Defence Staff (Ops) at the MoD. Tyneham still being denied to him, he settled on an estate at Moigne Coombe, near Dorchester. Here he threw himself into the management of the estate, restoring the woodlands, planting 60,000 trees and creating a daffodil garden.

There followed an unstinting life of service to his County. He was successively High Sheriff (1977) and Vice Lord-Lieutenant (1984-90), chairman of the Dorset Police Authority (1980-82) and the Wareham Bench (1984-1989) and vice-chairman of Dorset County Council (1981-85). He was also a lifelong servant of Dorset County Museum in his position as president of Dorset Natural History and Archaeological Society as well as chairman of the governors of Milton Abbey School, later serving as School's Visitor.

Mark Bond never married, but as a man of Dorset he was wedded to his county and a member of the Society of Dorset Men. Now, like his beloved Tyneham, he is lost to us but, again like Tyneham, he will never be forgotten.

A Blue Plaque for Mill Street

by David Forrester

Recognition for a truly special Christian man who, by his actions, was able to change the lives of so many people forever.

Mill Street, 'Thomas Hardy's Mixen Lane' was in 1900 a slum which was actually worse than the Gorbals in Glasgow, dirty, rat infested, lawless, indeed a den of iniquity. The houses such as they were had been badly built all on top of one another, their flagstone floors laying beneath the river level, leading to filthy water often flooding up between the flagstones. Open drains ran between the houses, many of which shared one outside tap. The Reverend Moule reported that in one area thirteen houses shared one outside toilet. The houses were built so close together that there was nowhere to get rid of the rubbish, therefore this was often thrown into the street or into the Mill Stream, which was often used for washing or even culinary purposes.

The majority of men, who did work, were in the water meadows, working in a variety of agricultural jobs. Some of the men were known as 'Drowners' an interesting title. These were the men who kept all the channels in the water meadows clear, when they had been trodden down by cattle or sheep. This was important if the meadows were to be flooded (drowned) at the right time of year. All the men were employed by the day, and were paid at the end of each day, it was usual for the men to stop at the pub on the way home. Therefore very little cash actually found its way into the wife's purse; this fact further aggravated the situation and added to the feeling of hopelessness. It was also the cause of more crime "if you want food you will have to thieve it" "there's no dinner, your dad drank it" was often to be heard.

Imagine the courage when in 1905 the 19 year old Alfred Harman Edwards came onto the scene, determined to bring about change. Alfred started two of the things which eventually brought about this change, although nothing changed overnight, things were heading in the right direction. The Mill Street Mission was set up in a small thatched cottage, here children learned from the Good Book, and received drinks, cake and biscuits as encouragement, the mission soon took off and grew at quite a rate. Next door Alfred opened another cottage as a Men's Club. The men were encouraged to go here after work instead of frequenting the pub; the men were entertained by a record player and games of various kinds. They also were given Tea, biscuits and cake as encouragement, very soon many of the men attended the club after work. This had a life changing effect at home, as the men reached home with their day's pay still in their pocket. Things for the women and children had finally started to improve.

Eventually, by 1926, Alfred realised that only an improvement in housing could bring about lasting change and by 1931 was instrumental, with the help of others, including Florence Hardy, Mr W J Fare (the Mayor) Miss E Williams, and other Proprietors from the town in starting the Mill Street Housing Society. Its aim was to improve those houses which were worth improving, or build new houses to be let at an affordable rent. These houses were to be built and paid for by either, donations, a payment for £1.00 ordinary shares, or purchase of 2.5% Loan Stock.

Backed by the great and good as they were, the money started to come in. By 1932 The Society was ready to invite the Mayor and Florence Hardy to the laying of the Foundation Stone of the first six, three bed roomed houses, to be built in Kings Road. These houses still stand in Kings Road as a Testament to all the hard work these people, led by A H Edwards put in.

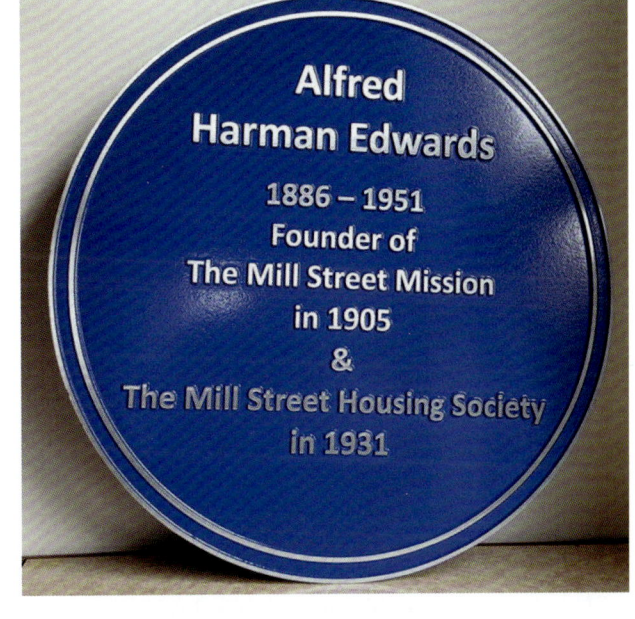

As recognition of Alfred's Achievements on the 18th October 2017 at 2.30 a blue plaque was unveiled in Mill Street, present were Sir Philip Williams, President of the Society, Rupert Edwards Chairman of the Society and Grandson of A H Edwards, also Julia Gibbs Granddaughter of A H Edwards. The unveiling was followed by short get together over tea and biscuits in St Georges Hall, where many old Mill Street residents swopped memories.

In writing my book Mill Street Thomas Hardy's Mixen Lane, published by Roving Press, I was constantly amazed by some of the story's I uncovered, and some which are still drifting to the surface! When I give talks around the County, many people say "and all this is not so long ago".

People talk of the 'Good Old Days' I'm not convinced they actually existed in Mill Street, although it's clear that there was a great community spirit. From my own memories Mill Street was known as the 'wrong end of town'. As children we were warned not to go there, people living there were looked down upon. Looking back on this, it was a great shame, perhaps we should like A H Edwards have shown more compassion. In the forties and fifties policemen would only travel into Fordington in pairs, they would meet up at the White Hart pub at the bottom of High West Street, before proceeding further together! This fact shows that the area was still far from perfect, even then.

Gentleman Pyrate, Henry Strangways, the Red Rover of the Channel

Fabyan Hodder

Henry Strangways, born about 1530 and part of the well known Dorset family became a pirate in 1552 operating in the Irish Sea where he was associated with fellow pirates, the Killigrews of Cornwall. They were all said to use Portland Castle to store their pillaged goods and certainly from about September 1556 until 29 May 1557 that was probably the case, as his brother George Strangways was the stand-in Captain of Portland Castle until John Leweston was reappointed.

In 1555 Henry Strangways is in the Tower of London, presumably as a pirate, but he manages to escape any punishment on that occasion. However he was arrested during 1559 with 80 of his men and condemned to death, though he again cheated the executioner and was set free.

The year had proved to be eventful for in August Lord Cecil writes "The Portugals that were robbed by Strangwish have brought letters from the King there requiring restitution, which is against all law and example." Strangwish is then accused in September of taking a Spanish ship. The Calendar of State Papers for Elizabeth says "His Orator, the Bishop of Aquila, will inform her how a Spanish merchant, Johannes de Bagnes, was plundered of his ship and stores by an English pirate, "Enrriex Tranguaz" [Henry Strangwish] of which restitution should be made. — Valladolid, 30 Sept. 1559. — Signed: Philippus [Philip II], - G. Perezius.

This is followed in January 1559/60 by "The pirate Estranguitz [Strangways], who has the command of a galley, has been informed by Captain Malbazart (a French prisoner of war in London, upon promise of deliverance) of the landing-places and harbours in Lower Normandy." Perhaps being a pirate ensured that he had good intelligence to trade with Cecil and others in Court informing them of what was happening in foreign ports and being a Gentleman by birth may have also helped to obtain his freedom.

It seems his piracy is fully confirmed and he is later imprisoned in December 1560 but then released on the promise of good conduct. In 1562 he died at Rouen as captain of an English ship in the Newhaven expedition on behalf of French Huguenots and was posthumously given a full pardon by Queen Elizabeth. While imprisoned in 1554 his fellow prisoner Gerlach Flicke, an artist, painted a portrait of Strangways, so we have at last the face of a true Dorset born pirate.

While searching for ballads about later Dorset pirates I came across a ballad to Henry Strangways praising his life.

A new balade of the worthy service of late

doen by Maister Strangwige in Fraunce, and of his death.

England hath lost a Soldiour of late
    Who Strangwige was to name:
    Although he was of meane estate
His deedes deserved fame.

¶ For as the Plowman plowes the ground
And toyleth to til for corne:
So Strangwige sought a deadly wound
For Brittaine where he was borne.

¶ In deede of birth he was borne bace
Although of worshipful kyn:
In youth he sought to runne the race
Where he might prowes wyn.

¶ In his yong yeares he walked wyde
And wandred oft a stray:
For why, blynd Cupid did him guyde
To walke that wyldsome way.

¶ Thus here & there I wot not where
He sounded where to ryde:
But happy haven he found no where
Nor harbour for to abyde.

¶ But when he had the course out run
Where Pyrates prict the Carde:
Twyse at the least, he thought undone
And looked for his rewarde.

¶ For by legall lawes he was condemd
Yet Mercy bare the mace
And in respect he wold amend
He found a Princes grace.

¶ And in that state he vowed to GOD
And to his righteous Queene:
He wold no more deserve such rod
Nor at Justice barre be seene.

¶ He thus contented for a whyle
And laughed Fortune to scorne:
Tyl weeds did worke by subtil guyle
To overgrow the corne.

¶ And then occasion served just
That Martiall men must trudge:
He vaunced himselfe with valiaunt lust
To go he did not grudge.

¶ And to the sea he sought a charge
Where he might take his chaunce:
And there with spred his sayles at large
To seke a porte in Fraunce.

¶ And passed by a warlyke towne
Where munition lay a land
He spoyld and cut their chaynes a down
And passed by strong hand.

¶ Where as he caught a deadly wound
Yet his courage never quayled:
But as he had ben safe and sound
On his way forth he sayled.

¶ And passed through even to that porte
Where he vowed to aryve:
And styl he did his men coumfort
And courage did them geve.

¶ Then ATROPOS did him assayle
That al Adams kynd doth call:
Against whose force may none prevayle
But subject to him all.

¶ This life (quod he) which was me lent
From judgement seat in perrill:
I came with heart for that entent
To spend in my Queenes quarell.

¶ Therfore this debt here wil I pay
This life which is not mine:
O Lord receyve my spirit to joy
That by Christes death is thine.

¶ All Subjects now, loke and foresee
That to trade the warres pretend:
Offendours eke (if any there bee)
Make ye no worse an end.

    FINIS. W. Birch.
Imprinted at London by Alexander
Lacy for William Owen, and are
to be sold at the little shop at
the north dore of Poules.

Horrocks & Webb
Fine Jewellers

35b Salisbury Street, Blandford Forum, Dorset, DT11 7PX
01258 452618 sales@horrocksandwebb.co.uk   /horrocksandwebb

The Western Front 1917 - Weymouth's Dead.

Greg Schofield

The Battles of Arras and Messines

The fighting on the Western Front in 1917 was overshadowed by the dreadful 3rd Battle of Ypres, sometimes known as the Passchendaele Campaign. But before that happened, events further south were to dominate the early part of the year and caused the death of 16 Weymouth men.

In February and March, the Germans withdrew to the Hindenburg Line, which was a specially designed and built, in depth, defensive position. The French Nivelle offensive planned for an attack against the German's original lines should have been cancelled, but now took place against the new German positions, with minimal gains and 180,000 dead, which, following the slaughter at Verdun the previous year, caused the French Army to mutiny.

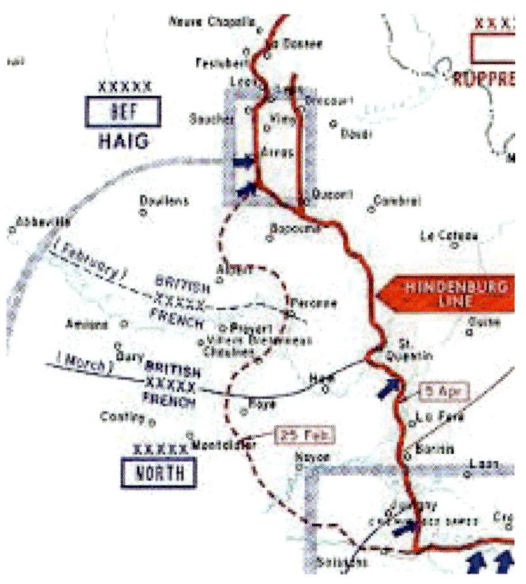

As an adjunct to the original French attack, on 1st April, the British launched an attack from Arras which resulted in the death of eight Weymouth men:-

George Thomas BURT
aged 47, died 12th April. Private, 6th Dorsetshires. 20, Ilchester Road.

Edgar William Sydney DAMEN
aged 26, died 7th April. Rifleman 1st/18th London Rifles (London Irish Rifles). Lived 29, Chelmsford Street. Reported missing, believe killed on that day.

Thomas ELLIS
aged 21, died 10th April. Private, 6th Duke of Cornwall's Light Infantry. Killed in action. Lived 22, Love Lane.

Thomas Henry HAWKER
aged 25, died 14th April. Private, 2nd Hampshires. Killed in action. Lived 'Verne House', Great George St. Sang in St Mary's Church choir.

Charles Joseph JACKET
aged 19, died 9th April. Private, 2nd Wiltshires. Killed in action Easter Monday. Three brothers also killed. Lived 20 Chickerell Road.

Harry G. KING
aged 20, died 13th April. Sergeant, 2nd Lancashire Fusiliers. Killed in action, had previously been wounded in the Dardanelles. Lived Maiden Street.

Charles Edwin PERRY
aged 22, died 25th March. Gunner, Royal Garrison Artillery. Killed in action. Lived 2, Clearmount Gardens, Rodwell.

A. V. SEABROOK
died 11th April. Sergeant, 20th Middlesex.

The situation in the French trenches was critical; through mutiny and desertion, so few French occupied their trenches, if the Germans found out, they could have walked straight through. Partly to distract the Germans from French weaknesses, on 23rd April the British launched the 2nd Battle of Arras (The Scarpe), during which six Weymouth men died:-

Frank CHAPMAN
aged 20, died 10th May. Gunner, Royal Field Artillery. Lived 146, Abbotsbury Road.

Frank COLES
aged 27, died 25th April. Sergeant, Royal Field Artillery. Nicknamed 'Cockney'. Employed as a checker by GWR.

Ernest MARTIN
died 14th May. Private 6th Dorsetshires. Killed in action.

Frank MELLISH
aged 36, died 23rd April. Private, 2nd Hampshires. Killed in action. Lived Lower Bond Street.

James PITMAN
aged 29, died 5th May. Private 1st/14th London Rifles (London Scottish). Died of wounds.

William Henry ROPER
aged 32, died 16th May. Private, 6th Dorsetshires. Killed in action. Lived 3, Walpole Street.

Events now moved north to the Ypres Salient where the British were planning a major campaign. As a prelude to that, it was decided to seize in June the Messine Ridge from the Germans in order to prevent them from firing into the southern flank of any British attacks. Organized by General Plumer, this was arguably the outstanding campaign of the war. Nineteen mines were exploded along the ridge and all objectives were achieved with minimal casualties, which nevertheless saw the death of two Weymouth men:-

A. J. ROPER
aged 35, died 25th June. Private, 3rd/4th The Queens (Royal West Surreys). Killed in action. Left a wife and 6 children under 10. Had originally been declared unfit for active service and put on garrison duties, but finally sent to the front.

William Richard TOWNSEND
aged 23, died 10th June. Private 5th Dorsetshires. Died of wounds. Had been wounded on four previous occasions.

3rd Battle of Ypres
The Passchendaele Campaign – Phase 1

CENTENARY OF PASSCHENDAELE
THE THIRD BATTLE OF YPRES

By 1917, the French Army was a shadow of its former self, having suffered horrific losses in 1916 at the Battle of Verdun, and this was followed by further catastrophic losses in early 1917 during the disastrous Nivelle Offensive. Their spirit broken, the French Army mutinied, and although it was brought back under control, any further offensive action was out of the question. This left the British Army as the main allied strike-force on the Western Front, having become a fully trained unit, and gained much valuable experience from the Somme campaign of the previous year.

The Allied Command decided to launch a major campaign at Ypres, break out of the salient and seize the major rail junction of Roulers which lay just behind the German lines. At a time when armies were so reliant on railways for transportation of men and supplies, such an action would cripple German communications, make possible the seizure of the U-boat pens at Zeebrugge and free up large areas of Belgium for recruitment and supplies.

The campaign was to be carried out by General Gough and the British 5th Army, which would have to break through three main lines of German defence, each based on the ridges of Hooge, Ghulevelt and Pilkem, climbing up to the top of the salient. But, there had been a two month delay since the successful Messines campaign, and the element of surprise had been lost, giving the Germans time to strengthen their defences.

The opening bombardment lasted 10 days, during which 4.5 million shells were fired to break down the German defences, but all it succeeded in doing was destroying the drainage systems which kept the land dry. The result of this was that when the first assaults took place in driving rain on the 31st July, it did so through thick mud and water filled shell-holes against German defences which were virtually intact, they failed. Two further attempts were made to break through, which were beaten back with fierce counter-attacks. At this point, the attacks were called off to allow the army time to regroup, and General Gough was replaced by General Plumer.

Nothing had been gained for the loss of 67,000 men, amongst which were 5 Weymouth men:-

Bertram Charles ARTER
Company Sergeant Major, 1st Wiltshire Regiment. Died 11th August, 1917 aged 35. Hit by a shell. Lived 'The Bungalow', Rocky Knaps, Dorchester Road.

Percy Albert HURFORD
Private, 12th Royal Sussex Regiment. Killed in action 31st July, 1917, aged 22.

Walter Frank LEGG
Private, 8th Royal Iniskilling Fusiliers. Killed in action 5th August, 1917, aged 19. One of three brothers fighting. Had worked for Biles Newsagents and then Weymouth Gas Company.

Frederick J. STEVENS
Private, Army Machine Gun Corps. Died 31st July, 1917.

Herbert WILSON
Corporal, Royal Engineers. Died 31st July, 1917, aged 29. Lived 6 Gordon Row, Chapelhay.

General Gough

3rd Battle of Ypres
The Passchendaele Campaign – Phase 2

The 3rd Battle of Ypres having started so disastrously, General Gough was dismissed

Ypres Mud

The Ypres Salient

General Plumer

Having been assured by the Army Meteorological office that he could expect two to three months of dry weather, Plumer planned accordingly. Throughout July and August the weather was dry and sunny and the ground dried out and became firm. Phase 2 of the battle began in September

and almost immediately it poured with rain, turning the ground into a quagmire once again. Nevertheless, Marshal Haig insisted the attack go ahead.

The mud had two affects; the tanks were quickly bogged down and played little part

and replaced by General Plumer and his 2nd Army, whose very successful campaigns were marked by meticulous pre-planning rather than brilliant sweeping attacks.

Throughout the rest of July and August, Plumer concentrated on reorganisation and retraining. Instead of achieving a massive break through, Plumer aimed to advance in small steps through coordinated attacks. The infantry would attack in company with tanks, and when enemy trenches were seized, artillery would be advanced to cover the next attack. Meanwhile, the new Bristol fighters, which could carry radio, would look out for German counter-attacks, let the artillery know the coordinates, and they would be shelled before the attacks could be launched.

in the battle, and the infantry was slowed right down, but progress was made and the 2nd Army slogged its way forward, gradually driving the Germans back up the slopes. However, it should not be thought that there was nothing but mud, some areas were firm underfoot and across these major attacks were launched at the Menin Road, Polygon Wood and Broodseinde, but mud was the dominant factor.

By 10th November, the British had finally captured the village of Passchendaele at the top of the ridge. It was not the original final objective, but the British Army was exhausted, and the German Army, despite

all expectations, was still very far from being broken. The campaign finally ground to a halt having advanced just 7 miles for the loss of nearly 245,000 men, amongst whom were 8 Weymouth men:-

Charles Francis BROOKES
Private, Army Service Corps (Canteens). Died 29th November, 1917, aged 33. Was Head Waiter at the 'Royal Hotel'.

A. CADDY
Private, Army Machine Gun Corps. Died 18th September, 1917, aged 29.

Alfred GARRET
Private, 6th Oxford & Bucks Light Infantry. Died 21st September, 1917, aged 35

Alec LOWE
Private, Canadian Infantry (Quebec Regiment). Died 6th November, 1917, aged 19. Lived 4, Gloucester Terrace, Weymouth.

Alan Douglas Rowland MENZIES
Gunner, Royal Garrison Artillery. Died of wounds 28th September, 1917, aged 21. Lived 24, Milton Road, Weymouth.

Sydney Robert ROGERS
Private, 15th Hampshire Regiment. Died of Wounds 24th September, 1917. Lived 25, St Thomas Street, Weymouth.

Arthur James VINE
Gunner, Royal Garrison Artillery. Died 30th October, 1917, aged 31. Lived 4, Turton Street, Weymouth.

Gordon WILSON
Bombardier, Royal Siege Artillery. Killed in action 12th November, 1917. Worked at the 'Beehive', men's outfitters.

Battle of Cambrai

The use of tanks on the battlefield first occurred towards the end of the Battle of the Somme in 1916. It was a last desperate throw of the dice to achieve a breakthrough, release the cavalry and roll up the German line. The impact of the tanks stunned the Germans and lifted the morale of the British troops, and created huge gaps in the German lines. It seemed that at last a breakthrough had been achieved, but there were two problems; firstly, the tanks were mechanically unreliable and those few that got through the lines soon broke down; secondly, the success had been unexpected and the troops to exploit the gaps were too far back, which gave the Germans time to fill the gaps and re-establish the defensive line.

In 1917 during the '3rd Battle of Ypres', tanks were used once again, but proved useless. Prolonged shelling had destroyed the land-drainage systems and created a sea of mud; the tanks sank into the mud up to their bellies, their tracks spinning uselessly around. Thus disabled, they were easy targets for German artillery.

Officers of the Tank Corps made a determined effort to promote the use of their cumbersome machines, insisting that they could bring about the much hoped for breakthrough by using tanks en masse on dry terrain as opposed to the muddy fields of Flanders. The Third Battle of Ypres was turning into a tragic failure, and Cambrai was chosen by British command as the scene for the offensive. The town, one of the principal railway intersections and German garrisons of the Western Front, lay on a vast chalky plain which was ideal terrain for the tanks. Preparations for the attack broke with recent military dogma: there would be no preliminary heavy shelling in order to preserve the element of surprise, hundreds of tanks would be used to open up a route through the defences, and air support would intervene at the German rear to check the arrival of reinforcements.

The attack began on 20 November at 6.20 a.m. along a ten kilometre wide front. The Tank Corps provided 476 tanks (of which 350 were armed) to lead six infantry divisions into the field. The bombardment which accompanied the attack was carefully timed and took the Germans by surprise. Preceded by a creeping barrage, the tanks made quick progress and soon reached the enemy's trenches. The Hindenburg Line had never before been so deeply penetrated. The surprise and terror provoked by the tanks among the German ranks caused several units to retreat and the British

took 8,000 prisoners on the first day of the offensive. Never had an attack advanced so quickly since 1914 and by the evening of 20 November the British vanguard had won nine kilometres of terrain and was closing in on Cambrai.

But once again the problem of capitalizing on the initial breakthrough reared its head. A fundamental problem was the tardy arrival of reinforcements caused by the heavy congestion on the roads: it took fifteen hours for troops to cover the final five kilometres to the front and the opportunity was lost.

The Germans set about assembling twenty divisions and by the morning of 30 November they were poised to launch a counter-attack. Their success was immediate and devastating. Supported by a barrage of poison gas shells, the Germans advanced more than five kilometres in two hours and, put into practice new methods of fighting which consisted of infiltrating the enemy's lines with small groups of highly-skilled and heavily-armed soldiers.

By the time the fighting had come to a close, on 4 December, the initial and unexpected success of the British Army had deteriorated into a total failure. All the terrain which had been won in the initial stages of the offensive had to be abandoned and the losses, although similar for both sides, were high. The Germans casualties amounted to 45,000 and the British had 44,000 killed, wounded and lost in action, amongst whom were the following five Weymouth men:-

Herbert Frederick BREWER
Private in the 2nd Hampshire Regiment. Shot by a sniper 21st November, 1917, aged 21.

Edward CORNICK
a private in 1st Northumberland Fusiliers. Killed in action 20th November, 1917, aged 30. Was a Captain in the 'Church Army' and lived at 9, Holly Road, Weymouth

Lionel Jack HULLETT
a Private in the Tank Corps. Died 23rd November 1917, aged 26.

Bertie Leopold PRINCE
Sergeant in 1st Royal Munster Fusiliers. Killed in action 20th November, 1917, aged 27. He had served for 12 years and been wounded 3 times. His brothers Joseph Ernest and Reginald Luke were also killed in the war. The Prince family of 12a, Governors Lane had 6 sons serving; 3 were killed and two were discharged as a result of wounds.

Charles Christopher STRANGE
Rifleman in the 1st/17th London Rifles. Killed in action 30th November, 1917, aged 39. He lived at Myrtle Terrace, Westham.

Sturminster Mill

Fran Gardner

The old mill stands
beside the slow moving stream.
Where willows dip their branches in the
coolness of water.
Studying the beauty of their reflections,
contented cows graze the lush green
of nearby fields.
Moss drapes the roof,
last night's rain permeating through
to hang jewel-like from
overhanging fronds.
Leaves spiral from autumn trees,
and dainty feathers float to earth
from birds singing high above.

Surdly Sam

David Downton

With acknowledgement to George Philip Rigney Pulman 1819-1890

Surdly Sam[I ban't bound ta tull ez reyle name] had a terrible antipathy

to all coxcuombes and sham anglers, and wadden very nice in ez talk to sitch voke. I can't say that I've got much wish ta be exter- civile to 'em myzull –

partic'ly to thease mighty knowin' ones who be more nice about vlies than trout can be- who v'e got sarts var every day an' hour, and know'th to a T th'

exact shade and number of ligs and zo v'oth, of every vly that can show ez nose in a zun- mote. Lord deliver all real anglers vrem the wondervully cliver chaps o' the sart !

They be var too knowin' and slyantific ver sich as I, and I 'spose th' reyson why they za sildom da catch a trout ez that the said trout be too daft to understand th' turrable larnin and knowin' that's a-heynde tawards 'em, er else be too unthankful to own to it.

I be only a-minded, at present, ta gie ee a annydote of th' wold Surdly Sam.

He was leaning auver Clap'n Bridge one fine marnin' watching the trout, when one of thease clivver dandy gin'l'men comed on, and zes ta Sam, zes he :-"Oh, my man, by what name do ee call ease river ?" "Caall'n ? "sez Sam,looking out under es gurt shaggy eye-brows as thof ee'd eyte en –"Call'n? We don't caall'n at all, there's no need o'et.

He da always come wi'out caallin'"

On first visiting Kingcombe Ponds, Toller Porcorum

David Downton

Early primroses, morning pale, glisten with dew and swaying willows are black with nesting crows.

Freshly lacquered kingcups rest their heads by the bank and a light breeze flirts with flag irises, modestly fluttering their eyelashes' before regaining military composure.

On this soft morning, the early sun gilds nearby farm buildings.

Through a dreamy haze on the ponds, glide black, shadowy carp like submarines waiting to strike.

A visiting squadron of Canada geese land noisily, upsetting residents and Red kites, in their new home, hover menacingly, relearning lost skills of scavenging.

Then a noise of machinery drifts across the valley, breaking nature's magic spell.

Dorchester – Stories from the Great War

Brian Bates

In 2014 I wrote an article in the Year Book about how Dorchester reacted to the outbreak of war 100 years earlier. Now 4 years later, and 100 years since the Armistice, it is an appropriate time to tell some of the stories of some of those Durnovarians who gave their lives during that terrible conflict. Just over 1000 Dorchester men enrolled in the armed forces to defend king and country during the Great War and almost a third (303) of them gave their lives. Those families that did not have a relative who was killed were lucky and some, like that of William and Georgina Rogers, of 35 Trinity Street, were exceptionally lucky. They had six sons who served in the War all of whom survived.

The names of most of those who did not survive appear on the war memorial at the bottom of South Street and on various church memorials. Every one of those recorded tells a unique story but the limitations of this article only allow me to highlight a few of them.

Two regular soldiers of the 1st Battalion Dorsets were the first to be killed. Sergeant William Cake was born in Owermoigne but married local girl Elsie Legg, 7 months before he went with his regiment to fight in France. He was killed in action on 25 August 1914 when the Dorsets were advancing towards Mons. Elsie's marriage had been a very short one and her grief was compounded when in the following April she was sent a Princess Mary gift box intended for her husband. For 7 years Elsie was anxious to know about what had happened to her husband's body and in 1921 there was a glimmer of hope when a broken watch was found which had belonged to him. But, despite correspondence between her and the authorities the result as to his whereabouts was inconclusive. There is, however, a gravestone in Houtrage Military Cemetery near Mons dedicated to him which bears the inscription, 'Believed to be buried in this cemetery'.

As a child William Ralph Teversham had been brought up with the Dorset Regiment. His father George was a Colour Sergeant and the family lived in quarters in the Depot Barracks. Given his upbringing there may have been greater pressure for William and his brothers to join the War. William was killed with the 1st Dorsets on the same day as William Cake. His brother Percy who served with the West Yorkshire Regiment was killed on 1 November 1917. A third brother, Lionel was discharged from the Army on 13 May 1915 due to the effects of poisonous gas and shell shock.

The Teversham's were not the only family to suffer multiple casualties. The Daily Mail on New Year's Day 1916 published, among its usual war portraits, a photo of Alfred Pope the Dorchester brewer and 9 of his sons, accompanied by the patriotic headline 'Nine in the Line'. With so many serving it is not surprising that some never survived the War.

Percy Paris Pope was the fifth child of Alfred and his wife Elizabeth. Educated at Winchester and New College Oxford Percy considered joining the Church but instead went for the law and was called to the Bar in 1907. The outbreak of hostilities in Europe found Percy taking a holiday in Paris but instead of returning home he decided to remain and see the War first hand. When his thoughts finally turned to how he might play a part in things his first reaction was to help the French by joining the Foreign Legion. Instead he returned to England in October, 1914 and was Commissioned second lieutenant in the Welsh Regiment, under the command of his elder brother Edward.

Percy Pope

During the afternoon of 1 October 1915 the officer commanding Percy's battalion called together his officers and told them that orders had been received to take a trench called Little Willie, at the point of the bayonet, regardless of cost. The attack was to be made after dark and in complete silence. Percy's company was in the middle of the line and what happened next was related to Alfred Pope in a letter from his son's battalion commander Lieutenant-Colonel Hoggen: "The timing was perfect – precisely at 8.00pm the 1st Welsh crept over the parapet like one man, officers in line with the men…so silently was the advance carried out that the regiment were within 100yds of the enemy before being discovered. Then, from both flanks machine guns opened fire, and the whole length of the opposing trench opened fire…In 20 seconds, there were 250 men and a proportion of officers on the floor – the remainder were in the trench, bayoneting those in the trench and firing on the retreating Prussian Guards.' Colonel Hoggen went on to describe how after the initial success things began to deteriorate and in the melee Percy's company had lost touch and the men in the trenches were running out of ammunition. The Welsh fought on in a bitter struggle until 2.30 in the afternoon and when the final count was made Percy was missing and it was hoped that he had been taken prisoner. It was not until August 1916 that his parents received official notification from the War Office that, 'The Army Council are regretfully constrained to conclude that Second Lieutenant Pope is dead, and that his death occurred on or since the 1st day of October, 1915.'

Charles Pope was a doctor and in 1915 offered himself for home service only. Given this, it must have been of considerable surprise to him when in 1917 he was ordered to Egypt and embarked

Charles Pope

on the troopship Transylvania with over 3,000 troops, hospital nurses and crew. Early in the morning of 4 May 1917 the ship left Marseilles and at 10.00am, as she was sailing in the Mediterranean, the captain saw a small sailing craft change course. From behind it appeared a German submarine which fired a torpedo at the transporter causing much damage when it hit but leaving the engines intact. The shore was about eight miles away and the captain thought that he might be able to beach his vessel. Then, a quarter of an hour later, another torpedo struck the engine room and the ship settled down and sunk in about 50 minutes.

Charles' fate was described by a fellow member of the R.A.M.C.: 'he was in charge of us on the Transylvania and was missing when we landed. He died as every British Officer likes to die – doing his duty, and went down with the ship whilst dressing the wounds of the poor fellows who were hit by the explosion. I happen to know this as I was working with him up to about 3 minutes before she sank, when he ordered me over the side. He was a good officer and we are all very sorry to lose him.' Charles is commemorated on the Savona Memorial, Italy.

When the Armistice was signed the Pope family, whilst grieving for their two lost sons, must also have breathed a sigh of relief. But, tragically, the gods of war had not quite finished with them yet. Born in Dorchester in 1875 Edward, known in the family as Alec, was the eldest son of Alfred and Elizabeth and his introduction to the Military came when at the age of 19 he obtained a Commission as second lieutenant with the Dorset Militia. Three years later he was transferred to the 3rd Welsh Regiment as a captain and then in 1899, on the outbreak of the Boer War, sailed with his battalion on the troopship Majestic, landing at Cape Town on 26 February 1900. But his service was cut short when he developed severe sciatica and had to be sent back to the UK. His return to Dorchester was something of an event. On his arrival he was met at the railway station by a large body of cheering men who proceeded to pull him in a carriage the three miles to Wrackleford, the procession headed by the Volunteer Band, and all this happening as church bells in the town pealed their welcome home.

Edward Pope

On 6 August 1914 Alec's old battalion was mobilized and he immediately joined up in Cardiff, where he was given the job of training those reservists and recruits that would replace the casualties of the original BEF. The following April he undertook the raising and training of the 12th Service Battalion, South Wales Borders and by November 1915 they were ready to join the other Welsh battalions forming the 119th Brigade in France, and in a report on the success of its formation the South Wales Argus gave a pen picture of Alec: 'Tall, finely built, a born leader, a stickler for discipline and efficiency, detesting all that smacks of slackness or denotes a slacker, he has instilled the soldierly spirit into those over whom he has command. He has won the respect and esteem of his officers and the admiration of his men...'

The first serious encounter the 12th Borderers had with the enemy came in April 1917 when they captured the formidable defences of Fifteen Ravine, southwest of Cambrai. Then, at the end of that same month he was forced to return home after being wounded and such was his health that subsequently he was passed fit for home service. It was whilst he was serving with the 3rd000 battalion in Chatham that he was admitted into Queen Alexandra's Hospital for Officers where he died, on 9 April 1919 from, 'disease contracted on active service.'

As the biggest employer in the town it was almost inevitable that the workforce at Alfred Pope's brewery would be depleted by the War. One such casualty was Arthur Prowse, who like his father worked at the brewery. Life must have been very difficult for his parents Robert and Caroline in the 1890's, who are trying to bring up their eight children in the overcrowded and unhealthy environment of Mill Street, Fordington. Robert worked at Eldridge Pope's brewery for over 30yrs and it was with the help of his employer that he was able to improve his family's circumstances by moving them to 1 St George's Rd. By the 1911 census we find that Caroline had produced 13 children, 11 of whom survived, and that the family were now residing at 18 Allington Rd.

Arthur was the fourth eldest son and In February, 1916 he joined the Army and proceeded to France in September. He was serving with the 165th Brigade Royal Field Artillery when he was killed on 15 April, 1917, during the Arras offensive. He was

Arthur Prowse

buried in Roclincourt Valley Cemetery. In a letter to the bereaved parents the officer in charge of his battery wrote, 'Your son was a very gallant and a very good soldier. He was in my section and one of the best men I had. I could always trust him to do anything and he always did his best.' The Chaplain of the unit wrote a very touching letter to Arthur's brother, in which he said, 'In a little grave near the gun which he served I laid to rest your brother with three of his comrades, all of whom were respected and loved by their officers and fellow men. The life and sacrifice of your brother will help us to love the things for which he died, and to hate with an ever-increasing hatred the things which caused his death' In remembrance of their son Robert and Caroline placed a notice in the 'In Memoriam' column of the Chronicle on the anniversary of his death, containing the following verse:

> 'He nobly answered duties' call,
> His life he gave for one and all.
> A loving son, a brother kind,
> A beautiful memory left behind.'

Dorchester Grammar school was very proud of its Officer Training Corps and each year in his prize-giving speech the headmaster referred to the report made by the military authorities following inspection. But, in July 1917 his speech had a more sombre tone. In addition to the usual plaudits to scholars and staff it contained a roll of honour to those former pupils who had become casualties of the War. On 24 April 1915 the Dorset County Chronicle in an outburst of patriotic language reported on 'par nobile fratrum,' referring to two former Grammar School boys who had joined the War. The lads concerned were Arthur Woolston and his younger brother Charles, and the Chronicle chose them as an example to 'many who still hold back' from joining the War and congratulated them for their 'promptness and wholeheartedness.'

Charles F. Woolston.

Although the Woolston family had left Dorchester a generation earlier the name returned to the town when Charles and his brother were sent to the Grammar School as boarders. After leaving school Charles took up farming, before enlisting into the 6th Battalion, East Kent Regiment (Buffs) in August 1914. As part of Kitchener's New Army Charles, together with 26 officers and 866 other ranks disembarked at Boulogne on 1 June 1915 and after a short stay at a rest camp moved to Bailleul, were the raw recruits were taught the basics of fighting, including loading and unloading their rifles and how to kill a German with a bayonet. They were toughened up with daily 8 mile route marches. This initiation lasted just ten days before they were on the move again, to Armentieres, where they were introduced to the trench and Charles, who had been promoted to corporal and his fellow NCOs attended lectures on trench warfare. The men of the 6th Battalion learned about life in the trenches at Ploegsteert Wood and Despierre Farm but nothing could prepare them for the terrible events that would soon be upon them.

On 13 October the newly promoted Sergeant Woolston sat in a trench waiting for the order to charge the German line running between Gun Trench and the Quarries, 3 miles to the north of the town of Loos. The Battle of Loos had been raging for some two and a half weeks and Charles would have been only too aware that he was about to traverse the same ground that the regiment's 6th Battalion had crossed on 26 September, sustaining 582 casualties, hardly a cheering thought for him and his section of machine gunners. At noon an artillery barrage open up on the enemy's trenches and what happened next is described in the battalion's war diary: 'At about 2.00pm all the smoke had cleared. At 2.15pm the order was given to charge…The men were met with a terrific fire of machine guns on three sides while the Germans were lying on their parapets giving rapid fire. The three companies were practically wiped out.' The attack had lasted just a few minutes and the troops had travelled barely 100yds. On their withdrawal it was found that there were 409 casualties, including Charles and two of his team. In a letter to his parents his Lieutenant said of him, 'He was in charge of one of our machine guns and was working it with great courage and coolness, when he was killed and two of his men with him. In Sergeant Woolston I have lost a most valued NCO, one whom I knew I could trust to carry out any enterprise, whatever the difficulties or dangers.' He is remembered on the Loos Memorial. Back in England the Society of Dorset Men in London, of which his father was a member, drank a toast to him at one of their meetings.

One of the most tragic stories of those on the Dorchester roll of honour involved a former Grammar School boy. John Brough and his brother Alan were both pupils and both went on to achieve senior rank in the Army. Their father William was a colonel in the Royal Horse Artillery and in 1901 was living at Vicarage Farm House, Pound Lane, Fordington, with his daughter Elizabeth, his wife Annie having died. In 1911 the 69 year old retired army officer was living at 56 High West St with two servants.

John, the eldest of the two brothers, was born in Punjab and had a diverse military career. He received his military training at the Royal Military Academies of Greenwich and Sandhurst, and before the War he served with the Royal Navy and was part of the West African Frontier Force which was set up to garrison British colonies in that area. He also served as a Royal Marines gunnery officer on several ships. In 1914 John was promoted from major to lieutenant colonel and took part in the West African Campaign, which was conducted in order to capture the German colonies of Togoland and Kamerun. At the end of the campaign, in 1916, he returned to the UK and was employed on special duty with the Heavy Section Machine Gun Corps, a very secret part of the Royal Artillery. The HSMGC was developing Britain's new weapon, the Tank, and John has been credited as the man who prepared the first force of them for action. As well as helping in the training and strategy of using this new mechanized assault unit he spent much of his time demonstrating the armoured vehicles to military leaders and dignitaries including King George V.

In 1916 the question arose as to whether the limited number of tanks produced so far should be used in the Somme offensive, or whether they should wait for more to be built. Field Marshall Douglas Haig decided to use what they had and John prepared to get the crews ready. However, for some unknown reason he was, in effect, sacked on the eve of their deployment and ended up with a desk job in London. Later, on 25th July 1917 John went with the 61st Division (2nd South Midlands) and joined the Fifth Army in Flanders as a staff officer. He helped with preparations for the Third Battle of Ypres and two days later presented a draft training schedule for the attack to his senior officers.

On 30 July a Lance Sergeant Gibbs was searching the French countryside for a missing British officer who had disappeared without reason, when he came across a body in a hedgerow. It was that of John Brough, who was holding his service revolver in his hand and had a gunshot wound in his temple. On 31 July a court of enquiry commenced where the medical officer, Capt. Scanlon reported that two bullets had been found indicating that John had twice pulled the trigger. The reason for his action was not known. There was no suicide note, though some witnesses close to him testified that he had become worried about his work and appeared very morose and dejected. From the Army point of view, soldiers only committed suicide if they were mad or cowards and John had proved to be no coward, having been mentioned three times in Despatches while serving in Africa. The court of inquiry chose the other option and concluded that he shot himself whilst temporarily insane, caused by worry. The date of his death was recorded as 29 January and he was buried in Longuenesse (St Omer) Souvenir Cemetery. His medals were sent to his sister Elizabeth.

John's father received the usual telegram from the War Office at the Junction Hotel, in Dorchester and this was shortly followed by a letter stating that his son had died of self-inflicted wounds. The implications were unthinkable. John would not be listed among the fallen because he had died a dishonourable death. His father immediately wrote to the War Office asking them to state in the public record that he had died of wounds, but his pleadings were rejected, a pencil note being scribbled on the letter that if he wanted that then he would have to publish his own notices in the newspapers. Locally, William was treated more kindly, the Chronicle reporting, simply, that his son had died of wounds. This was echoed in the obituary that appeared in the 1917/18 Dorset Year Book.

Great War memorials take many forms, from the plain to the statuesque. Many schools and churches have Rolls of Honour instead, whilst others have Remembrance Books. Lloyd's Bank published a Memorial Album, which consists of photographs of its staff, who died, with a note of where they worked. One of the photographs in the album is that of Walter Paull.

Walter was the eldest son of Laura and William Paull of Puddletown, where William was the local postmaster. Walter

W. R. PAULL.
Bridport.

was sent to Dorchester Grammar School and after he left joined Lloyd's Bank as a clerk in their Bridport branch. On 27 September 1916 he enlisted into the Royal Navy and trained as a Signalman. Before he could join a ship he had to be able to able to send and receive semaphore at eight words per minute, read Morse flags and use an Aldis lamp, as well as have a working knowledge of naval flags and pennants. After reaching the required standards Walter was posted to HM Trawler Charles Astie which had been requisitioned for military duties. On 26 June 1917 the trawler was escorting the steamer Hartland from Tory Island, off the northwest coast of Ireland to Inishowen on the mainland, when it collided with a mine which had been laid off Fanad Point by the German submarine U-79. All 17 members of the crew perished. Walter was just aged 18.

Another sailor was John Pitfield, who was killed just off the Devon coast. John lived with his family at 'Chapel Lawn,' 114 Maumbury Way, Dorchester and like his father William was employed on the railway but then decided on a career change and joined the merchant navy as an engineer. At just after midnight on the morning of 21 March 1917 the villagers of Salcombe in Devon were woken by the sound of motorboats moving into the estuary and they were asked to bring blankets and clothing to the survivors of a ship that had been torpedoed off the coast. The vessel concerned was the hospital ship Asturias which was on passage to its home port of Southampton after discharging about 900 wounded at Avonmouth. The single torpedo, which came from the German submarine UC 66, damaged the rudder and entered the engine room where John would normally have been working. The Captain grounded the ship in Starehole Bay, whilst those on board climbed into the boats but John was not among the survivors. He was one of the 42 crew members who were either killed outright or died of their wounds after being brought ashore. His body was returned to Dorchester and buried in Weymouth Avenue Cemetery. [Insert photo: Pitfield grave- Caption: 'John Pitfield's grave in Dorchester Cemetery'.

As one can imagine the attack on the hospital ship caused considerable outrage and was widely reported in the British and American press. According to a member of the Royal Army Medical Corps on board, the ship was sailing with full navigation lights and the large red crosses on the sides of the vessel were clearly visible. A statement of apology was issued by the German Ambassador, who claimed that the ship was mistaken as a troop transporter, as she carried the normal navigation lights of a steamer and the crosses on her sides were not illuminated.

Today, people still remember Parsons grocery store, known for the aroma of roasting coffee that emanated from its doorway in High East St. Ernest Parsons was the second generation to run the shop and in 1901 his first son Willie was born. Willie attended the Dorchester Commercial School which, as well as providing the basic curriculum, taught those skills required for office work and business. Willie's school report for 1909 shows that he was particularly strong in English and his conduct was excellent, and the Chronicle described him as, 'One of the brightest and most promising scholars that Mr Victor Dodderidge ever had.' Despite receiving an education geared for commerce Willie's real interests and talent lay in mechanical science and he became quite an expert at operating the school's telegraph system.

The Commercial School had its own scout troop, of which Willie was a member and he went on to receive the coveted award of King's Scout.

Parson's shop

Willie Parsons

In 1914 Willie was not old enough to go to war, so instead drove his father's motor car, petrol restrictions permitting, collecting and delivering orders. Keen to help his Country in its hour of need, his membership of the Scouts enabled him to do his bit on the Home Front, be it at some cost to his education. Ernest Parsons received a letter, in September 1914, from the Commandant of the Dorset National Reserve, pointing out that the scouts were due back at school after carrying out duties for the military since the beginning of the War, and that Mr Dodderidge, the headmaster, had decided to leave it to each parent to decide whether their son should continue their studies or continue, 'to help the officers who are working almost night and day at their military duties,' also adding, 'Therefore I write to beg you on patriotic grounds to allow your son to go on as he is doing. He is giving valuable help to the Country in this tremendous crisis in her history by doing work which would otherwise have to be performed by a young soldier, to the detriment of his military training.'

Given Willie's penchant for things mechanical it was probably of no surprise to his parents that when he was old enough he informed them that he wished to join the Royal Flying Corps as a mechanic. Ernest applied on behalf of his son on 3 November 1917 and was informed that Willie just fell into the qualifying age bracket for taking on suitable lads, which was 15 to 17 ½. Having satisfied the educational requirements and given satisfactory references Willie was accepted into the RFC as a boy mechanic and set off for its School for Technical Training at Haldon Camp, Tring, in Hertfordshire.

The early letters between Willie and his parents give no indication of the problem that would beset him and the family were clearly looking forward to Christmas when their son would come home on leave. His mother wrote to Willie that she had not told her younger children of their brother's visit and that he should not get too excited in case he gets a headache. Being a mother, she also told him to keep his feet dry and to that effect, that she was preparing a parcel of socks for him. 'Pater,' as Ernest signs himself in a letter dated 23 December, tells his son about the busy run up to Christmas in the shop although, 'we had no oranges like last year, else we should have taken more, but still we had a good day We had a nice lot of chocolate from Frys.'

According to the Adjutant at Haldon Camp the first indication that all was not well with Willie was when he reported sick on 10 January 1918 with a cold and then on the 18th with what was diagnosed as Impetigo. He again parade before the MO on the 23rd with a swollen face and showing signs of Albumin in his urine. It was only then that it was recognised that there might be something seriously wrong with the young recruit and he was admitted to the Isolation Hospital the next day. In a letter from Willie to his parents, which appears to have been written the day after he went into hospital, he is quite matter of fact about his illness and cheerful, although the degree of his pain and discomfort is evident. After describing his ward, telling them that that he was on a milk diet and that he had too many blankets, which made him sweat, he informs them that he, 'Woke up this morning at 8 o'clock feeling a little better in myself although my limbs ache so very much.' He ends the letter by asking his parents to send him two or three eggs.

There appeared to be little reason for Ernest and Emma to be unduly anxious about their son but then on Saturday 26 January they received a telegram informing them that Willie was dangerously ill. Ernest immediately left for Tring, where he arrived the following day, in time to be with his son during the last few hours of his young life. He died the same day of Scarlett Fever.

On Wednesday 6 February the 5.34 evening train pulled into Dorchester West

Station carrying a coffin that contained the body of Willie Parsons, which was taken to the Weymouth Avenue Cemetery where it lay until the funeral the next day. The service was conducted by a missionary of the Plymouth Brethren to Central Africa and was attended by a large number of people from the town. The days that followed brought many letters of sympathy, including one from Willie's commanding officer saying, 'It has been a great blow to the section, for he was universally liked – and the whole flight have expressed their desire to be present at the funeral.'

Among all the letters of condolences sent to the parents there was one which stood out among the rest. It came from a colleague of Willie's, Lance/Corporal Dunkerley, who slept in the same hut. In the letter he tells them that his friend reported sick every morning for eight days before he was admitted to hospital and that, 'The Medical Officer ought to have known his case was serious before all that time passed. They don't seem to care much.' By writing such a letter Dunkerley had committed what in the eyes of the authorities was an offence and he asked not to be mentioned in any subsequent complaint. We do not know how far it went but it appears that Ernest made some representations, the evidence for which is contained in two letters. The first was from the Adjutant at Haldon who, in replying to an enquiry from Ernest, said that an investigation had taken place but gave no indication of any conclusion arrived at. The second letter was sent to Ernest from Willie's schoolmaster, Mr Medway, in which he wrote, 'I am very sorry to think that his bright career has been cut off by the carelessness of those whose duty it was to have given him every attention.' Willie's sad story ends there. His family remained in Dorchester, a Jack Parsons becoming mayor. The Parson's shop finally closed in the 1980's, after moving into Cornhill, and with it went part of Dorchester's history.

For some Dorchester men being plucked from a quiet country town to some far off theatre of war must have been quite a shock. Places like Mesopotamia, India, Egypt and Palestine carried threats of illness and disease unknown of at home. Then, there was the terrible heat. The high temperatures in these places were a real problem for the British army. For instance, the Dorsets regimental history records that out of a draft of 60 sent up the river in Mesopotamia, in June 1916, only 11 reached the Battalion, the remainder suffered from the effects of the sun. One of those who was hospitalised and subsequently died was Dorchester man Frederick Read. Another local man's death was caused also by unbearable heat.

Reg (left) and his brother Birtie in tropical uniform

The two men posing before the photographer wore British Army tropical uniform comprising tunic, shorts and topi. Behind them was an appropriate backdrop painted with palms and ancient ruins and to one side was a table covered in a leopard skin. Thousands of soldiers had similar photographs taken, the backdrop changing with the theatre of war. The two men in this particular piece of artwork were brothers Bertie and Reginald Dabinett, both of whom served in India with the 1/4th Dorsets and were two of the eight sons of George, a house painter and his wife Louisa. The family were well known in the town, especially Reginald who, as the Chronicle pointed out was, "in the front rank of local footballers and popularly known as 'Little Titch', he was one of the most skilful components of the winter game in the district, and had been selected to play for the county." Before joining up Bertie worked for some time at Holy Trinity Church Rectory and Reginald was a carriage painter at Channons, coach builders. Reg's occupation was to of some use to him in India. In a letter, he told his brother Arthur that he had been excused duty for two weeks whilst he painted the Captain's gig. Reg definitely had an eye for the main chance. When he enlisted he gave his religion as C of E and consequently paraded in the Indian heat with the other soldiers of his denomination and marched the two miles to the local church carrying rifle and 20 rounds of ammunition. He then decided to change his religion to that of Chapel, not because of some spiritual revelation but simply because the local chapel was only 100yds from the barracks. As he pointed out, 'you have to be artful in the army'.

Reg and Bertie were both regular letter writers while in India and their missives make interesting reading. Bertie's letters mainly concern themselves with life back home, the Dorchester boys he came across in the course of his duty and the telegraphy course he was sent on. Reg's indicate his interest in the local life, like the 'curious habit' of the Sikhs, who took off their shoes before entering a house, or the women who went out of their way to avoid contact; the myriad of insects waiting to strike a man down and the plethora of half wild dogs. One thing that they both complained about, incessantly, was terrible heat. Bertie, somewhat graphically, wrote, 'You will not see any of the fellows very fat out here, as you sweat the fatness out of you, you are sweating more or less from the time you get up in the morning until last thing at night.' Reg explained that sometimes the heat was so bad at night he had to take his bed outside to sleep.

The brothers were stationed together in Jullundur, until Reg was drafted to Mesopotamia in the autumn of 1916, where he was attached to the 2nd Battalion. Inevitably, because the battalion was frequently on the move, his letter writing decreased but he continued to write postcards to Bertie who passed on the news of his brother to their parents. The reason for Reg returning to India is not clear. He may have been one of the regular group of soldiers returning from Mesopotamia to rest or possibly the cause was more serious. On 31 July 1917 he wrote a letter to his parents from the military hospital in Poona. As well as admitting patients with the usual illnesses and injuries the Kirkee hospital was the only one in the area that dealt with cases of men who had been bitten by animals. Reg had been bitten on the face one night by a prowling jackal while sleeping outside but his letter indicated that there was little reason for his parents to be anxious about because he was on the mend and was looking forward to an extended period of leave in Bangalore, where the weather was much cooler. He also said that he would have liked to have sent home to his sister Cissie one of the beautiful large butterflies prevalent around the hospital. A month later his parents received the terrible news that their son had died of rabies, on 22 August. His brother Bertie returned to Dorchester, married and worked in the town as a painter and decorator.

Accidents were always likely to happen and a particularly tragic one befell Frank Adams. Charles and Ada Adams married in 1896 and in 1901 were living with their son Frank and daughter Dorothy at 28, High St, Fordington. Unfortunately, Ada died in 1909 and Frank and his sister were taken under the wing of William and Ellen Holley, of 6 Salisbury Terrace. The death of his wife was not the only tragedy in Charles' life.

On the 31August, 1914, young Frank appeared before the recruiting sergeant in Dorchester to enrol with the Dorsets. As part of the process he was required to answer a number of questions, including one about his age, which he gave as 19 years 2 months. The figure standing before him, weighing just 7stones 12 pounds and measuring only 5ft, 2inches in height might have put some doubt in the Sergeant's mind about Frank's true age but, nevertheless, he was recruited into the 3rd Battalion.

As a Special Reserve Battalion the role of the 3rd Dorsets during the Great War was to raise and train drafts of soldiers for the front. As part of their training the men were required to guard important strategic places and installations and whilst the majority of the 3rd Battalion marched off in early August from the Depot Barracks to Wyke Regis, the Company that Frank was to join was destined for Upton Camp, Ringstead, with the job of, among other things, guarding Weymouth waterworks.

Five months after Frank joined his Company the following headline appeared in the Chronicle, "Fatal accident at Upton Camp." The report that followed was of an inquest that had taken place into the circumstances of Frank's death. Through the graphic testimony of several witnesses a terrible tragedy unfolded.

Two days before the day of the inquest Frank and his fellow recruits returned to their barracks, after a day of musketry training, using blank bullets. The inquest jury heard from a Private Harry Belcombe, that at about 8.30pm he was getting into bed and saw Frank and his good friend, named Stevens, larking about with a rifle. He said to Stevens, 'You had better put that rifle down, or something will happen,' to which Stevens answered, 'alright'. What Harry did not see was Stevens pick up a bullet and load it into the rifle, which he then pointed at Frank and pulled the trigger. His friend immediately fell to the ground with a wound to his left breast. A Sergeant Major Searle, who was in the canteen when the incident occurred, was immediately summoned and when he arrived at the hut he found the young private laying on the ground, unconscious, his heart beating feebly. He then asked Stevens if he had shot Frank, to which he replied, 'Yes, quite by accident, having picked up a live cartridge instead of a dummy one'. The dozen or so men present confirmed that Frank and Stevens were good friends and the shooting had been a complete accident. Dr T A Walker told the inquest that when he arrived on the scene the casualty was quite dead. The bullet had entered the centre of left breast and struck the spine, breaking three or four ribs before it passed out of the body. Stevens took the accident very badly, was admitted into hospital the same night and was assessed to be too ill to attend the inquest to give evidence.

As if Frank's death was not disastrous enough Melpomene, the Muse of tragedy played a last card, when his father informed the Coroner that his son had celebrated his sixteenth birthday a month before his death. In answer to a question from the Coroner, Sergeant Major Searle said that according to the official papers Frank was nineteen years and that his real age did not concern the Army. Fortunately, Frank's service record survives and the section on the form showing his age is very telling.

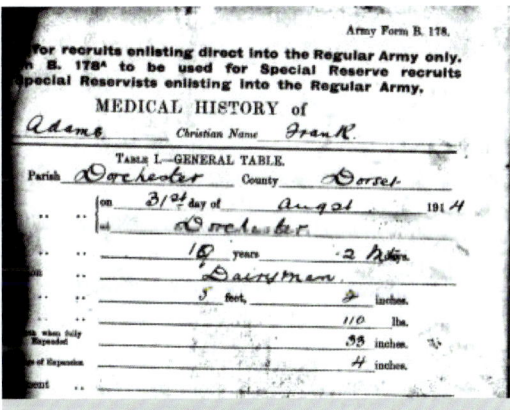

Extract from Frank's service record shows clearly that his age was altered (Image reproduced by kind permission of Ancestry.com Operations Inc)

The handwritten age of 19 yrs 2 months had clearly overwritten a previous entry that suspiciously looks like the figure 16.

The funeral cortège must have made an impressive sight. Frank's coffin was borne on a gun carriage from the Hampshire Royal Field Artillery Battery and was draped in a Union Jack upon which were his cap and badge. Present was the full regimental band, which played funeral music, as the procession wound its way slowly through the streets of Weymouth to Melcombe Regis Cemetery, accompanied by a large body of Dorsets with arms reversed. On arrival at the cemetery Frank's body was lowered into its grave to the sound of the last post played on the bugle, followed by three sharp rifle volleys. Ironically, the coffin bore the inscription, "Frank Adams, died 19th January, 1915, aged 19 years."

Another young lad who died through an accident was Frederick Benjafield. At the lower end of Monmouth Road there is a terrace of nine houses and although their addresses now form part of Monmouth Road a plaque on the wall states that they were once known as Railway Terrace. Built in 1889 by the London and South Western Railway there were originally ten houses, but number one has since been extended into the Baker's Arms public house. In 1901 this house was both the home and the place from which Thomas Benjafield, baker, ran his business, and if you go into the pub today you can still see the bread ovens he used.

The Benjafield family consisted of Thomas, his wife Elizabeth, three sons Reginald, Frederick and William, and their daughter Ethel. By 1911 the family had moved to 7 Alfred Place and the boys were all gainfully employed, Reginald as a cab driver and Frederick following his father's trade as a baker.

William, who was born in 1895, was still living with his parents but spent much of his time travelling around the countryside as a cook with a steam plough team. In January 1913 he decided to join the Dorsets as a Reservist and signed up with the Colours for six years. Unfortunately, his introduction to military life was not without incident.

William Benjafield

William was put on active service on 24 October, 1914 and joined the 1st Battalion in France. Following the battle of Armentieres, the Dorsets were operating in an area about eleven and a half kilometres south of Ypres. It was a quiet period for the troops, who were alternating between being in the front line and in billets in Dranoutre. But even in quiet periods soldiers succumbed to enemy snipers or shellfire and William was killed on 3 December while the battalion was being relieved in the trenches by the Norfolks. He is buried in R. E. Farm Cemetery, Wytschaete. The news of his death was received by his parents at their new address at 4 Colliton Street.

Frederick Benjafield

Napoleon Bonaparte is quoted as saying that, 'An army marches on its stomach,' and the British Army in the Great War was no exception. It was no surprise therefore that when William Benjafield's older brother Frederick, who was a baker, enlisted into the Army Service Corps to bake bread for the troops.

Born in 1894, Frederick worked for Buglar's and Son, bakers at 1 Prince's Street. He then moved to Winton in Bournemouth, where he was similarly employed and where he met and became engaged to a Miss Squires, of Corfe Mullen. His army record shows that he enlisted, in Bournemouth, on 12 January 1915 and after attending the Military Workshop in Aldershot, where he had to prove his competence, he was posted to the 51st Field Bakery in Alexandria, as a Third Hand Baker.

On 6 July, 1915 Fred and some of his friends were bathing in Dock Q of the port, which was not surprising when one considers how hot and uncomfortable it must have been for them working with bread ovens at the height of an Egyptian summer. What happened next cannot be more graphically described than the through the words contained in the depositions of two witnesses submitted to an inquest into Frederick's death. The first witness was Private Raymond Barnett, and reads, "The deponent was bathing with several other soldiers, when he heard a shout, 'Freddie has gone down'. He made for the spot where Private Frederick Benjafield was seen to sink. He at once dived together with Private James Drummond and several other soldiers but could not see any sign of Private Benjafield. They remained on the spot for three quarters of an hour trying to find him but had to give it up. After sinking, Frederick Benjafield did not come to the surface again; if he had they could have saved him. About two minutes before hearing the shout, he warned Private Benjafield to keep to the shallow water, he replied, all right Ray, I will. He could swim only a little."

Private James Drummond also heard the cry for help, 'he turned round to see what was wrong and all he could see were ten fingers disappearing under the water. He shouted to Barnett to come, then he dived but it was too late, when he came up he learned that it was his friend Frederick Benjafield that was down. By this time Barnett had dived but he too was unsuccessful. There were several other soldiers and a sailor and they all tried their best for about an hour. He gave up hope of getting Benjafield that night. He went down so sudden that no one got a chance of getting near him. How he came to be out of his depth no one knows. He only gave one cry then disappeared and never came up again. He was 21 and liked by everyone.'

Frederick's body was not recovered until the afternoon of the following day and the verdict of the Court was that he met his death by misadventure, drowning most probably as the result of a sudden attack of cramp. The Coroner also added that both Barnett and Drummond did their best to rescue their comrade and deserved a word of commendation.

As well as receiving the usual medals, plaque and scroll, Frederick's personal belongings, which consisted of a fountain pen, a safety razor, 3 books, a bundle of letters, a pair of mittens and 10 handkerchiefs, were received by his parents. In addition, their son's commanding officer wrote them a letter, which read, 'I feel it my duty to pay tribute to your son's sterling qualities. While under my command he led a clean upright life, and although circumstances were often trying, he never failed to perform all his duties in a thoroughly satisfactory manner. His loss we deeply deplore, and feel we have lost a good comrade.' Frederick is buried on 8 July, with full military honours, at Alexandria (Chatby) Military and War Memorial Cemetery.

When the War finished it was time for Dorchester to take stock of its losses. It had been decreed as early as mid-1915 that no bodies would be repatriated from the war zones, and as a consequence, communities throughout the land sought ways of remembering those who had fallen. In Dorchester the process of determining some form of town memorial would turn out to be a protracted one. The idea of creating something that would be a memorial to the sacrifice made by the people of the town was first discussed publically at a meeting at the Corn Exchange, on 14 March 1919, when the mayor said that they had a duty to erect some memorial to 'the gallant Dorchester men who had so nobly sacrificed their lives for King and Country.' There was no paucity of ideas forthcoming at the meeting; Mrs Logan suggested a swimming pool for children and Mr Kibbey a workingman's institute.

Other suggestions included a rest home for soldiers and sailors, the endowment of scholarships for the sons of working class men and a convalescent home for children. Then, Major Cosens got to his feet and made an appeal to the assembled, saying, 'Don't for goodness sake talk about a hall for the working man, or also something for the babies, or washhouses for one section of the population.' In his opinion no particular section of the community should be singled out and that what was required was something that reminded posterity of the sacrifice made. Presented with such a diversity of suggestions the meeting decided to appoint a committee of 24 persons to deal with the matter.

Not surprisingly, with so many members the committee could not agree on a single proposal and instead presented both a minority and a majority report. The majority report proposed a monument located at the junction of South St and Trinity St, outside Ernest Tilley's shop and in addition, the erection of a memorial institute and victory hall, providing the money to pay for it could be found. The minority report agreed with the idea of the memorial but not the site and did not consider that funds could be raised for the memorial hall. Matters got a little personal at the meeting between Cosens, who was clearly against the idea of erecting a hall, and a supporter of the idea. Cosens asked the man whether his 'class' would be willing to make financial contributions, in reply to which the man said that his class had always been generous when it came to giving money to good causes. Mrs Logan stepped in and told them to stop squabbling, and get on with the business in hand. The meeting finally decided to defer the item until public subscriptions showed what funds were available for the project.

Things came to an impasse at that point and any idea of a memorial might have been mothballed forever it had not been for the Dorchester Comrades of the Great War who, in January 1920 wrote to the Town Council and asked for the scheme to be resuscitated. The matter was duly resurrected and it was finally agreed that a monument should be built on its present position at the corner of South St and South Walks. Even at this late stage alternative proposals were still being sent in, including an interesting one from John Acland, consisting of an arch gate to be placed in the Borough Gardens.

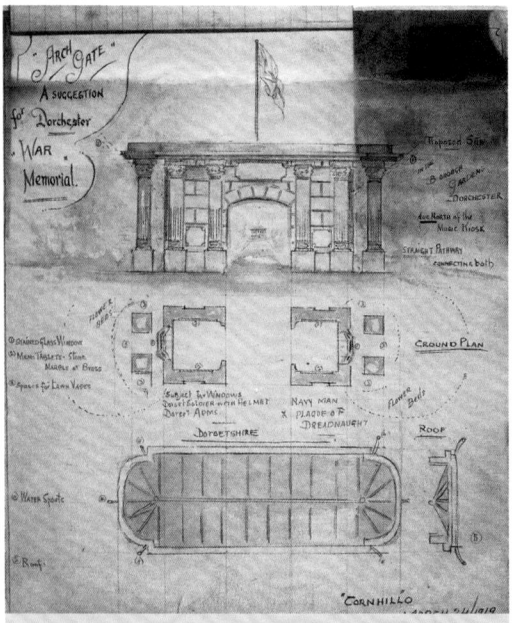

John Acland's proposed memorial to be placed in the Borough Gardens. (Source: Dorset History Centre).

When it came to the design for the monument the Council looked to Sir Edwin Lutyens, the designer of the Cenotaph in Whitehall and wrote to him, asking if the design was copyrighted. His office replied that it was but they were sure that he would not object to it being copied, providing he supervised the work. The expenses of employing such a renowned architect were too much for the council so, instead, they sought estimates from local firms for the design, carving and erection of a monument. The winning tender was that of Algernon Grassby, monumental mason, of Maumbury Way, at a cost of £400. To accommodate the structure some of the chestnut trees in the Walks had to be removed and the kerb re-aligned. Made of Portland whitbed stone the monument is 15ft high and weighs 17 tons. Both back and front are decorated by relief panels, with a carved laurel leaf and crusader's sword, with the dates 1914-1918 on a scroll. Attached to the front of the memorial are the bronze plaques that bear the names of the fallen.

The process of collecting names was done through public advertisement; with notices inserted in newspapers and posters appearing around the town. Letters were also sent to local churches asking if they had any nominations for inclusion. Except for a couple of complaints about omissions everyone seemed to be happy with the result. 239 names are listed, including 16 sets of brothers, three cases where both father and son died, one of uncle and nephew and one of two cousins. One woman, Nurse Constance Hodges, appears on the memorial. Constance was the daughter of Sara and John Hodges who ran a wine importing business in High East Street. One of 11 children Constance died of blood poisoning on 22 June 1917 whilst serving at Urmston Hospital, in Sussex.

Unveiling the war memorial on Empire Day, 1921. The nurses to the left background were from Dorchester's military hospitals.

At the forefront of the multitude gathered before the cenotaph, on the day of unveiling, 24 May 1921, were the mourners. The remainder of the congregation included local dignitaries, Red Cross nurses, representatives of the Dorset Regiment and the Royal Field Artillery, the Girl Guides, Boys' Brigade and the Church Lads' Brigade, as well as a contingent of the Grammar School Officer Training Corps. An approach had been made to the Prince of Wales, through the Deputy Lieutenant of the county, requesting him to do the unveiling but as he was not available, so the job fell to the Right Hon. Lord Ellenborough, who had served with the 2nd Dorsets in the Boer War and had worked tirelessly in the recent conflict. After the singing of several hymns, addresses by local clergy and a reminder to all about the sacrifice that had been made, the Last Post was played and Dorchester's Great War dead were finally put to rest.

The stories in this article are among nearly 300 that can be found in Brian Bates' book, Dorchester Remembers the Great War. Copies can be bought, priced £12.99, from local outlets, or at a discounted price of £10, plus p&p, from the author. (Telephone: 01305 263824. E-mail: brianbates@trayfoot.co.uk. All proceeds from sales go to the charities Sense and Sightsavers). Brian has also written a book about Dorchester's Great War prisoner of war camp. Entitled, Living with the Enemy, it is similarly available, priced, £10.

TALKS BY BRIAN BATES

I give talks on aspects of Dorchester's rich history. Each talk lasts an hour, but can usually be modified to meet individual requirements. They are fully illustrated. I ask for a donation of £35 to charity, plus travelling expenses of 30 pence per mile. I can be contacted by phone, on 01305 263824, or by e-mail, brianbates@trayfoot.co.uk

Talk 1 – An Imaginary Walk through 17th Century Dorchester
In the early 17th century Dorchester was seen my many as a hotbed of puritan revolution. Through an imaginary walk through the town we will see how Durnovarians were affected by, and contributed to, the cataclysmic national events that would eventually lead to the English Civil War. We will also see how the high and the low born dealt with the every day tribulations of hunger, sickness and crime.

Talk 2 - Dorchester Remembers the Great War.
As a garrison town, the outbreak of WW1 had more significance for the inhabitants of Dorchester than most other towns. At the end of conflict 285 names were added to the town's various war memorials. Through the stories of some of those who perished in that terrible conflict this talk shows how their families and the local community dealt with the tragic losses.

Talk 3 - When the Germans Invaded Dorchester
The invasion began in August, 1914, when 18 German prisoners arrived in Dorchester. By March, 1919 4,500 foreign nationals were incarcerated in one of Britain's largest POW camps, situated on the outskirts of the town. We will see what life was like in the camp and how Durnovarians dealt with the extraordinary situation in which they found themselves.

Talk 4 – Lives around the Borough Gardens
Dorchester's Borough Gardens is a fine example of Victorian pride. This talk illustrates a history of the gardens and then takes a peek through the curtains of some of the splendid villas surrounding the gardens, to view the people who lived in them during the Edwardian period.

Talk 5 – Dorchester Now and Then.
In this talk we take a tour around Dorchester today, comparing places as they are now and how they were 100 years ago.

Talk 6 – Discovering your Great War Ancestors.
Find out where to look for information about your ancestor who took part in the Great War and how to interpret what you find.

Talk 7 – Annie Keats – A WW1 Nurse.
Annie Keats served as a nurse in one of Dorchester's military hospitals. In this talk you will discover what life was like for a nurse during the War and have the chance to see the extraordinary contents of three autograph books, including poems, sketches, cartoons and paintings.

Talk 8 – Dorset People and Places
A trip round the county looking at some of its lesser known characters and stories.

Talk 9 - Dorchester Now and Then (Part 2)
Another photographic tour showing Dorchester now and then.

Robert Hudson
The Man Who Saved the Ryder Cup

Peter Fry

Robert Hudson is best known for resurrecting the Ryder Cup matches after a lapse of ten years owing to the conflict of World War II. However that special highlight overlooks his various other accomplishments in the world of golf. The author realised that Robert Hudson played a prominent role in promoting golf on both sides of the Atlantic and yet had so little written about his efforts beyond brief articles. Accordingly he set out to plug this gap in golfing history.

For this story, the author researched assiduously with the particular assistance of Portland Golf Club and a specialist Portland genealogist. A visit to Portland endorsed the author's commitment to the project and gained him much extra material at the same time.

Robert Hudson's family background is carefully chronicled as is how he set up his successful wholesale grocery business as a young man. His character is portrayed as being hard working, outgoing and occasionally forthright. Acquiring the Oregon franchise of the

Piggly Wiggly grocery stores is documented as is Hudson's involvement with the hazelnut trade. Gradually his business expanded as the American Northwest's leading wholesale grocery concern. After 65 years in operation, liquidation followed and is reported upon blow by blow.

Hudson's success in business led to him becoming one of golf's greatest benefactors. The book relates his generous sponsorship of four Portland Open tournaments, the 1946 US PGA Championship, the 1955 Western Open and, especially, the 1947 Ryder Cup matches. Additionally he gave his name to one regional tournament in Oregon and another for friends in far-off England.

The story is completed with Hudson's little-known roles as a committee man and lists the many honours bestowed on him for his various golfing achievements.

The book will compliment the existing books relating to the history of the famous Ryder Cup matches and complete the story. The foreword has been kindly contributed by the Portland resident and two-time Ryder Cup player, Peter Jacobsen, who is fully appreciative of Robert Hudson's efforts in promoting golf from a regional, national and international point of view.

The publication consists of 140 pages which include 20 full colour and 100 black and white illustrations. The printing is of the highest quality using Essential Velvet paper.

The Author

Peter Fry has taken on various golfing roles from being a golf club secretary to being an author of golf history books. Peter is possibly best known for his full-length biography of Samuel Ryder, the donor of the Ryder Cup (www.samuelryderstory.co.uk), which includes a foreword by the former Ryder Cup captain Bernard Gallacher. Later he had the pleasure of writing the centenary history of Samuel Ryder's home golf club of Verulam Golf Club at St Albans. One of Peter's overriding considerations is that the history of any subject is researched thoroughly and documented accurately. He has endeavoured to do this with this publication and hopes that Robert Hudson can now take his rightful place in golf history.

Society of Dorset Men member Peter Fry continues to promote the history of the Ryder Cup ever since the time he met Samuel Ryder's eldest daughter, Marjorie, while researching the history of Came Down Golf Club. She recalled how the family regularly visited Weymouth for their holidays. Samuel Ryder became a country member of the Came Down club and was impressed by the play of the Whitcombe brothers who were professionals at the club. Marjorie told Peter that this was the catalyst for her father founding the Ryder Cup matches and went on to record this fact in writing with privately produced booklets. In happy memory of those days, Marjorie gave Peter a large sepia picture of her father which is now hanging in pride of place in the lounge at Came Down Golf Club.

Peter went on to write the only full length biography of Samuel Ryder which, significantly, includes how Came Down Golf Club became the birthplace of the Ryder Cup. With his latest book, Peter has produced a biography of the businessman from Portland, Oregon, USA who actually resurrected the Ryder Cup after the conflict of World War II when money was desperately short. Peter hopes that media interest will recognise Came Down's crucial part in the founding of the iconic Ryder Cup. Peter can be contacted on 01305 833276.

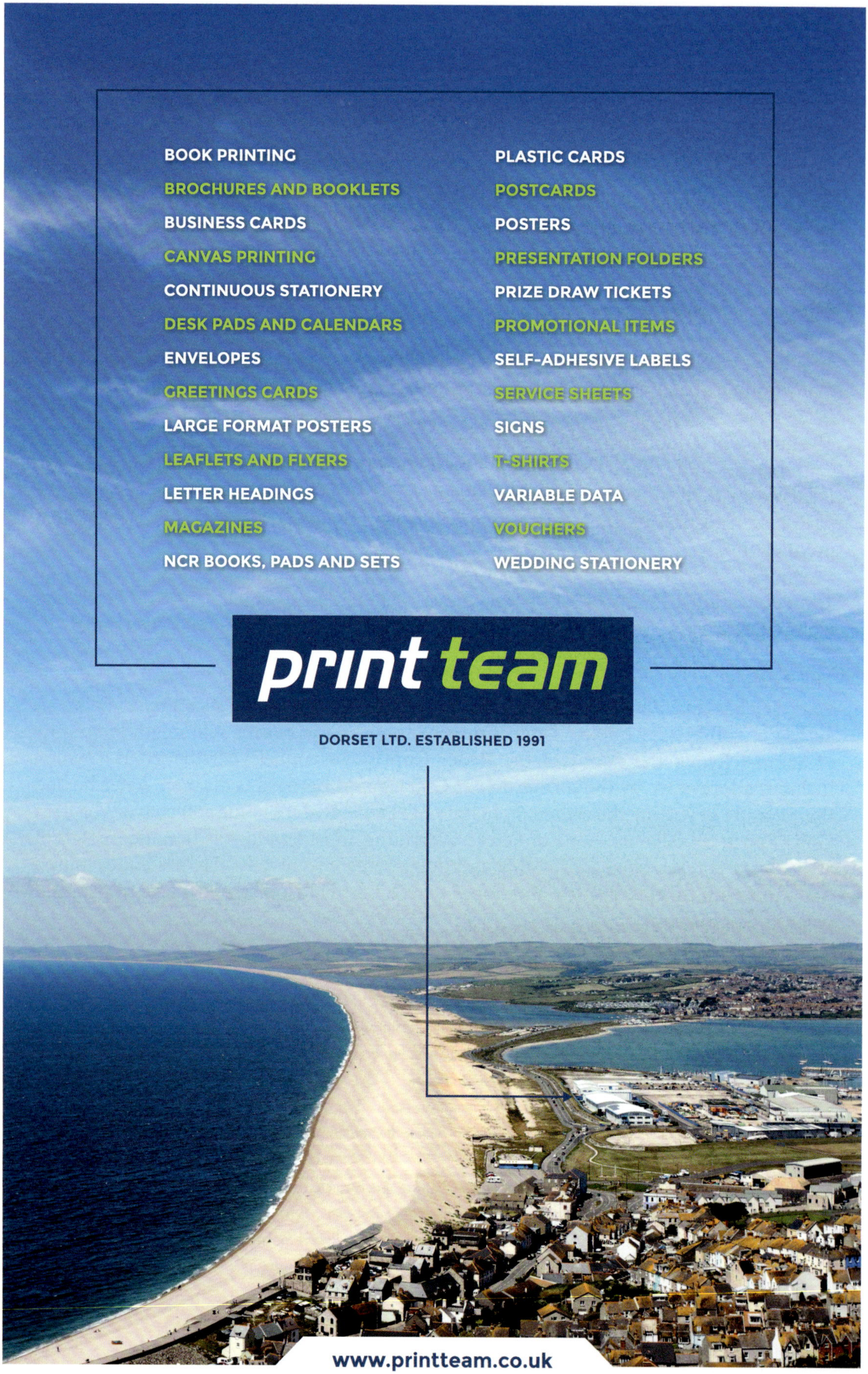

BOOK PRINTING	PLASTIC CARDS
BROCHURES AND BOOKLETS	POSTCARDS
BUSINESS CARDS	POSTERS
CANVAS PRINTING	PRESENTATION FOLDERS
CONTINUOUS STATIONERY	PRIZE DRAW TICKETS
DESK PADS AND CALENDARS	PROMOTIONAL ITEMS
ENVELOPES	SELF-ADHESIVE LABELS
GREETINGS CARDS	SERVICE SHEETS
LARGE FORMAT POSTERS	SIGNS
LEAFLETS AND FLYERS	T-SHIRTS
LETTER HEADINGS	VARIABLE DATA
MAGAZINES	VOUCHERS
NCR BOOKS, PADS AND SETS	WEDDING STATIONERY

print team

DORSET LTD. ESTABLISHED 1991

www.printteam.co.uk

County Dinner 2017

The County Dinner, the highlight of the Society's year and possibly the only occasion of its kind left in the Dorset calendar was once again held at the George Albert Hotel, Evershot.

Attended by no less than 214 members, together with partners and guests, it was without doubt a resounding success. Under the patronage of our President Lord Fellowes and joined by his guests which included the Lord Lieutenant Captain Angus Campbell and the High Sheriff Mr John Young MC JP DL, proceedings followed long held tradition.

Member Noel Spreadbury MBE read the dialect poem which pays homage to the Dorset Blue Viny cheese, and also in dialect, the loyal message to H M The Queen was read by the Hon Sec. This was followed by the presentation of the Challis Cup to member Trevor Bond for recruiting the most new members and the Hambro Golf Cup to Mike Smeaton.

Our speaker this year was Kate Adie OBE DL who will of course be known from her time as the BBC's Chief War Correspondent from 1989 until 2002 and now the presenter of "From Our Own Correspondent" on Radio 4.

She gave us a fascinating account of her life, having been born in Sunderland where she grew up with memories of the shipbuilding and mining industries but where at the time no women were employed. She had a happy childhood, despite Sunderland being the fourth most bombed city in WW II and one bomb demolishing their greenhouse!

She eventually went to Newcastle University where she obtained a degree in Swedish and Icelandic studies and then joined the local BBC radio station in Durham. She felt extremely lucky that it was there that she obtained a thorough grounding of broadcasting, being expected to undertake every task even reporting on the weather which involved opening a window to see what it was like outside!

After seven years in local radio, including a final period with Radio Bristol she became a BBC TV news correspondent. She said that she has never ceased to be amazed that it is the people not the reporter who have the stories to tell and they remain resourceful and resilient despite the awful situations they find themselves in and surrounded by terrible scenes of destruction.

She now lives quietly in Dorset which she has grown to love although she does go back to Sunderland quite regularly being a supporter of Sunderland Football Club. She said it gave her great pleasure to propose the toast "Dorset our County".

This very successful evening was then drawn to a close by the President.

NEW for Christmas 2017...

Dorset men and women through original poetry, prose, and illustration: poems and prose by award-winning local author, poet and performer, Sue Worth. New this December, this charming selection of Sue's work is accompanied by illustrations by local artists Naomi Price and Liz Poulain.

"Sue Worth's 'Dorset Ophelier' is a wonderfully imagined exercise in how Dorset country women would have reacted to Ophelia. Fab!"
Jane McKell, Artistic Director, AsOne Theatre Company

THE COWS who PLAYED BINGO
DORSET in POETRY, ART and TALE
by
Sue Worth

ISBN 978-0-9551633-4-0
Cover price £7.95 GBP • 46 pages • colour illustrations
For more information, email info@boredbooks.co.uk

IN MEMORIAM

The President and Members mourn the loss of the following worthy fellow Dorsets and tender their sincere sympathy to their relatives.

Name	Membership	Date
TONY SKIDMORE (Wimborne)	Ordinary Member	December '16
DR W.H. BEESLEY MD MCh FRCS (Iwerne Minster)	Overseas Member	2015
GRAHAM GATEHOUSE (Shaftesbury)	Life Member	January 2016
WILLIAM THORPE (Bryanston)	Overseas Member	2016
MAJ GEN C T SHORTIS CB CBE (Shaftesbury)	Life Member	2016
BERNARD (BIM) DOWNES (Broadmayne)	Ordinary Member	20/2/17
ERIC GOSNEY (Swanage)	Ordinary Member	1/3/17
GRAHAM COOKE (Dorchester)	Ordinary Member	1/3/17
WILLIAM FINUCANE (Compton Abbas)	Ordinary Member	2/3/17
RICHARD BURLEIGH FSA (Broadwindsor)	Ordinary Member	23/2/17
DAVID BIDDLECOMBE (Weymouth)	Vice President	20/3/17
MAJ GEN HENRY BOND OBE DL JP (Owermoigne)	Ordinary Member	27/3/17
PETER BURRIDGE (Gillingham)	Ordinary Member	29/12/16
NIGEL BARNES (Arne)	Ordinary Member	February 2017
RODNEY MARTIN (Durweston)	Life Member	31/3/17
JOHN LANGHAM CBE (Melcombe Bingham)	Life Member	May 2017
NIGEL SIMS (Sherborne)	Ordinary Member	11/6/16
JOHN DICKINSON (Weymouth)	Ordinary Member	4/6/17
HENRY DRAX DL (Charborough Park)	Life Member	June 2017
C.R. SMITH (Swanage)	Ordinary Member	14/7/17
DAVID BETTS (Winterborne Whitechurch)	Ordinary Member	11/8/17
FRANK HEELS (Motcombe)	Ordinary Member	24/8/17
PETER JUKES (Gillingham)	Ordinary Member	16/10/17

RULES OF THE SOCIETY
(Incorporating the alterations passed at the Special General Meeting of the Society held on 23rd April, 2017)

NAME
1. The name of the Society shall be "THE SOCIETY OF DORSET MEN."

OBJECTS
2. The objects of the Society shall be:
   To make and to renew personal friendships and associations, to promote good fellowship among Dorset men wherever they may reside, to foster love of County and pride in its history and traditions, and to assist by every means in its power, natives of Dorset who may stand in need of the influence and help of the Society.

MEMBERSHIP
3. The Society shall consist of a President, Deputy Presidents and Honorary Deputy Presidents if desired, Life Members and Members.

QUALIFICATIONS
4. Any person connected with the County of Dorset by birth, descent, marriage, property or past or present residence in the County, shall be eligible to be elected to membership.

MODE OF ELECTION AND TERMINATION OF MEMBERSHIP
5. (i) The names of all candidates for election shall be submitted to the Committee, who shall have full power to deal with the same.

   (ii) The Committee shall have power to remove from the list of Members the name of any Member whose subscription is in arrear for 12 months.

   (iii) The Committee may also at any time in their discretion terminate the membership of any person without furnishing reasons for their action, in which event a pro rata proportion of the subscription will be returned.

SUBSCRIPTIONS
6. The Subscriptions to the Society shall be:

   (a) Life Member - one payment £200.00
   (b) Ordinary Member- per annum (payable on the 1st October) . . .£15.00
   These subscriptions will apply whether the member is residing in the UK or overseas.

OFFICERS

7. The Officers of the Society shall be:
Chairman, Deputy Chairman, Honorary Treasurer, Honorary Editor, Honorary Secretary, Honorary Membership Secretary and Honorary Newsletter Editor and they, together with the President and Deputy Presidents, if desired, shall be elected at the Annual General Meeting each year.
The Committee shall have the power to fill any vacancy arising during the year.

COMMITTEE

8. (i) The Society shall be governed by a Committee not exceeding twenty in number, to be elected from the Members at the Annual General Meeting. In addition, the Officers of the Society shall be ex-officio Members of the Committee. Seven shall form a quorum.
   (ii) The Committee may delegate any of their powers to a Sub-Committee.
   (iii) The Committee shall retire annually, but shall be eligible for re-election.
   (iv) Not less than twelve days before the Annual General Meeting the Honorary Secretary shall send to every Member a notice of the Meeting. The Notice shall also intimate to the Members that any two Members may nominate one or more Members for election as Officers or to the Committee, and that such nomination must be sent to the Honorary Secretary not less than four days before the Meeting.
   (v) The Committee shall have power to fill any vacancy arising during the year.

MEETINGS

9. (i) The Annual General Meeting will be held on a date to be decided by the Committee.
   (ii) The Committee may at any time convene a Special General Meeting and they shall do so within six weeks of the Honorary Secretary receiving a written requisition signed by not less than twenty Members. Members requiring such Meeting shall state in their requisition the subject or subjects to be discussed, and the resolution or resolutions to be submitted thereat. Notice of the date and place of all Special Meetings shall be sent by the Honorary Secretary to each Member twelve clear days prior to the date fixed for the holding of a Meeting, and such notice shall state the object or purpose for which such Meeting is convened.

BOOKS AND RECORDS TO BE KEPT

10. Proper Books of Account, showing all receipts and expenditure, shall be kept by the Honorary Treasurer, and the Honorary Secretary shall record and keep Minutes of all Meetings of the Committee. The Membership Secretary shall record and maintain a list of members.

EXAMINATION OF ACCOUNTS

11. At each Annual General Meeting two Examiners shall be elected to examine the Accounts of the Society for presentation to the members at the next Annual General Meeting.

ALTERATION OF RULES

12. These Rules may be amended, altered, or varied by a majority of two-thirds of the Members voting at a Special General Meeting.

COMMITTEE CHAIRMAN:
STUART ADAM
Court Barton, West Bagber, Taunton, TA4 3EQ. Tel: (01823) 432076
Email: stu.adam@outlook.com

MEMBERS OF COMMITTEE:
P. ASHDOWN, G. KING, S. CREGAN, A. HUTCHINGS,
A. PROWSE, J. ROUSELL, P. SNOW, S. WOODCOCK

OFFICERS:
Hon. Secretary: H. C. RUSSELL,
34 Brunel Drive, Preston, Weymouth, DT3 6NX. Tel: (01305) 833700
E-mail: hrussell@gotadsl.co.uk

Hon. Assistant and Membership Secretary: P. LUSH
25 Maumbury Square, Dorchester, DT1 1TY. Tel: (01305) 260039
E-mail: peterlush3@hotmail.com

Hon. Treasurer: I. MORTON
1 Wainwright Close, Preston, Weymouth, DT3 6NS. Tel: 01305 832722
E-mail: ianvalmorton@fsmail.net

Hon. Editor "The Dorset Year Book": S. WILLIAMS
41 Everest Road, Weymouth, DT4 0DQ. Tel 07805 884786
E-mail: selles.macuquina@btinternet.com

Hon. Newsletter Editor: M. L. HOOPER-IMMINS,
2 Waverley Court, Radipole, Weymouth, DT3 5EE. Tel: (01305) 779705
Email: hooperimmins@btopenworld.com

Society Archivist and Historian: REV. DR. J. TRAVELL
44 Cornwall Road, Dorchester, DT1 1RY. Tel: 01305 264681
E-mail: johntravell@outlook.com